EACH ONE MUST SHINE

EACH ONE MUST SHINE

The educational legacy of V. A. Sukhomlinsky

Alan Cockerill

EJR Language Service Pty. Ltd.
Brisbane, Australia

Cataloguing Data

(based on Library of Congress cataloguing-in-publication data
for the edition published by Peter Lang, New York, in 1999.)

Cockerill, Alan.
Each one must shine: the educational legacy of V. A. Sukhomlinsky / Alan Cockerill
Includes bibliographical references (p. 221)
1. Sukhomlinsky, Vasily Aleksandrovich. 2. Educators—Soviet Union—Biography.
3. Educational Philosophy. 4. Education—Soviet Union—History
LB880.S842C65   370'.1—dc21   97-39384
ISBN 978-0-9945625-9-3

This 2017 edition is essentially a reprint of the 1999 edition
published by Peter Lang in New York.

Copyright has reverted to the author by permission of Peter Lang.

This 2017 edition is published by EJR Language Service Pty. Ltd.
181 Oxley Road, Graceville, QLD 4075 Australia
www.ejr.com.au

For other publications see http://www.ejr.com.au/publications

Cover photo of Vasily Aleksandrovich Sukhomlinsky
reprinted by permission of Olga Sukhomlyns'ka

Copyright © 2017 EJR Language Service Pty. Ltd. All rights reserved.
No part of this publication shall be reproduced, stored in or introduced into a retrieval
system, or transmitted in any form or by any means
(electronic, mechanical, photocopying, recording, scanning or otherwise),
without the prior permission of the copyright owner and publisher of this book.

The internal design of the 1999 edition by Paul Howson
has been imported into this edition.

Cover Design by Alan Cockerill

TABLE OF CONTENTS

Preface vii

Introduction 1

Chapter 1 V.A. Sukhomlinsky—Life and Legend 7

Chapter 2 The School at Pavlysh 25

Chapter 3 A Foundation in Health and Values 49

Chapter 4 Intellectual, Vocational and Aesthetic Development . 71

Chapter 5 Education of the Heart 103

Chapter 6 Civic Responsibility 137

Chapter 7 Sukhomlinsky's Influence 155

Chapter 8 Sukhomlinsky's Successors 181

Chapter 9 Sukhomlinsky's Relevance to the West 209

Selected Bibliography 221

Index 225

V. A. Sukhomlinsky

(reprinted by permission of Anna Ivanovna Sukhomlinskaia,
Olga Vasilievna Sukhomlinskaia, and Sergei Vasilievich Sukhomlinsky)

PREFACE

THIS BOOK is the fruit of doctoral studies undertaken at The University of Queensland, Australia, from 1987 to 1993. It is the product of two converging interests: an interest in Russian studies fostered at the University of Melbourne and the University of Queensland, and an interest in holistic education inspired by the work of the Australian educator Vijayadev Yogendra.

At the outset, I intended to make a more general study of moral education in the Soviet Union in the light of the 1984 reforms, and I undertook preliminary research in that area. Several people helped me to find my bearings in the field, including Dr Colin Collins from The University of Queensland and Mrs Nina Christesen, my former teacher at the University of Melbourne, who helped me to make contact with several authorities on Soviet studies. In the course of my preliminary research I came across Sukhomlinsky's name quite frequently, and chanced to purchase a five-volume collection of his works in Melbourne. I found his writing so compelling that I determined to devote the whole thesis to a study of his educational thought.

Several years of study only served to increase my sense of excitement about Sukhomlinsky's work, and my long-suffering supervisor, John McNair, had to battle to contain my "missionary zeal", lest it cloud my sense of objectivity. I am very grateful for his untiring help throughout the project, and for his many thoughtful suggestions. I fear the missionary zeal remains, but hope that some readers, at least, will consider it justified. I hope readers will also forgive me the extent to which I have included lengthy verbatim quotations from Sukhomlinsky's work. I had teachers in mind when I wrote the study, and wished to allow Sukhomlinsky to speak for himself as far as possible. I hope something of the tone of his writing will come through in my translations. The same applies to quotations in chapter eight from the work of Sukhomlinsky's successors. Most of the material translated is not available in English.

It was necessary to make a trip to the Soviet Union to collect material for the thesis, and in 1987 and 1988 I spent a most stimulating ten months at the Pushkin Institute of Russian Language in Moscow, where a supervisor was appointed to assist me with my research. Vera Sergeevna Deviataikina gave me invaluable help, organising meetings with Sukhomlinsky's daughter, with the publicist Simon Soloveichik, and with Mikhail Boguslavsky, who had himself recently completed a dissertation on Sukhomlinsky. She also arranged for me to attend a progressive Moscow school, headed by Evgeny Yamburg, where for several months I assisted with English language classes and acquired some experience of the Soviet education system. Subsequently Sukhomlinsky's daughter, Olga Sukhomlinskaia, gave significant help, replying to several letters and sending me valuable material.

While I was in Russia there was considerable public interest in the work of the "teacher-innovators", and I have devoted some attention to them in Chapter 8 of the study, where I have attempted to show a relationship between them and Sukhomlinsky.

It was a great privilege to be able to devote so much time to pursuing an interest, and I would like to thank the University of Queensland, for providing a scholarship and a tutorial assistantship, and the Australia-USSR Society for providing a scholarship to study in Moscow. I am grateful to Irene Kobald-Karabut and Sandra Mikula, who generously helped in making notes from Erika Gartmann's German-language study of Sukhomlinsky.

Finally, my deepest thanks go to my wife Hiroko, who has supported my involvement in this study throughout.

INTRODUCTION

There should not be any nobodies—specks of dust cast upon the wind. Each one must shine, just as billions upon billions of galaxies shine in the heavens.[1]

V. A. Sukhomlinsky

A STUDY devoted to the work of Sukhomlinsky may be justified on two grounds. The first is that such a study is indispensable to an understanding of Soviet education in the post-war period. Joseph Zajda suggests that Sukhomlinsky was "the most influential Soviet educationist during the 1960s and 1970s".[2] It may truly be said of Sukhomlinsky that he became a legend in his own lifetime. The school of which he was principal was an educational mecca visited by thousands of Soviet teachers. He was a prolific writer and his publications ran into millions of copies. His personal correspondence was prodigious. After his premature death at the age of 51 he became even more well known and was regarded by many with something akin to reverence. In the minds of some Soviet educators he came to eclipse Makarenko as the leading exponent of Soviet educational ideals. In a survey of teachers conducted in the Donetsk region of the Ukraine in 1988, Sukhomlinsky's name was the one most often given in reply to the question "Outstanding personalities of our times who have influenced or are influencing the formation of your educational ideals and practice." (460 out of 1,048 respondents).[3]

The second reason for studying Sukhomlinsky's work is that much of it is close in spirit to that of progressive Western educators. While still believing, like Makarenko, in the educational power of the collective, he made the individual, rather than the collective, the focus of education. For him education was a deeply personal endeavour, and the most important educational relationship was the archetypal one between the teacher and the individual pupil. It will be suggested in this study that Sukhomlinsky belongs to a European humanistic tradition in education inspired by such educators as Vittorino da Feltre, Comenius and Pestalozzi. If this is so, Sukhomlinsky's work may be relevant to teachers and parents in English-speaking countries, as well as to those with a special interest in Soviet education.

Sukhomlinsky was working within a very different social context to our own, however, and the influence of communist ideology on his work may mask its relevance. Some effort will be made to explain such ideological influences in a way that makes Sukhomlinsky's experience more easily assimilated, and to highlight those features of his work which are of more universal significance. In order to bridge the gap between the Soviet educational experience and our own, an attempt will be made in this introduction to define a humanistic educational ideal which derives from European antecedents shared by the Soviet Union and the West.

Humanism is a concept which emerged during the Renaissance. Renaissance humanism was characterised by a blend of Classical and Christian ideals, of rationalism and spirituality, of individual concerns and civic responsibility. The humanism of Petrarch, Erasmus and More owed as much to Christianity as to the study of the Classics. It is in this balance of spiritual and material concerns that we should seek the spirit of humanism.

Towards the end of the Second World War the eminent classical scholar Gilbert Murray delivered a lecture on "Myths and Ethics", subtitled "Humanism and the World's Need". He was interested in finding an ethical basis to unite people, in the face of myths which divided. He called this common ethical basis "humanism".

For Murray there were two attributes which distinguished the people he would call humanists:

> In every one of them I recognise first an acceptance, beyond all other duties, of a duty to the welfare of Humanity, and secondly, of a choice of sincerity of thought, with all its sacrifices, as better than all the psychological flesh-pots of conformity …
>
> … By a Humanist I mean essentially one who accepts it as the special duty of Man, whether he has a "Friend behind phenomena" or not, to raise life to some higher level and redeem the world from its misery.[4]

Murray's plea for humanity and truth was conditioned by his having witnessed the increasing inhumanity of two world wars, with their attendant suppression of truth. He affirmed, though, that

> ... this inhumanity and deceit are all the time essentially repugnant to human nature ... Much more significant ... long periods of intense war tend to be followed by intense reactions towards ideal justice, humanity, and truth. The present struggle has been called a Thirty Years' War, from 1914 to 1944, with an uneasy truce in the middle. The Thirty Years' War that devastated Europe from 1618 to 1648 was marked by hideous crimes and lawlessness, including even cannibalism: but it was followed by the idealist movement in education associated specially with Comenius, and by Grotius's great book, *De Jure Pacis et Belli*, calling on a maddened world to remember that there is a Natural Law with authority over princes and nations, as much in war as in peace.[5]

Murray notes that a similar idealistic movement followed the Twenty-Eight Years War which divided the Greek world from 432 to 404 BC. This movement gave rise to the great philosophic schools which concentrated "on the individual soul of man as of incalculably more value than States and armies."

> It would be easy to point out abundant manifestations of the same spirit today ... these desires or ideals exist; they are a fact. In Comenius and Grotius they clothed themselves in Christian language; in the Stoics and Plato they used that of the current polytheism. In China they will be Buddhist or Confucian. The desire for some higher moral perfection or beauty is almost ineradicable in the human race ... It may be differently analysed by different thinkers, but for certain it exists, and innumerable religions and sects and philosophies, and even political parties, testify to its existence.[6]

In the same year in which Gilbert Murray delivered this lecture, a Ukrainian school teacher, Vasily Sukhomlinsky, returned to the region where he was born, which had recently been freed from German occupation, and set about helping to rebuild a normal life for himself and his community. For him the "desire for some higher moral perfection" clothed itself in the language of communism, but it burnt no less brightly for all that. He dreamt of a society which existed to develop the human potential of everyone within it. During the 'fifties and 'sixties all his efforts were dedicated to developing an educational methodology to meet the needs of such a society. This book is dedicated to his efforts and his achievement.

It would appear that the idealism prevalent in the post-war decades has been followed by a period of reaction. In the 'nineties the spirit of economic rationalism seems to dominate nearly every facet of our lives. Even our universities, which should be the guardians of humanistic traditions, are forced to justify their existence in economic terms. Russia in the 'nineties has demonstrated instances of crass materialism even more extreme than those found in the West. It may be a good time, then, to reflect on ideals of human development which transcend the grossly materialistic, and to dream with Sukhomlinsky of a society dedicated to the development of human potential.

In the former Soviet society, as in our society, the perception of what it meant to be human was largely a product of the evolution of two interacting traditions: the Christian and the Classical. For all its attempts to break with the past, Soviet Marxism, too, evolved from these traditions and never entirely broke free from them.

One of the most prophetic of Russian poets, Alexander Blok, wrote a poem about the revolution entitled *The Twelve*. In it he created a powerful image of an unruly band of red soldiers tramping the streets of St Petersburg, intent on overturning the old world order. They are scornful of a priest:

> Do you remember how you used
> To walk, belly first,
> And how, with the cross,
> Your belly shone at the people? …

They are ready to fire on "sacred Russia". The closing passage of the poem seems to suggest, however, that the moral impulse which guided the leaders of the revolution derived from Christianity. The soldiers are unable to discern who is bearing the red flag in front of them in the raging blizzard. Only in the final words of the poem does Blok reveal who it is:

> … And so they march along—
> Behind them—a hungry dog,

> In front — with bloodied flag,
> Invisible in the blizzard,
> Unharmed by bullet,
> With gentle step above the storm,
> Sprinkling pearl-like drops of snow,
> In a white crown of roses —
> In front — is Jesus Christ.[7]

In spite of attempts by communist regimes to promote atheism, Russia in 1988 celebrated the 1000th anniversary of the adoption of Christianity with pomp and ceremony.

Nor is it difficult to discern classical antecedents in the Soviet experiment, which could be viewed as an attempt to give practical expression to concepts put forward by Plato in *The Republic*. The oft-stated goal of Soviet education, the "roundly developed personality", is an ideal which derives from classical sources and which flourished during the Renaissance.

In defining a humanistic educational ideal, then, we shall draw on the Christian and Classical heritage of Western civilisation. For the purposes of this study, humanism will be taken to mean an approach that is inspired by the ideal of the rounded development of the whole person, that reveres life and is thus humane in both end and means, and that fosters a sense of civic responsibility which may be extended to a concern for the welfare of all of humanity. In the West, the ideal of holistic development has Greek origins. It was revived in the Renaissance in the notion of *humanitas*. It may be interpreted as the harmonious development of all human faculties, including reason, in the pursuit of truth, beauty and goodness. The ideal of humaneness derives from the Christian ideal of love and compassion, and is common to other religious and spiritual traditions. The ideal of civic responsibility is typically Roman, and was also revived during the Renaissance. In its highest form it merges with the Stoic ideal of striving for a universal outlook and a sense of world citizenship.

These three ideals are all expressed in Sukhomlinsky's work, and the exposition of Sukhomlinsky's educational ideas contained in this study is structured around this threefold ideal. Following the first chapter, which is biographical, chapters two, three and four examine the ideal of holistic development as it was practised at Sukhomlinsky's school in the Ukrainian country town of Pavlysh. They show the interrelationship between physical education, moral education, intellectual education, vocational education and aesthetic education as practised at Pavlysh. Chapter five focuses on Sukhomlinsky's attempts to inculcate humane values in his pupils—to educate the heart. Chapter six is an attempt to throw light on Sukhomlinsky's approach to educating a sense of civic responsibility and also addresses the issue of ideological influences in his work.

Chapters seven and eight attempt to trace Sukhomlinsky's influence on Soviet education. The concluding chapter will suggest, in broad outline, Sukhomlinsky's relevance to Western educators. It is hoped that the study as a whole may serve as a general introduction to Sukhomlinsky's work.

Notes

1 Sukhomlinsky, V.S., *Pis'ma k synu [Letters to my son]*, Moscow: Prosveshchenie, 1987, p. 53.
2 Zajda, J.I., *Education in the* USSR, Oxford: Pergamon Press, 1980, p. 158.
3 Goncharova, T., Goncharov, I., "Portret uchitelia [Portrait of a teacher]", Pravda, 16 August, 1988, p. 3.
4 Murray, Gilbert., *Myths and Ethics*, London, Watts & Co., 1944, pp. 2–3.
5 Ibid, pp. 15–16.
6 Ibid, pp. 17–18.
7 Translated from Blok, A., *Stikhotvoreniia i poemy*, Vostochno-sibirskoe knizhnoe izdatel'stvo, 1970, pp. 178, 187.

CHAPTER 1

V.A. Sukhomlinsky—Life and Legend

> What was most fundamental in Vasily Aleksandrovich's character … what enabled him to accomplish so much in a comparatively short period of time? Firstly, an unusual love of hard work. He worked forgetful of self. In the last decade of his life he did not take a break in the normal sense. There were no days off, holidays, annual leave — he devoted them to creative work. He hastened to live, in the highest sense of the word. He strove to do as much as possible, to pass on the fruits of his experience, his ideas to others. The second feature of his character was an inner concentration of his energies. He was strong in spirit, and strong-willed. Outwardly gentle, slow, at times shy, especially in the company of unfamiliar people, there dwelt in him so much vital energy that its power permitted him to accomplish the seemingly impossible.
>
> Anna Ivanovna Sukhomlinskaia[1]
(Sukhomlinsky's wife)

THERE CAN BE few fields of endeavour where the impact of the individual personality and character are more important than education. Education in its broadest sense is the result of the personal relationship between student and teacher, and the teacher's influence on the student is in proportion to his ability to inspire the student's respect and desire to emulate him. As Sukhomlinsky himself put it:

> We educate, first and foremost, not with this or that variety of methods or techniques, but through the influence of our own personality, of our individuality.[2]

The best introduction to Sukhomlinsky's ideas is an account of his life and character. Indeed, it is difficult to separate theory and practice in Sukhomlinsky's work, as each continually gave rise to the other: all his theories were a result of his practical teaching experience and all his practical work was directed by the convictions born of his ideological and theoretical quest. Each lesson he gave was part of an on-going experiment which continued for the duration of his working life.

Sukhomlinsky was born on 28 September 1918, and grew up in the village of Vasilievka, some 40 km from the city of Kremenchug in the southern Ukraine. His early life coincided with a particularly turbulent period of history in a region that, during his first 25 years, suffered civil war, the excesses of collectivisation and the ravages of Nazi occupation. His whole life's work could be viewed as an heroic response to the suffering which he witnessed and experienced during this period.

Sukhomlinsky's father was a carpenter who, until the revolution, carried out piecework for landowners and peasant farmers. After the revolution he was an active supporter of the new Soviet government, participating in the management of the local cooperative farm and consumers' cooperative, writing newspaper articles as a rural correspondent and teaching carpentry at the local 7-year school. Sukhomlinsky's mother worked at home and on the collective farm and also as a seamstress. Vasily had an older brother (Ivan) and a younger brother (Sergei) and sister (Malania), all of whom became village school teachers, teaching Ukrainian language and literature.

The fact that Sukhomlinsky's father actively supported the process of collectivisation, and was even shot at for his pains, helps to explain why Vasily became committed to the communist cause, despite witnessing the famine which came in the wake of collectivisation. Respect for parents and family loyalty had always been strong values in the Ukraine.

Vasily attended the 7-year school at Vasilievka from 1926 until 1933, and excelled in his studies. He liked to read and to draw, and was prepared to go to great lengths to achieve his goals. In order to obtain paper on which to draw he gathered acacia seeds in the forest, and as a twelve-year-old he once walked 40 kilometres to the city of Kremenchug to buy some paints.

His talent for relating to young children manifested itself while he was still at school. As he later recollected:

Once on the way home from school I saw a group of about 20 youngsters — children from 3 to 7 years old. I felt an urge to play with them. I showed them how to make a snowman. They squealed with delight. The next day the youngsters were waiting for me long before lessons finished. Gradually it became their custom: before lessons had even finished the youngsters would be waiting by the school.[3]

When the snow melted Vasily and the young children found new activities in the surrounding forests and meadows, exploring waterways and gullies. These "journeys into nature" were later to become an integral part of his teaching approach, and he developed a theoretical basis for using such outings to develop the language and thinking skills of his pupils. He would later contend that the emotions of wonder stimulated by outings in nature in their turn stimulated intellectual inquiry and motivated language development and that they were crucial to the development of a young child's thinking processes. At this early age, however, it was just an enjoyable way to spend his time:

> The thought never entered my mind that I had become some sort of supervisor or organiser of children. It was just something I wanted to do myself, for my own pleasure.[4]

By the time he finished his schooling he had decided to become a teacher. He seems never to have doubted his vocation, and the remainder of his life was devoted to developing an educational theory and practice to meet the needs of the community into which he was born. He does not even seem to have experienced any urge to travel beyond the rural area in which he grew up. With the exception of the war years and the last few years of his life (when he made several brief trips to other countries to give lectures on education), he lived and worked in the district of Onufrievka: in the town of Onufrievka itself and in the villages of Vasilievka, Zybkovka and Pavlysh. His ability to concentrate all his energies on a single purpose no doubt had a lot to do with the success he enjoyed and the influence he came to have.

His geographical isolation may also have contributed to the originality of his thought and his relative independence from passing fads in Soviet education. Sukhomlinsky's daughter commented in conversation that at a time when it was popular to extol the virtues of moral lectures and explanations as a means of moral education, her father was emphasising the need for moral principles to find expression in practical activities which rendered a real service to the community. Later, when it became fashionable to criticise "verbal" means of moral education, Sukhomlinsky wrote of the power of carefully chosen words, and the need to use words sensitively to respond to the inner needs of the child.

Upon completing his schooling in Vasilievka Sukhomlinsky undertook further studies in Kremenchug to prepare for the entrance exam at Kremenchug Pedagogical Institute, where in 1934 he enrolled in the faculty of Ukrainian Language and Literature. He was the first member of his family ever to have undertaken tertiary studies and, according to Tartakovsky, upon whose authoritative biography much of this chapter is based, his attitude was like that of a pilgrim entering a sacred temple.

His capacity for hard work and independent thought attracted the attention of his teachers, but in 1935 he had to discontinue his studies due to serious illness. He had a tendency to make heavy demands on himself even when unwell, and disregarded a doctor's advice to rest in order to recover from a bout of influenza. An acute case of pleurisy forced him to withdraw from his course and travel to the Black Sea to recuperate.

It was a major disappointment for him, but the circumstances which resulted from his illness may have helped to establish the work patterns which he maintained for the rest of his life—a combination of practical teaching experience and simultaneous study and research. When he had recovered from his illness, he commenced work as a teacher at the Vasilievka 7-year school, where he had himself recently been a pupil. He worked there and at the Zybkovka 7-year school until 1938, while at the same time completing his teacher training by correspondence at the Poltava Pedagogical Institute. Upon graduating from this institute (from which, incidentally, Makarenko[5] also graduated), he became qualified to teach at secondary level, and took up a post at Onufrievka High School. Onufrievka was the district centre for the villages of Vasilievka and Zybkovka, and also for the town of Pavlysh, which he was later to make famous in Soviet educational circles.

During his first teaching experience at the school in Vasilievka he began to develop the style of teaching which he later described in his books. Paramount to his approach was the personal relationship of the teacher with each individual child. He considered that the teacher should be a companion to the children outside school hours and should be keenly interested in each individual, especially those who experienced difficulty in studying. He began to keep a diary where he reflected on the experience of each day and analysed problems faced by the children. He would later write:

> In front of you are forty youngsters—at first glance they seem very similar to each other even in their external features, but by the third, fourth or fifth day, after several walks to forest and field, you become convinced that each child is a world in themselves, unique and never to be repeated. If this world reveals itself to you, if you sense the individuality within each child, if the joys and sorrows of each child find a response in your heart, in your thoughts, cares and concerns—then you may confidently choose as your profession the noble work of a teacher and you will find in it the joy of creativity. For creativity in our work ... is first and foremost the process of coming to know, of discovering a human being, of experiencing wonder at the many facets and inexhaustibility of human nature.[6]

He continued his earlier pattern of joining in the children's games, and during summer holidays would organise camps and excursions for them. He also conducted some school lessons outdoors, setting the pattern for his later "lessons in nature". In this he was influenced in part by one of his own former teachers, a certain Anna Samoilovna, whose nature study lessons had made a great impression on him.

The vice-principal of the school, Vladimir Viktorovich Zubkovsky, though sometimes bemused by Sukhomlinsky's approach, encouraged him to develop his own style of teaching and helped him to find a theoretical basis for it, pointing to the link between emotion and thought. He also lent moral support and on one occasion quoted Virgil to the young teacher, advising that "whatever happens, with patience and will we can overcome all obstacles."[7]

When, having graduated from Poltava Pedagogical Institute, Sukhomlinsky commenced work at Onufrievka High School, he was hardly 20 years old, but already had some firm convictions about education which he was prepared to defend. He believed, for instance, that no matter how erudite a teacher, or how clear his presentation of his material, he could not be a good teacher unless he could understand and respond to the needs of each individual pupil, unless he could relate to the inner worlds of his charges. He believed in inspiration rather than coercion—that unless the inner resources of the child were mobilised in a quest for self-education, the teacher's efforts would in the long term be fruitless. Coercion aborted the process of self-education. The teacher must have faith in the pupil and in the power of education. Lack of trust eroded faith and sapped initiative.

Despite his youth, only a year after he commenced work at the school he was appointed vice-principal—at the suggestion of the retiring vice-principal and with the blessing of the Communist Party. In this new position of supervision he found himself in conflict with some of the more experienced teachers, who had a more formal and authoritarian approach, and who resented being corrected by one so young. One went so far as to complain to the local education authorities that Sukhomlinsky was giving unrealistic and apolitical advice to the teachers. In consequence, an inspector was sent to the school to investigate the work of the vice-principal. He conducted tests in several classes and found that in classes where Sukhomlinsky's guidelines had been implemented, the number of pupils who had failed to master the program had dropped from 14% in the previous testing period to 6%, whereas the failure rate in the class of the teacher who had lodged the complaint had increased. Criticism of his approach was thus deflected for the time being. Later in his career, when his ideas gained prominence, he would again have to defend them against certain ideologues who accused him in the press of "abstract humanism".[8]

In 1941, Sukhomlinsky's educational career was interrupted by the war, which laid waste the region where he lived and worked, and which brought him great personal hardship. The war played a crucial role in shaping his world view and his educational philosophy. Henceforth he was to view the world as a battleground where the forces of socialism and fascism fought for supremacy. He identified socialism with the forces of progress and humanity which would foster the all-round development of the individual. Against them were arraigned the forces of reaction, which subordinated human values to those of commercial gain.

Sukhomlinsky was called up immediately at the outbreak of war, which coincided with the end of the school year in June 1941. Events developed so precipitously that he did not have time to say farewell to his young wife, Vera Povsha, whom he had been planning to join in her native village at the end of the school term. After several weeks' training near Moscow, he joined a battalion not far from Smolensk as a 'politruk' —a junior officer responsible for the political education of the troops. He fought in several battles as the Soviet forces first retreated to Moscow and then went on the offensive.

In February 1942 he was seriously wounded in a battle near Rzhev. His left arm was almost severed at the shoulder, and pieces of shrapnel entered his chest. Some were too close to his heart to be removed by surgery, and remained there until his death, to which they contributed. He never fully regained the use of his left arm. After five months in an army hospital, he recovered sufficiently to take up duties as a teacher, having been pronounced unfit for active service.

As the southern Ukraine was still occupied by German forces, he took up a position in unoccupied territory as principal of the secondary school at Uva, a small town in the western Urals, not far from Izhevsk. Here he was concerned not only with educating the children, but also with the plight of families who suffered privation, hardship and grief during the war.

He, in his turn, had to experience the grief of losing loved ones. When, in 1944, the southern Ukraine was freed from German occupation, he received news in Uva of the death of his father and of his young wife. The circumstances of his wife's death, of which he learnt later, affected him profoundly. Upon returning to the Ukraine he learnt from the testimony of a witness that she had been arrested by the Gestapo for helping the Ukrainian resistance. She had been tortured and had given birth to a child while being held in detention. A Gestapo officer had threatened to kill the child if she did not reveal the names of other members of the resistance. When she remained silent the child was killed in front of her and then she herself was further tortured and hanged. Many years later, in an afterword to the German edition of his most highly acclaimed book, *My Heart I Give to Children*, he wrote about the grief and anger he had experienced on learning of the fate of his wife and child:

> After I returned to the village I wanted to go and fight again. I wanted to meet that animal of a Gestapo officer face to face. I wanted to

> understand how it could happen that such animals were born of human mothers. But I was not able to serve in the army any more — not one board would recognise me as fit even for 'limited duties'.
>
> I returned to work at school. Work, work and more work — in that I found at least some degree of relief from my grief. All day I was with children. At night I woke up at two or three in the morning and could not get back to sleep — I worked. I waited impatiently for the morning, when the chorus of children's voices would ring out. Even now I wait every morning for the children. With them is my happiness.[9]

It was a characteristic response to seek an outlet for his grief and anger through work. For the remainder of his life, he was to maintain an extraordinary work routine, using the early hours of the morning to learn foreign languages and to write, and the remainder of the day to carry out the duties of teacher and school principal. A routine of working at his desk every morning from 4.00 till 8.00 explains his prolific output of articles and books.

In 1944, Sukhomlinsky returned to Onufrievka, bringing with him a wife, Anna Ivanovna, who had been a school inspector at Uva. His second marriage was by all accounts a very close one. He and his wife worked together at the school at Pavlysh for 23 years and brought up two children. Tartakovsky indicates that Anna Ivanovna gave considerable support to her husband throughout this period, during much of which Sukhomlinsky suffered from serious illness.

On his return to Onufrievka, Sukhomlinsky took up a position as head of the district office of the Department of Education and was responsible for overseeing the restoration of schools in an area devastated by the occupation. Not only was it necessary to rebuild and refurnish many schools; teachers were faced with the task of healing the psychological wounds sustained by children during the war. A high proportion had lost one or both parents, and children were also affected by the general breakdown in normal social relations. Some children did not know who their fathers were, and others had parents who had been involved in profiteering or other criminal activities. Nearly all needed in some sense to regain their childhood. While working as an administrator, Sukhomlinsky continued to do some teaching, and in 1948 he was, at his own request, appointed principal of the combined primary and secondary school in the town of Pavlysh, a position he was to occupy until his death in 1970.

The 23 years at Pavlysh were the most productive of his life. His formative years were behind him, and he set about the long and painstaking task of attempting to realise his educational ideals in practice.

We may assume that his efforts to reequip the burnt-out and damaged school began while he was still working as head of the district office of the Department of Education. Although he was by nature quiet and reflective, he was determined, and apparently capable of mobilising community resources and obtaining support from Communist Party officials when the need arose. He was himself actively involved in community service and the Party. He was, on and off, a member of the Party's district committee from 1947 to 1968, and from 1949 to 1969 he was a member of the District Council of Workers' Deputies. It is apparent from his books that, as the school developed, the children and staff, with community support, played an increasing role in creating and maintaining the material resources of the school. This was done through activities that included the construction of buildings, gardening and horticulture, production of lathes and power tools, and cleaning and maintenance.[10] Sukhomlinsky believed that work education should include projects which rendered genuine assistance to the school and to the wider community, and that the pupils should feel responsible for the environment in which they studied.

In addressing the emotional problems of children in the aftermath of the war, Sukhomlinsky emphasised the need to be aware of their special needs:

> I considered that the most important task at that time was to gain the acceptance of my educational convictions by all the teachers … I tried to convince them that many of our problems could only be overcome through genuine humanity.[11]

This sometimes involved individual discussions lasting as much as two or three hours at a time:

> Individual, friendly, open, heart-to-heart chats are the main method in the principal's work with teachers. Education, after all, is a most subtle activity involving the inner person. I would liken the influence of an educator on a student with the influence of music. "To

attempt to influence the inner life by force", wrote L.N. Tolstoy, "is like trying to catch the rays of the sun. Whatever you cover them with, they always come out on top." ... I did not write a single instruction regarding the process of education ... that is completely futile. Neither did I air differences of opinion with teachers at staff meetings.[12]

In individual conversations however, he could be relentless in opposing approaches he saw as being detrimental to the children's development:

> Once while checking homework in year 5 the literature teacher called on a weak pupil. She didn't like a sentence he had composed by himself. Without saying a word she dismissed him with a wave of her hand ... and the boy wept for a whole evening ... It was necessary to discuss this incident for a long time to prove to the teacher that she had been in error, to explain that her gesture had expressed her educational attitude — indifference to the pupil, lack of faith that he could do something well, acceptance of the notion that a poor student will remain a poor student ... Only when I am able to convince a teacher and he begins to demonstrate his conviction practically in his work (this is achieved, of course, not by a single conversation and not through conversation alone), only then do I consider that I have fulfilled my mission as a principal.[13]

Faith in the child, in the teacher, and in the existence of solutions to complex problems underlay all his work at Pavlysh. He could never simply accept the inevitability of problems which seemed to dog teachers everywhere. He would always seek a solution, and call on the staff as a whole to pool their experience and help in the search.

First he would become aware of a problem — for instance that many children did not enjoy study, and that their language in class was lifeless and stilted. Reflection would lead him to some conclusion — in this case, that the pupils were just being fed information from books, but not being taught how to think, how to relate what they read to their own experience, or how to apply what they learnt. He would share his concern with the other teachers at a staff meeting and they would discuss the problem on the basis of their varied experience. Collectively, they would seek solutions, and he and other teachers would experiment with various approaches.[14] Activities generated in response to the above issue included nature walks, on which children studied cause-and-effect relationships and developed language skills as they tried to capture in words the complexities and subtleties they observed in nature, and after-school activities in various clubs where children could apply their knowledge in scientific, technical, agricultural and artistic pursuits. Teachers who experienced successes would pass these on to other staff members and the school as a whole gradually developed an exceptionally creative approach to teaching.

When Sukhomlinsky was satisfied that some significant progress had been made in addressing a particular issue, he would write about the school's experience in articles or monographs. His first articles on education appeared in the local (district and regional) press from 1945 onwards, and from 1949 his articles began to appear in the national press. In 1951 he was invited by the head of the Ukrainian Educational Research Institute in Kiev to undertake post-graduate studies there, with a view to writing a thesis on the role of the school principal in the educational process. This he did concurrently with his other duties, and in 1955 he successfully defended his thesis at Kiev University, receiving his Candidate's Degree.[15]

In 1951 he also decided to combine the work of principal with that of class teacher. He was not satisfied with a chiefly administrative role, and felt that he could not properly train his staff unless they could see him performing the same duties as themselves. He also sought the closer relationship with children which work as a class teacher would bring. He later wrote of this decision:

> Just as the head doctor of a hospital cannot be a genuine doctor unless he has his own patients, so the principal of a school cannot direct the staff unless he has his own pupils.[16]

He thus established a pattern of work which combined practical experience as a class teacher, teacher education, administration, research and writing. Simon Soloveichik, an educational journalist and enthusiastic promoter of Sukhomlinsky's ideas, has written of Sukhomlinsky's capacity for work in sustaining such a program:

> When one talks with teachers at Pavlysh School, one gets the impression that Sukhomlinsky did nothing else but educate teachers. When he visited lessons he would visit 10 or 15 in succession ... and would first analyse each individual lesson and then the "system of lessons" as

a whole. If he was beginning to train a young teacher, he would visit his lessons, set assignments, conduct open lessons for him alone ... and would do this ... over a period of six or eight years ... [under Sukhomlinsky's influence] nearly all the teachers produced scholarly articles ... And yet with the same thoroughness, seriousness and extraordinary demands on himself, he worked as a class teacher, directed the school, gave lessons, wrote books and articles, worked with parents ... [17]

A survey of Sukhomlinsky's main published works gives some idea of the central concerns which motivated Sukhomlinsky at Pavlysh. We can see that the dominant orientation in the 'fifties was a social one — creating a cohesive school community and preparing children for citizenship and work. In the 'sixties he focuses more on the individual, on problems of psychological development and on moral issues. The works published from 1967 onwards are review works which attempt to generalise from his total experience and provide the most comprehensive picture of the educational system which evolved during his 23 years at Pavlysh.

One of the key issues which interested him increasingly as the years went by was education in the family. A collection of essays published under the title *Parental Pedagogy*[18] reflects this interest. He had two children of his own, a son (Sergei) and a daughter (Olga), both born shortly after the war. Sukhomlinsky attached great importance to the preschool years, citing Tolstoy's belief that the child learnt more in its first five years than in the rest of its life. Throughout the child's schooling, the family continued to mould attitudes and character, building on the foundation of the preschool years. Sukhomlinsky came to the conclusion that the only system of education which could successfully foster positive character development was one in which the school and the family cooperated. He felt that the school should initiate this process, and that those teachers with the deepest understanding of the processes of human development should offer guidance to all parents in the upbringing of their children.

To this end Sukhomlinsky organised lectures on child development and family life which were attended by school parents twice a month. He gained wide support for this program, which parents would commence two years before their children enrolled at the school. Parents sustained this commitment for twelve years, or until their children completed their schooling. In his later years Sukhomlinsky also organised courses on family life and parenting for students in the senior classes at his school, lamenting the fact that the national school curriculum did not include any such program:

> For several years now we have been teaching our young men and women how to morally prepare themselves for marriage and family life, about the nature of refined human relationships, how to educate one's children. Of course teaching this important subject when there is no time allocated to it in the programme is no easy matter. But whatever the difficulties, we must overcome them, because this subject is no less important than mathematics, physics or chemistry...
>
> I hope people will not think that I am denigrating the role of mathematics and other natural sciences. Without a knowledge of these subjects it is impossible to gain entry even to the threshold of science. But knowledge of human nature is even more important. And if not in today's then in tomorrow's school curriculum a subject about the refinement of human relations will take pride of place, because we are living in the age of humanity.[19]

No doubt as a result of Sukhomlinsky's efforts and of those who thought like him, such a course was indeed introduced as a part of the educational reforms initiated in 1984. An anthology published for that course contains some of Sukhomlinsky's writing: two letters from *Letters to My Son* and several shorter quotations.[20]

Sukhomlinsky's views on family upbringing and his educational approach in general were greatly influenced by traditional practices in the Ukrainian family. His daughter suggested in conversation that many key elements in his approach—respect for grandparents and parents (especially for mothers), closeness to nature, love of music and fairy stories—have a strong Ukrainian flavour, that there is a strong folk element in his educational legacy. Sukhomlinsky's grandmother played a very significant role in his own upbringing, and he always considered that the mother was the moral authority in the family and should be respected as such. He believed that children should be involved as early as possible in work around the home. He approved of Ukrainian folk sayings about family life and ethics, such as: "The wife supports three corners of the home and the husband the fourth", or "He who does not work should not expect to eat". He also liked to repeat the moral tales his grandmother had told him to illustrate points to his students, and composed many such tales of his own.

Another aspect of his research not evident from a cursory survey of the titles of his published works concerned the education of children with severe learning difficulties, particularly those relating to poor memory. He made studies both of the causes of such learning difficulties and of the methods needed to assist such children to complete the normal school program. He had considerable practical success in this area, and a number of the children he worked with even gained entry to tertiary institutes. This aspect of his work may receive closer attention if an unpublished manuscript devoted to the subject sees the light of day.[21]

By the late 'fifties, Sukhomlinsky had become well known in educational circles and frequently received visitors and delegations at the school. He received many letters in response to his articles. He also gained considerable official recognition. In 1957 he was elected a corresponding member of the Academy of Pedagogical Sciences of the RSFSR. In 1958 he was awarded the title of Distinguished Teacher of the Ukrainian Republic, in 1960 he received the Order of Lenin and in 1965 he was awarded the Makarenko Medal. In 1968 he was elected a corresponding member of the Academy of Pedagogical Sciences of the USSR and awarded the title of Hero of Socialist Labour.[22]

With these honours came invitations to travel to other socialist countries to lecture on education. In 1961 he visited Cuba, in 1964 Bulgaria, in 1965 East Germany and in 1969 Hungary.[23]

Recognition and fame also brought with them an element of controversy. There were quite a few in the educational establishment, especially academics somewhat removed from the daily practice of teaching, who had reservations about his approach, and some went so far as to attack him in the press. Even at the time when his first monographs appeared, the use of a word like "spirituality" offended some orthodox Marxists, and his recommendation of a system of education without punishment was sometimes interpreted as a form of "non-resistance to evil". At a discussion at the RSFSR Academy of Pedagogical Sciences in 1962, Sukhomlinsky's latest publication, *The Formation of Communist Convictions in the Younger Generation*, came in for considerable criticism, and he had to defend his ideas.[24]

The most serious attack on his ideas came towards the end of his life. In 1967, following the publication in the journal *Narodnoe obrazovanie [National Education]* of a series of essays entitled "Essays on Communist Education"[25], Sukhomlinsky was taken to task in an article in *Uchitel'skaia gazeta [The Teacher's Newspaper]*. This article, entitled "We need a campaign, not a sermon"[26], was written by B.Likhachev, senior lecturer at the Department of Pedagogy and Psychology at Vologda Pedagogical Institute. He accused Sukhomlinsky of "abstract humanism", of advocating universal forgiveness, of opposing Makarenko's ideas and of laying emphasis on the individual at the expense of the collective. The editorial board of *Narodnoe Obrazovanie* were quick to spring to Sukhomlinsky's defence, accusing Likhachev of "outright distortion" of Sukhomlinsky's statements and views.[27] This controversy, which was taken up by other writers and continued well after Sukhomlinsky's death, has been dealt with in more detail in chapter seven. For the time being we shall limit ourselves to pointing out that the attacks in the press to which Sukhomlinsky was subjected in the late 'sixties must have placed additional strain on him at a time when his health was rapidly failing. Sukhomlinsky himself wrote of his reaction to Likhachev's article:

> Having read it from beginning to end, I tried to be firm with myself, to tell myself that nothing had happened, but I didn't have sufficient will power ... I can't agree that a child should be loved circumspectly, that in humanity, sensitivity, affection and warmth there is some kind of danger ... A third of a century working in schools has convinced me that ... an absolutely normal education is one without shouting, without threats ... not merely an education without punishment, but an education without the need for punishment. I firmly believe that a time will come when a human being will not know what it is to strike another human being, to insult him.[28]

Sukhomlinsky continues this passage with recollections of his wartime experience, revealing the link between his feelings of tenderness for all children and his recollection of the horrors of the war.

Overwork had compounded the health problems he faced as a result of his war injuries, and he had been hospitalised more than once since the war. Metal fragments remained in his lungs, some dangerously near his heart. In addition he suffered from kidney failure and thrombosis. In 1966 he was gravely ill, but he ignored doctors' warnings that he should rest, and set his mind on completing several major works. Nor was he prepared to give up his work as principal of Pavlysh School. That he knew his life was near its end is shown by a letter he wrote to his publisher in Kiev on October 18, 1968, quoted by Soloveichik. In it he wrote:

> Due to an incurable disease and the inevitable cessation in the near future of my educational research activities, I ask the Radianska Shkola publishing house to accept the gift of all my published works … In addition … those of my manuscripts which are completed and ready for publishing.[29]

According to Soloveichik there follows a list of 18 manuscripts. A similar letter was sent to A.E. Boim, deputy editor of *Narodnoe obrazovanie*, in 1970, as Sukhomlinsky attempted to ensure that his final, and, in his view, most important works would see the light of day. It is the works completed during his astonishingly productive last three years which have secured his reputation. They include *Pavlysh School, My Heart I Give to Children, The Birth of a Citizen, How to Educate a True Human Being, Methodology for Educating the Collective,* 100 *Pieces of Advice for Teachers, Letters to My Son* and *A Book about Love*. Most of these works were published posthumously. Another interesting work from this period which attempts a theoretical summary of his life's work is *Issues in the All-round Development of the Personality*. This was written from October 1969 to April 1970 as a report on his major works, to be defended for the degree of Doctor of Pedagogical Sciences. It would appear he did not have time to defend it before his death.

Sukhomlinsky continued working right up until his death at the start of the new school year in September, 1970. Doctors who operated on him in an attempt to save his life found his condition to be hopeless and expressed surprise that he had been able to live as long as he had, let alone work with a heart in such a condition. The operation confirmed a diagnosis of gangrene of the heart due to thrombosis. Sukhomlinsky did not regain consciousness after the operation.

The whole village turned out to honour Sukhomlinsky at his funeral and children led the procession to his grave, strewing the ground with petals. It was the stuff of which legends are made, and writers such as

V.A. Sukhomlinsky — Life and Legend

Simon Soloveichik, who did much to popularise Sukhomlinsky's ideas, made considerable use of biographical accounts to increase the impact of their articles. Biographies by Tartakovsky, Borisovsky and others presented the reading public with a more comprehensive, if eulogistic, picture of his life than could be gleaned from Sukhomlinsky's own works. Thus, the details from Sukhomlinsky's life, briefly sketched out in this chapter, lent moral authority to his ideas, and contributed in no small way to the influence which he came to enjoy.

Notes

1 "Serdtse otdaiu detiam" — Rekomendatel'nyi ukazatel' literatury o zhizni i tvorchestve V.A. Sukhomlinskogo ["My Heart I Give to Children" — A Guide to Literature about the Life and Work of V.A. Sukhomlinsky], Moscow, 1984, pp. 24,25.
2 See "Metodika vospitaniia kollektiva [Methodology for educating the Collective]", in Sukhomlinsky, V.A., Izbrannye proizvedeniia v piati tomakh [Collected Works in Five Volumes], Kiev, Radianska shkola, 1979–80, Vol. 1, p.618.
3 Sukhomlinsky, V.A., "O dobrom serdtse", Ogonek, 1963, No. 42, pp. 3–4. (Quoted in Borisovsky, A.M., V.A. Sukhomlinsky, Moscow, Prosveshchenie, 1985, p. 6.)
4 Ibid.
5 Anton Semienovich Makarenko (1888–1939) described his experience as an educator in communities for homeless youths in several widely-read books. For several decades he was regarded as the foremost authority on communist educational ideals, particularly for his formulation of principles of education through the collective.
6 from "Sto sovetov uchiteliu [100 pieces of advice for teachers]", Sukhomlinsky, V.A., Izbrannye proizvedeniia v piati tomakh [Collected Works in Five Volumes], Kiev, Radianska shkola, 1979–80, Vol. 2, p.451.
7 Tartakovsky, B.S., Povest' ob uchitele Sukhomlinskom [The Story of the Teacher Sukhomlinsky], Moscow, Molodaia gvardiia, 1972, p. 62.
8 See Chapter 7 of this study for more details.
9 Quoted in Grigoriev, K., Khandros, B., Pavlysh — prodolzhenie legendy [Pavlysh — the continuation of a legend], Moscow, Znanie, 1976, p. 13.
10 See, for instance, "Pavlyshskaia sredniaia shkola", in Sukhomlinsky, V.A., Izbrannye pedagogicheskie sochineniia v trekh tomakh [Selected pedagogical works in three volumes], Moscow, Pedagogika, 1979–81, Volume 2, pp.71–2.
11 "Pavlyshskaia sredniaia shkola", in Sukhomlinsky, V.A., Izbrannye proizvedeniia v piati tomakh [Collected Works in Five Volumes], Kiev, Radianska shkola, 1979–80, Vol. 4, p.40.
12 Ibid., p. 41.
13 Ibid.
14 See, for instance Borisovsky, A.M., V.A. Sukhomlinsky, Moscow, Prosveshchenie, 1985, pp. 36–7.

15 Sukhomlinsky, V.A., *Direktor shkoly — rukovoditel' uchebno-vospitatel'noi raboty [The school principal as a supervisor of educational work]*, Dissertation for the degree of Candidate of Pedagogical Sciences, Kiev, 1955.

16 "Serdtse otdaiu detiam [My heart I give to children]", in Sukhomlinsky, V.A., *Izbrannye proizvedeniia v piati tomakh [Collected Works in Five Volumes]*, Kiev, Radianska shkola, 1979-80, Vol. 3, p.13.

17 Soloveichik, S., "Vospitanie, vospitatel' [Education and the educator]", in Sukhomlinsky, V.A., *O vospitanii [On education]*, 6th edition, Moscow, Politizdat, 1988, p. 9.

18 See Sukhomlinsky, V.A., *Izbrannye pedagogicheskie sochineniia v trekh tomakh [Selected pedagogical works in three volumes]*, Moscow, Pedagogika, 1979-81, Volume 3, pp.395-578. (also published as Sukhomlinsky, V.A., *Mudrost' roditel'skoi liubvi [The wisdom of parental love]*, Moscow, Molodaia gvardiia, 1988.)

19 Ibid., p. 401.

20 See Grebennikov, I.V., Kovin'ko, L.V., compilers, *Krestomatiia po etike i psikhologii semeinoi zhizni [An anthology on the ethics and psychology of family life]*, Moscow, Prosveshchenie, 1986.

21 See Sukhomlinsky, V.A., "Uchitel' — sovest' naroda [The teacher is the nation's conscience]", *Narodnoe obrazovanie*, 1988, No. 9: pp. 78-9, for a list of unpublished manuscripts. (This list is included in Chapter 7 of this study.)

22 See Sukhomlinskaia, A.I., Sukhomlinskaia, O.V., *V.A. Sukhomlinsky: Biobibliografiia*, Kiev, Radianska shkola, 1987, pp.254-5.

23 Ibid.

24 See "Obsuzhdenie knigi V.A. Sukhomlinskogo 'Formirovanie kommunisticheskikh ubezhdenii molodogo pokoleniia'[Discussion of V.A. Sukhomlinsky's book 'The formation of communist convictions in the younger generation']", *Sovetskaia pedagogika*, 1962, No. 9: pp. 156-160.

25 in *Narodnoe obrazovanie*, 1967, No. 2: 38-46, No. 4: 44-50, No. 6: 37-43, No. 8: 51-56, No. 9: 28-33, No. 10: 54-59, No. 12: 40-43.

26 *Uchitel'skaia gazeta*, 18 May, 1967.

27 *Narodnoe obrazovanie*, 1967, No. 12: p. 43.

28 Quoted in Soloveichik, S., "Rasskazyvaite o Sukhomlinskom [Talk about Sukhomlinsky]", *Yunost'*, 1971, No. 3, p. 84.

29 Ibid. p. 85.

CHAPTER 2

The School at Pavlysh

"All-round Development" and "The Harmony of Educational Influences"

IN THIS chapter and the two that follow, we shall be considering the ideal of holistic education as it was manifested in Sukhomlinsky's work. The Soviet term which best corresponds to holistic education is "vsestoronnee razvitie"(all-round development). We shall examine various aspects of holistic education relating to health, moral development, intellectual development, aesthetic development and vocational development, and shall attempt to explain how these various aspects were addressed at the school in Pavlysh.

The Russian word which corresponds most closely to the English word "education" is "obrazovanie". This refers to the formal process which young people pass through at schools, colleges and universities. There is, however, another Russian word used very frequently in Soviet educational writing, and that is "vospitanie". "Vospitanie" is used when referring to preschool education and education in the family, and also when referring to those educational influences at school which effect the development of a pupil's personality and character. It was this deeper aspect of education, coexisting with the formal process of study, which was of particular concern to Sukhomlinsky. "Vospitanie" is frequently translated as "upbringing" in order to differentiate it from "obrazovanie", but in this study it has been simply rendered as "education". It frequently appears in combination with a qualifying adjective in phrases such as "moral education", "aesthetic education" and "work education". These are key concepts in Sukhomlinsky's work and he uses the word "vospitanie" far more than "obrazovanie". His use of the term also reflects the central importance of character development in Soviet educational thought.

Sukhomlinsky's most comprehensive exposition of his educational system is contained in *Pavlysh School*. While not as popular as the more lyrical *My Heart I Give to Children*, which focuses on the interaction between a teacher and his pupils, it, more than any other work, explains how the various components of his system were coordinated in an attempt to bring about the integrated development of each pupil. As he writes in the introduction, he attempted to show the work of the school "as far as possible from all angles, not only to explain the methods used, but to reveal their internal links and interdependencies."[1]

Sukhomlinsky first explains the aims and ideals of the school, and then goes on in successive chapters to examine staff organisation, the school facilities and environment, health and physical education, moral education, intellectual education, work education and aesthetic education. As we progress through his treatment of these topics it becomes evident that these various aspects of education were not addressed separately, but through an integrated approach, where the central concerns were for the health and the moral and psychological development of the child. One and the same educational activity often served many functions in educating the child and extra-curricular activities were often just as significant as formal studies.

Let us take an example typical of Sukhomlinsky's approach. A group of children is participating in an agricultural project involving soil improvement, the cultivation of a crop and plant breeding. The activity will contribute to each of the above-mentioned facets of the child's development (physical, moral, intellectual, vocational and aesthetic), provided it is well executed and takes place in a context of previous experiences which have prepared the group to gain the most from the activity.

In order for such an activity to contribute optimally to the health and physical development of each child, it should take place in a context where general measures have already been taken to ensure sound health (what this entailed at Sukhomlinsky's school we shall see later), and in an atmosphere of emotional uplift so as to be enjoyed as if it were a sport. Sukhomlinsky viewed both work and sport as means of physical education:

> Physical work plays just as important a role in the development of physical perfection as sport ... There are many work procedures in which the harmonious, graceful, coordinated movements of the human body may be compared to gymnastic exercises ... (cutting hay by hand, the laying of brick walls). Young people perform such physical work with great pleasure, especially in a group.[2]

Such a statement is in the Tolstoyan tradition of the nobility of simple labour. Sukhomlinsky also suggests that if such work is combined with camping in the open air, with the pleasures of campfires and of sleeping in hay under the open sky, it contributes even more to health. (Sukhomlinsky was nothing if not a romantic.)

In order for the activity to contribute effectively to moral education, a context of previous involvement in socially useful work is required. From their earliest years children should be given many experiences of finding joy in work. This work could be anything from helping one's mother around the house to tending to a sick animal or collecting seed for the local collective farm. It should also take place against a background of making children aware that the good things of life enjoyed by them are the result of the unseen labour of countless people. This context is necessary to give the activity moral significance in the child's consciousness.

To contribute to intellectual development our agricultural activity requires a context in which students have thought about the natural and technical processes involved and can relate their practical work to scientific and theoretical issues of interest to them. It does not much matter whether these issues are part of the school curriculum. Sukhomlinsky thought that one of the best ways to make study easier was for students to read widely and to extend their interests far beyond the curriculum. Work activities, in his experience, were one of the best ways to stimulate such wider interests.

Work education, in Sukhomlinsky's view, is inseparable from moral and intellectual education. We might say, however, that our hypothetical activity is contributing optimally to work education as such if it gives all students confidence in the basic work skills involved and allows some students to uncover special skills and talents which indicate a possible vocation. To uncover their unique talents students need to be exposed to a great variety of work activities.

Finally, the activity will contribute to the aesthetic education of the children if they have been educated from an early age to appreciate the beauty in nature, in physical work gracefully executed, and in human relationships founded on mutual ideals.

This dependence of the effectiveness of an educational activity upon the educational context in which it occurs is a recurrent theme in Sukhomlinsky's work. In *My Heart I Give to Children* he writes:

> Discussion of the lives of particular children and their fates led us to the issue of *the harmony of educational influences*… The essence of this concept, which expresses one of the most important laws of education, is as follows: The educational effect of each means of influencing the personality depends on how well thought through, well-directed and effective all the other means are …
>
> … Between educational influences there exist tens, hundreds, thousands of interdependencies and conditioning relationships. The effectiveness of education in the final analysis is determined by how these interdependencies and conditioning relationships … work out in practice.[3]

The ramifications of this idea are far-reaching. It is not enough for a teacher to conduct recommended activities competently. The teacher's efforts will only be effective if the children's previous experiences have prepared them for those activities.[4] This is patently obvious in academic disciplines such as mathematics, but not so clear in an area such as character development.

Moreover, despite the obvious need for educational activities to be carefully sequenced, staffing procedures often hamper continuity of educational practice. It is often the case (particularly in schools run by the state) that procedures for promoting staff to positions with greater responsibility and higher salaries encourage staff to change schools. This works against stability and continuity within schools, conditions necessary for ensuring that teachers adopt a long term perspective on the child's development. For this reason it may be difficult for a government school to develop a coherent philosophy and set of policies. While the principal's tenure may be lengthy, he or she generally has little say in choosing staff, who are constantly changing.[5] We shall return to this issue of continuity when we come to consider staffing at Sukhomlinsky's school.

In *Pavlysh School*, then, Sukhomlinsky attempted to describe an integrated system of education aimed at the all-round development of the personality. The many aspects of the process of education were seen to form an organic whole, just as the many petals of a flower form one whole:

> Studies are just one of the petals of that flower which we call education in the wider sense. In education there is nothing major or minor, just as there is no main petal among the many petals which create the beauty of a flower. In education everything is important—the lessons, the development of diverse interests outside lessons, and the relationships between students in the group.[6]

The Aims and Philosophy of Pavlysh School

Sukhomlinsky opens *Pavlysh School* with a discussion of aims. He was a committed member of the Communist Party and he takes the Party guidelines on education as his starting point. The concept of "the all-round development of personality" and the "moral code of the builder of communism" are central to his discussion, though he does offer a fairly elaborate interpretation of these guidelines.

As in *Issues in the all-round development of the personality*,[7] he suggests that moral values must be central to any ideal of all-round development. He highlights the orientation towards the future that is implicit in any educational endeavour. He suggests that the school should prepare a person for a lifetime of work, study and social activity, and that to achieve this goal it is necessary to instil moral values, a love of work and a thirst for knowledge. Any attempt to cram too much information into the heads of pupils may create an aversion to learning and be counterproductive in the long run, and an approach which relies on words more than on deeds may encourage hypocrisy.

The life of the school should prepare pupils for all the responsibilities of adult life, and, according to Sukhomlinsky, this is best done if the school is a microcosm incorporating many features of adult life, the most important of which are productive work and responsibility for others. It is in the marriage of productive work and intellectual endeavour—both harnessed to the social good—that Sukhomlinsky sees the basis of happiness. The ultimate aim is to educate future builders of communism, an ideal which, in his mind, conjures up quite concrete images.

In *Letters to My Son*[8] Sukhomlinsky describes his vision of the future communist person. He thought that certain individuals with whom he was acquainted were already living according to the ideals of communism and demonstrating what it meant to be a "builder of communism". He considered that a communist was someone who found the meaning of life in working for the common good. He cites the example of an acquaintance who spends his spare time growing grapes, distributing the fruit and cuttings to the many children and adults who frequently visit him. He is regarded by the villagers as somewhat of a crank for not selling his produce, but is well loved, in contrast to another enthusiastic grape grower who protects his crop with barbed wire and dogs and has grown rich on his sales. Another positive example cited by Sukhomlinsky is that of a man who spends all his summer working with children. His home has become a recreational centre where children come and "build radio sets, play, sing and learn to play the violin." In Sukhomlinsky's glowing vision of communism, kindness will be the most important characteristic of the person of the future:

> Under communism a person will, in my opinion, above all be kind. Sensitivity towards another human being, an inner need for human fellowship—that, in my view, will be the main quality of the person of the future. A deep personal concern that every person, each fellow citizen, should be spiritually rich, endowed with moral beauty, intelligent, industrious. An ability to value, respect and love the the most valuable thing in our life—a human being.[9]

Conversely, the greatest vices in Sukhomlinsky's eyes are inhumanity, indifference to others, cruelty. These, he acknowledges, are still rife in Soviet society, despite the official view that the social conditions giving rise to cruelty no longer exist. He lays the blame on poor upbringing and feels that unless this is corrected communism will remain a dream.[10]

In trying to educate future builders of communism, Sukhomlinsky thought it of critical importance that children should very early learn to find joy in work:

> We have made the following rule the basis of our educational work: a child must find joy in work, in enriching his or her knowledge, in creating things of material and psychological value for people, for our socialist society.[11]

Study was seen as a form of work, and in order for students to find joy in study, teachers were expected to be considerate in their methods of instruction and assessment. Children were never to be made to feel that they were incapable of success. Very young children were never to be given a failing grade (1 or 2 on the Soviet scale). If they had not reached the required standard, no grade would be awarded; instead they would be given more time to master the material. Also, bearing in mind the variation in abilities, the effort made by the child, and not only the level of achievement, was to be taken into account. A positive attitude to study was in itself considered to be the best guarantee that a child would perform at the highest possible level.

Even more important for Sukhomlinsky than the joy which accompanies success, was that based on feelings of mutual concern and affection:

> In our view the joy of work and the interest in work, comes from the maintenance of deeply humane relations between young workers, where the prime motivating principle in the work is the creation of happiness and joy for individuals and for society. It is this which imparts to life a higher morality.[12]

There should be a reciprocal relationship between word and deed. Stories of heroism or of selfless activity should be accompanied by practical opportunities for students to practise altruistic deeds. If feelings are stirred by tales of noble deeds and the student has no practical outlet for those feelings, the result is what Sukhomlinsky calls a "blank shot".[13] The more of these "blank shots" students experience, the less ideas will stir them to action and the more insensitive they will become to the teacher's influence.

Sukhomlinsky was aware of the ineffectiveness of the noisy slogans and empty talk which passed for moral education in many Soviet schools during his time, and which persisted until the demise of the Soviet Union. The gulf between word and deed which was for so long a part of public life in the Soviet Union was no doubt responsible for much of the widespread cynicism and apathy which had developed by the 'eighties.

These issues were not unique to Soviet education. Educators in the West also have had occasion to ponder the effects of an almost exclusive emphasis on words and intellect in moral education. Jonathan Kozol criticised American schools for involving children in lengthy discussions of moral and social issues, while often discouraging them from acting on conclusions reached. The result, in his view, was to produce highly articulate people who failed to act on their expressed convictions. A cathartic effect was experienced when a problem had been diagnosed and a (possibly radical) solution suggested, but no action followed.[14]

Sukhomlinsky and his staff endeavoured to ensure that from the time children began to attend school they were involved in practical activities which enriched the lives of their family and friends. It was a tradition at the school that during their first year children planted an apple tree for each member of their family. After caring for the trees over a period of years they brought the first fruit which the trees bore to their mother or father, brother or sister.

Sukhomlinsky believed that the most effective character education was that which resulted from close cooperation between school and family. During the early years of Khrushchev's leadership, there had been moves to expand the system of boarding schools and reduce the role of the family in education. Sukhomlinsky, with his very traditional views of family life, found such moves completely unacceptable.[15] He did feel, however, that the school should play a role in advising parents on how best to educate their children. At his school this was effected principally through twice-monthly seminars held for parents. These addressed issues of developmental psychology and family life. They were for parents of pupils-to-be as well as for those of existing pupils, since Sukhomlinsky and his staff regarded the preschool years as critical in the child's physical, moral, intellectual and aesthetic development.[16]

Given Sukhomlinsky's emphasis on the importance of work in the all-round development of personality and as a foundation for the individual's happiness, it is natural that one of the goals his school set was to help each child to find a vocation, to discover where his or her greatest talents lay:

We view our task as being to ensure that each of our students in adolescence and early youth consciously finds themselves, discovers themselves, selects that path in life where their work can attain the highest degree of mastery — creativity. The key to achieving this is to discern in each child their greatest strength, to find that 'golden vein' from which can flow individual development, to ensure that the child achieves outstanding success for its age in that activity which most clearly expresses and reveals its natural talents.[17]

As will be seen later, an extremely important factor in attempting to realise this goal was a very extensive array of extra-curricular activities from which children could choose. Because of the importance attached to these activities and to stimulating an impulse towards self-education, the staff adopted a rule that children should have at least as much free time to pursue their own interests as they spent in classes at school.

Sukhomlinsky maintained that there is no real education without self-education. The impulse to educate oneself was considered important both in order to release the student's maximum potential while at school and also to ensure that education did not end when schooling ended. It was considered that the rapid changes in work practices and lifestyle brought about by the scientific and technological revolution meant that study must become a lifetime habit. Perhaps of even greater significance to Sukhomlinsky was the intrinsic value of continued intellectual and cultural endeavour for a person's quality of life and sense of self-worth. He often defended the place in the school syllabus of subjects which in all likelihood would have no application in the workplace. He felt that students should be able to study subjects such as astronomy, foreign languages or literature for their intrinsic interest and because in some sense they enabled a person to become more fully human.

Another aspect of the school's educational philosophy was a strong emphasis on the education of feelings. Sukhomlinsky believed that all education had an emotional as well as an intellectual component, since children related both objectively and subjectively to what they learned. Sensitivity and empathy were key qualities to be developed:

> A genuine human being is unthinkable without kindly feelings. Education, in essence, begins with the development of personal sensitivity — the ability to respond with heart, thoughts and feelings

to everything which happens in the world around us. Personal sensitivity provides a general background for harmonious development, against which any human quality—intelligence, industry, talent—acquires its true meaning, finds its most vibrant expression.[18]

The basis of emotional education lay in the child's relationships with family and friends. Attitudes of care and concern, qualities of empathy and sympathy had their basis in these primary relationships. Where the family did not provide the necessary nurturing relationships, the school —teacher and classmates—should attempt to make up the deficit. For Sukhomlinsky this was the great power of the "collective"—to provide a milieu which nurtured the individual, refined the emotions and stimulated the intellect. From these primary relationships with family and friends were developed wider feelings of concern for others in the village, in the nation as a whole and in the world at large.

In giving priority to the character-forming and moral ends of education, Sukhomlinsky found that in consequence academic goals were more easily achievable. As his concern was primarily to develop attitudes such as dutifulness, empathy, care, industry and love of learning, and as for him it was intolerable to in any way demoralise students who applied themselves conscientiously, his pupils had an exceptionally high success rate in their studies. He maintained that all children other than those with severe mental retardation were capable of completing secondary school:

> The power and potential of education are inexhaustible. All children without exception, as long as they have no pathological defects in intellectual development, may successfully complete secondary education … The school's task is not only to give each the knowledge necessary for a vocation and worthwhile social activity, but also to give each happiness in their own inner life.[19]

Sukhomlinsky and his staff endeavoured to organise the life of the school in such a way that no students should feel that they were lacking in ability. In the case of students who could not excel in studies, every effort was made to find some activity in which they could excel: grafting fruit trees for example, or electronics.[20] Success in such activities gave the confidence needed to overcome difficulties in studies. The result was that almost the only children who needed to repeat a year

School Year	Number of Children at the School	Had to Repeat Year	Illness the Cause of Repeating (2-4 months)	Success rate as %
1955/56	418	15	12	96.5
1956/57	406	14	12	96.6
1957/58	407	9	6	97.8
1958/59	422	6	4	98.5
1959/60	463	6	5	98.7
1960/61	477	5	4	99.0
1961/62	516	4	3	99.3
1962/63	560	3	3	99.5
1963/64	614	3	2	99.6
1964/65	640	2	2	99.8
1965/66	630	4	3	99.4
1966/67	570	2	2	99.7

of study were those who had been ill for extended periods. The figures above are taken from the introduction to *Pavlysh School*.[21]

It might be suggested that such figures are merely a manifestation of "percentomania" (the practice of always passing about 98% of pupils in order to avoid criticism of teaching standards) and that any school in the Soviet Union could produce similar figures. However, given the degree of scrutiny to which Pavlysh became subjected, and the enthusiastic responses of thousands of visitors, it seems likely that they are no mere smokescreen. There is further evidence suggesting a high level of scholastic achievement at Pavlysh. According to figures supplied by Sukhomlinsky, 64.7% of pupils graduating from Pavlysh between 1949 and 1966 went on to study in universities and other higher educational institutions—an exceptionally high rate for any school, but especially for a rural one.[22]

The figures raise another issue addressed at Pavlysh Secondary School—that of the health of the students. Sukhomlinsky believed that this was the single most important factor influencing success in studies, and, as will be seen shortly, very considerable efforts were made to ensure that all children enjoyed good health.

The Staff at Pavlysh

Having discussed the aims and philosophy of his school in the introduction to *Pavlysh School*, Sukhomlinsky turns, in the first chapter of that book, to a discussion of the staff and how they cooperated to try and achieve the school's aims. Topics examined include the role of the principal, the qualities of a good teacher, staff organisation and the role of the school council, the need for stability and continuity of staffing, the importance of staff health, the need to ensure that teachers have sufficient free time, how to provide all pupils with individual attention (what we might call "pastoral care"), and cooperation between staff and parents.

Sukhomlinsky felt that the most important consideration in managing the staff of a school is to ensure that they have a rich intellectual and cultural life themselves, that their approach is constantly being renewed through study, research and cultural activities. Only by living such a life themselves can they inspire their students with a love of learning:

> Education in the broad sense is the constant spiritual enrichment and renewal both of those who are educated and of those who educate …
>
> … The experience of many years shows that a most important condition for the all-round development of the children is that the intellectual life of the staff should be rich and varied, [characterised by] diverse interests, breadth of outlook, keen investigation, sensitivity to new developments in science and scholarship.[23]

Teachers set the tone of the school through their interest and enthusiasm and win the respect of their students through their erudition. Sukhomlinsky repeated in several different works the idea that teachers need to know many times more than what is on the school syllabus and should endeavour to keep abreast of latest developments both in their own discipline and in educational thought. He himself, as principal, made sure he was familiar with all subjects taught at the school and kept a file on each discipline, where he kept articles from newspapers and journals concerning latest developments. In this way he was in a position to discuss each teacher's subject with them, and to stimulate a process of exchange between teachers, who were encouraged to give talks to the staff on innovations in their field.

Sukhomlinsky believed that the most precious thing for a teacher was free time. This was needed in order to rest from the heavy mental and emotional demands placed on teachers, in order to read, and in order to spend time informally with children in interest groups. There was a strict rule at his school that a teacher should not attend staff meetings of any nature on more than one day of the week.[24] Soviet teachers frequently had very heavy demands placed on them outside normal school hours. They were expected to attend meetings, visit parents, conduct extra-curricular activities and supervise work brigades during school holidays. In the context of common practices—particularly in village schools—Sukhomlinsky's efforts to ensure that teachers had sufficient rest and recreation were quite significant. Another rule observed at his school was that apart from two months' annual leave teachers were to have at least twenty days' rest per year during other holiday times.[25]

Sukhomlinsky felt it was very important that the staff achieved a high degree of cooperation and were collectively responsible for each child's welfare. He expected each teacher to know every child in the school by name. It was an article of faith with him that no child was a hopeless case, and it was not uncommon for a staff meeting to devote time to discussion of problems faced by an individual child. An effort would be made to find out which of the teachers were best able to relate to the child—often through having some hobby or interest in common.

Staff meetings were generally devoted to educational rather than administrative issues. (Sukhomlinsky himself tried to limit his involvement in economic management and maintenance to fifteen minutes per day in discussion with the bursar.) Sometimes a discussion of teaching methods would generate a wave of interest in a particular theme and stimulate what Sukhomlinsky called "collective research", where the staff as a whole experimented with an idea and pooled experience. This collective approach was only possible if teachers individually had a high level of interest and enthusiasm:

> When each teacher day after day goes ever deeper into the details and subtleties of the education process, analysing their work and the men-

tal work of their pupils, there is, figuratively speaking, a kindling of living thought among the staff ... [26]

In such a climate one teacher's idea could initiate a wave of experimentation:

> An idea inspires the staff and there begins the most interesting and necessary thing in the life of the school—collective research.[27]

While Sukhomlinsky no doubt played a leading role in stimulating this process, it would seem that all the staff worked collectively to develop the educational theory and practice which is described in his books. The frequent use of the first person plural in his work expresses this collective "we" and is not merely a stylistic device. When he wishes to refer to himself in the singular he does not hesitate to do so.

Sukhomlinsky was proud of the way his staff worked together and felt that the degree of cooperation they achieved, and the resulting atmosphere at the school, were only possible if there were stability and continuity of staffing. At the time of writing *Pavlysh School* there were thirty-five teachers on the staff, twenty-five of whom had been there for ten years or more. Eight had been there for more than twenty years, though the average age of the staff was only thirty-nine.[28] Approximately half the children at the school had parents who had been educated there. In the light of these figures it is not so surprising that teachers were expected to know every child. The moderate size of the school (around 500 in years 1 to 10) was also significant in this respect.

It was a common practice in the Soviet Union for teachers to visit the homes of children shortly before they commenced school. At Pavlysh, parents attended courses on child education for two years before their children commenced school. At the age of four, children in the area were given a medical examination so that there would be time to address any health problems before their admission to the school.[29] Responsibility for overseeing these medical examinations lay with the school council, which was made up of all the teachers, seven parent representatives, a doctor and supervisors of various functions associated with the school (library, after school program, etc.).

Another of the functions of the school council was to elect the principal—an unusual practice, as appointment to this post was normally effected by the local office of the education department. During the period of *glasnost'*, with moves towards the "democratisation" of Soviet society, election to such positions by subordinates became increasingly common.[30]

As well as introducing the practice of electing the principal, Sukhomlinsky obtained the unusual privilege of being able to appoint teachers to the school, thus ensuring that the spirit and philosophy of the school could be maintained.[31] Demands on teachers at the school were high, but Sukhomlinsky felt that there were sufficient people in the community with the potential to be good teachers if one sought them out.

He looked for four main attributes in teachers. Firstly, and most importantly, they should like children, enjoy their company, empathise with them and have faith in their innate potential for goodness. Secondly, they should be in love with their subject and keep abreast of latest developments in it. Thirdly, they should be well versed in psychology and educational thought, and fourthly they should have some work skill which they could pass on to children. (The last requirement shows the exceptional importance which Sukhomlinsky attached to work education within the school.) He did not expect teachers just commencing work at the school to be masters of their craft, but they should have at least the potential to develop the above four attributes:

> A teacher's didactic and methodological inexperience is no cause for alarm; gaps in knowledge are not either, if a person is industrious and has a thirst for knowledge … If, however, the teacher has no faith in the child, if he becomes depressed and disillusioned at the slightest failure, if he is convinced that nothing will come of the child, he has no business to be in a school: he will only torment the children and himself be tormented throughout his life.[32]

During a period of twenty years, Sukhomlinsky writes, five teachers had agreed to withdraw from the school on the recommendation of the school council. Presumably Sukhomlinsky had the deciding voice, though he insists that such a decision would not come into force unless it was unanimous and agreed to by the teacher concerned. He also maintains that in each of the five cases the teachers found another vocation more to their liking.

An acknowledged problem in Soviet schools was the absence of men in the teaching profession. Sukhomlinsky considered it important that there be a reasonable balance between male and female staff members and thought it preferable that teachers have children of their own. At Pavlysh at the time of writing there were fifteen men and twenty women teachers and all but two had families. Many of his staff had started teaching at an early age (the most senior at 17–20 years) and subsequently upgraded their qualifications through external studies.

Pastoral care was effected through the normal system of class teachers, but, perhaps more importantly, also through the many interest groups which teachers conducted with children. There were approximately 45 of these groups devoted to a variety of activities such as creative writing, science fiction literature, plant breeding, mechanics, local geography, electronics and nature conservation.[33] Sukhomlinsky considered these groups particularly important for children who were withdrawn or alienated or who experienced difficulties with their studies. The key role of these groups was to kindle an interest which would awaken the student's creativity and sense of discovery. This interest would also form a basis for forming friendships with other students and with teachers, a teacher who was regarded as a friend being in a position to help a child in difficulty. Often the interest in some club or activity also stimulated interest in reading and had a beneficial influence on studies.

Problems with "difficult children" generally could be traced to problems in the family. Sukhomlinsky returned repeatedly to this issue, convinced that the school had a responsibility to educate parents — present and future. The twice-monthly discussions for parents were conducted by the principal and by senior teachers. They were divided into five groups according to the age of the children under discussion: Preschool (aged 5–7), Grades 1 and 2, Grades 3 and 4, Grades 5–7, and Grades 8–10. Over a period of twelve years parents attended a course of 250 hours' duration, covering topics related to developmental psychology and education, family relations, values and lifestyle.

"Everybody should study pedagogy", wrote Sukhomlinsky, and as well as conducting courses for school parents he made time in senior classes for discussion of parenthood and family life.[34] He complained at having to steal time from other subjects for this purpose, as he thought that a course on family life should be part of the regular curriculum. In this, as on several other issues, he foreshadowed the educational reforms of 1984.

Sukhomlinsky concludes his discussion of the staff at Pavlysh with a description of the traditions which grew up during the previous 20 years as a result of the stability and continuity in staffing and overall philosophy. Various celebrations and rites were associated with the beginning and end of the school year, with the changing of the seasons, harvest times, and public holidays. These traditions were aimed at generating reverence for study and work, family and school.

The School Environment and Facilities

Sukhomlinsky turns from the staff to an examination of the material base of the school, its buildings, grounds and environment. It is a hallmark of his approach that nothing is considered unimportant. Everything that surrounds children educates them, "from the equipment in the physics laboratory to the toilets".[35]

In order to understand the importance Sukhomlinsky placed on the environment in which children were educated, it is helpful to turn to some comments he made in *The Birth of a Citizen*. In it he talks of two sources of education: conscious and unconscious. On the one hand there are intentional educational activities, and on the other hand the unintentional, though constant influence of the total environment —physical and social—which is all the more potent for being unconscious. The unconscious impact of the environment has the power to completely undermine conscious educational efforts. If, for example, the physical environment bespeaks carelessness and neglect, if the attitudes and habits of the people surrounding the child fall far short of those which the teacher wishes to instil, then the teacher has an uphill battle:

> ... in everything that surrounds a child (not only people, but also objects and phenomena), it sees, in a materialised form, human attitudes, judgments, habits and intentions.[36]

The minutiae of daily life, like fine dust, penetrate into the depths of children's consciousness. This constant flow of information is organised by the unconscious and gives rise to what Sukhomlinsky calls "social instincts".[37] To illustrate this point, he describes a scene in the school canteen, where many small incidents witnessed by the children make nonsense of the outward forms of courtesy which they are required to observe. The children's ritual "thank you" addressed to the kitchen staff is not even heard, as the staff are being berated by a sanitary inspector. Here, instead of a "harmony of educational influences" we have what Sukhomlinsky calls "dissonance":

> The sharper the dissonance between the planned, intended means of education and those unplanned influences which provide a setting for the formation of a person's social instincts, the harder it is to form what we call in practice the *voice of conscience* … A conscience is unthinkable without a constant accumulation in the subconscious of information about noble human conduct.[38]

Sukhomlinsky worked to remove this dissonance by actively involving children in improving the environment in which they were educated, both at school and at home, by employing them in the *creation* of an optimum environment:

> In order to create a harmony between the two sources of education [elemental/spontaneous and planned/intended] it is necessary to direct the pupils' activity towards the creation of circumstances, the creation of an environment, which might reinforce the action of the planned, intended means of education.[39]

The school thus took on a reforming role in the community. The children became examples to each other through their efforts to transform their environment. The school became an example to the community and the children carried its influence into the home. It is in the light of such attitudes that we should consider the school facilities developed at Pavlysh.

Pavlysh Secondary School was situated on approximately five hectares of slightly hilly ground on the edge of the town. The grounds were surrounded by forest, by the fields of the collective farm and, to the south, by the river Omel'nik, a small tributary of the Dnieper which had been dammed at that point to create a reservoir. Sukhomlinsky describes the role of the pupils' work in improving the grounds and the surrounding countryside:

> Our children's efforts … have, in the space of a relatively short time —two decades—significantly changed and transformed the sur-

rounding environment. During these twenty years we have converted 40 hectares of infertile clay soil into lush meadows and flowering orchards.[40]

As well as providing an arena in which the children could develop their attitudes, values and talents, this transformation of the environment was aimed at providing optimum conditions for health and aesthetic development. Great emphasis was laid on ensuring that the vegetation surrounding the school was abundant and included those species which, in Sukhomlinsky's view, had the most beneficial influence upon the air the children breathed:

> In the organism of a child who breathes air saturated with the oxygen of forest and field the metabolism is activated, preventing illness. For our part, we do everything we can to ensure that the air is enriched with phytoncides which kill microorganisms. The school grounds are luxuriant with plantings of nut, cherry, apricot, chestnut and fir trees — they are particularly good sources of phytoncides; in a hazelnut grove, for instance, there are never any flies. All of this has been created by our children's hands, and may be created in any school.[41]

According to the *Great Soviet Encyclopaedia*[42], phytoncides are biologically active substances secreted by plants and capable of suppressing the vital activity of microorganisms and insects. Their potency varies from one plant species to another, with garlic, onion and horseradish producing particularly potent forms. Eucalypts and conifers are among the species which produce large quantities. The action of phytoncides may render the air in a coniferous forest practically sterile (200–300 bacterial cells per cubic metre).

Sukhomlinsky goes on to describe how the vegetation around the school gives rise to a specific micro-climate, and the beneficial influence this has on the health of the children. There is a common perception that living in the countryside is healthy, but Sukhomlinsky's approach is noteworthy for the degree to which he consciously used various plants and trees to create a healthy environment, and for the degree to which he utilised the children's energies in transforming the environment. He thought that all schools could apply these methods:

> One can't help thinking that the school of the future should fully utilise all nature's gifts and all means of ensuring that nature serves

human interests, in order to further the harmonious development of human beings.[43]

Sukhomlinsky shows a sensitivity to aesthetic and psychological considerations in the layout of the school grounds. He rejects the common practice of having a large open school yard, writing that "a school does not need a huge yard, from which the wind carries clouds of dust in at the windows".[44] Instead he favours grounds which are broken up by trees and shrubs into many small clearings, dotted with flowers. His is a design not for noisy crowds, but for smaller, more intimate groups or for individuals seeking a place for quiet reflection. Most school principals would avoid such a layout because of the difficulty it would present for supervising all the children, but this was not considered a problem at Pavlysh, where an extraordinary degree of trust existed between teachers and students. There was in fact an unwritten law that certain areas were not to be intruded upon by teachers:

> Each corner [of the school grounds] belongs by tradition to a particular age group. The youngest children frequent the grape bower; the year-eight pupils love the roses and hollyhocks; among the weeping willows is the alley of youth. We, the teachers, carefully protect the right of adolescents and young people to privacy, to that which is deeply personal, intimate and untouchable. A teacher considers it tactless to go to an area which has become a traditional place of retreat for senior pupils. In gratitude for this the senior pupils also guard our right to peaceful rest and solitude. In the school grounds there are a few nooks which pupils never visit ... All of this has come about not in consequence of some special agreement, but of itself.[45]

Such a degree of trust and emotional maturity was not reached overnight. Tartakovsky describes Sukhomlinsky's first attempt to build a glass house at the school and how panels were frequently smashed by children.[46] It required a great deal of perseverance by Sukhomlinsky and his staff to reach a point where it was no longer necessary to replace broken panes of glass or restore vandalised trees and flower beds. During those early years Sukhomlinsky regarded the greenhouse as a symbol of the health of the school. A broken pane was a sign of malaise. Behind the glowing picture which Sukhomlinsky paints of his school in the late 'sixties was twenty years of tenacious application to improving human relationships within the school.

Buildings were positioned and used in such a way as to reduce to a minimum the bedlam associated with school yards and which Sukhomlinsky considered so wearing on young children's nerves. The secondary section (years 5–10) was housed in the main building, which had been built before the revolution, and the primary classes were housed in three smaller buildings, linked to the main building by covered walk-ways. As well as being linked to the main building, these smaller buildings opened outwards on to grassed play areas, a feature which removed the necessity for the youngest children to jostle with older children during breaks. This facilitated the adjustment of young children to school life, as initially they mixed with a comparatively small group of children within their own building. Only gradually were they drawn into the larger school community.

The four buildings in which classes took place were in themselves nothing out of the ordinary. The main building had been built before the revolution to house a school run by the local *zemstvo* (a prerevolutionary form of local council). Many rooms were allocated special functions. These included a mathematics room, a music room, a literature room, a foreign languages room, a radio room (the school had its own radio station for broadcasts within the school), a photographic laboratory, reading rooms, a quiet room (for reading and reflection) and a room for parents. Wide use was made of visual displays and stands of a thought-provoking nature, posters, placards and students' art work. Students were responsible for most of the cleaning, a task made considerably easier by a procedure which ensured that children entered the school only after their shoes were thoroughly wiped.

Surrounding these four buildings were a number of other structures — mostly built by, or with the participation of, the students — where various specialist activities were carried on. We have already mentioned the importance Sukhomlinsky attached to providing a wide variety of vocational and other extra-curricular activities. Some 30 or 40 metres from the main corpus was a building housing physics, chemistry, biology and soil laboratories, and workshops for mechanics, electronics, woodwork and metalwork. Adjoining this building was a structure housing electricity generators and a small "foundry" and "smithy". Nearly all the equipment in these various rooms was made by the teachers and students. Sufficient metal-working lathes were produced to meet the needs of other schools as well as their own.

Another building housed the school library and several workshops. One feature of the workshops was the provision of miniature tools and lathes, fitted with special safety devices, for the younger children. Activity groups accommodated a variety of ages so that younger children could learn from older children, and older children had the responsibility of guiding youngsters. This facilitated the early detection of special talents which might lead to a vocation. An orchard, a vineyard, greenhouses, hot-beds, experimental plots, an apiary and a rabbit farm were also situated in the school grounds and provided opportunities for a variety of work and study activities. A small section of a nearby dairy farm was used by students for work experience.

A hall for drama and films was built in the northern part of the grounds and beyond it was a sports area. In the western section of the grounds was a shed where building materials were prepared for use by the school and next to it was a small weather station. There was a small "factory" where the children produced fertiliser for use on experimental grain crops. Seed was produced for the local collective farm. A nursery produced fruit trees, half of which were distributed free of charge to families, amateur gardeners and other schools, the other half being sold to raise money for school equipment. A garage housed two cars and two tractors, which belonged to the school. Another smaller garage housed two miniature cars built by one of the school clubs for the younger children. Significantly, the principal's flat was located in the main school building, reflecting Sukhomlinsky's total involvement in the school.

In summary, we might say that key features of the school's material base were: an accent on naturally beautiful and health-giving surroundings, a wide range of facilities to ensure a variety of work experiences, maximum involvement of the students in creating and maintaining the school's material base, and attention to small details, reflecting an awareness of the subconscious influence of the environment on character formation.

Notes

1. Sukhomlinsky, V.A., "Pavlyshskaia sredniaia shkola", *Izbrannye proizvedeniia v piati tomakh [Collected Works in Five Volumes]*, Kiev, Radianska shkola, 1979-80, Vol. 4, p. 7.
2. Ibid., p. 144.
3. Sukhomlinsky, V.A., *Izbrannye pedagogicheskie sochineniia v trekh tomakh [Selected pedagogical works in three volumes]*, Moscow, Pedagogika, 1979-81, Vol. 1, p.235.
4. See Sukhomlinsky, V.A., "Problemy vospitaniia vsestoronne razvitoi lichnosti", *Izbrannye proizvedeniia v piati tomakh [Collected Works in Five Volumes]*, Kiev, Radianska shkola, 1979-80, Vol. 1, p.77.
5. The author of this book taught at one school in Australia where a new building was constructed to house most of the school's 600 children. It was designed on an "open plan" principle, in accordance with the philosophy of teaching espoused by the staff at the time of planning. Unfortunately, by the time the building was completed the complexion of the staff had changed, and the building was regarded by most teachers as a liability.
6. Sukhomlinsky, V.A., "Serdtse otdaiu detiam", *Izbrannye proizvedeniia v piati tomakh [Collected Works in Five Volumes]*, Kiev, Radianska shkola, 1979-80, Vol. 3, p.13.
7. Sukhomlinsky, V.A., "Problemy vospitaniia vsestoronne razvitoi lichnosti", *Izbrannye proizvedeniia v piati tomakh [Collected Works in Five Volumes]*, Kiev, Radianska shkola, 1979-80, Vol. 1, p. 78.
8. Sukhomlinsky, V.A., *Pis'ma k synu*, 2nd edition, Moscow, Prosveshchenie, 1987, p. 116.
9. Ibid., p. 117.
10. Ibid., p. 118-119.
11. Sukhomlinsky, V.A., "Pavlyshskaia sredniaia shkola", *Izbrannye proizvedeniia v piati tomakh [Collected Works in Five Volumes]*, Kiev, Radianska shkola, 1979-80, Vol. 4, p. 9.
12. Ibid., p. 10.
13. Ibid., p. 12.
14. Kozol, J., *The Night is Dark and I Am Far from Home*, Boston, 1975.
15. See Sukhomlinsky, V.A., "K voprosu ob organizatsii shkol-internatov [On the question of the organisation of boarding schools]", *Sovetskaia pedagogika*, 1988, No. 12, pp. 82-88.
16. Sukhomlinsky, V.A., "Pavlyshskaia sredniaia shkola", *Izbrannye proizvedeniia v piati tomakh [Collected Works in Five Volumes]*, Kiev, Radianska shkola, 1979-80, Vol. 4, p. 13.
17. Ibid., p. 19.
18. Ibid., p. 25.
19. Ibid., p. 15.
20. Ibid., p. 29.
21. Ibid., p. 30.
22. Ibid., pp. 340/341.
23. Ibid., p. 53.
24. Ibid., p. 77.

25 Ibid., p. 71.
26 Ibid., p. 78.
27 Ibid.
28 Ibid., p. 54.
29 Ibid., p. 70.
30 See "Shkola — nasha nadezhda [The school is our hope]", *Pravda*, 1 September, 1988, p. 1.
31 Sukhomlinsky, V.A., "Pavlyshskaia sredniaia shkola", *Izbrannye proizvedeniia v piati tomakh [Collected Works in Five Volumes]*, Kiev, Radianska shkola, 1979-80, Vol. 4, p. 53.
32 Ibid., pp. 55/56.
33 Ibid., p. 342.
34 Ibid., p. 45.
35 Sukhomlinsky, V.A., "Rozhdenie grazhdanina", *Izbrannye pedagogicheskie sochineniia v trekh tomakh [Selected pedagogical works in three volumes]*, Moscow, Pedagogika, 1979-81, Vol. 1, p. 287.
36 Ibid., p. 281.
37 Ibid., p. 282/283.
38 Ibid., p. 283.
39 Ibid.
40 Sukhomlinsky, V.A., "Pavlyshskaia sredniaia shkola", *Izbrannye proizvedeniia v piati tomakh [Collected Works in Five Volumes]*, Kiev, Radianska shkola, 1979-80, Vol. 4, p. 96.
41 Ibid., p. 95.
42 *Bol'shaia sovetskaia entsiklopediia*, 3rd edition, Moscow, 1977, Vol. 27, p. 475.
43 Sukhomlinsky, V.A., "Pavlyshskaia sredniaia shkola", *Izbrannye proizvedeniia v piati tomakh [Collected Works in Five Volumes]*, Kiev, Radianska shkola, 1979-80, Vol. 4, p. 96.
44 Ibid., p. 117.
45 Ibid., p. 120.
46 Tartakovsky, B.S., *Povest' ob uchitele Sukhomlinskom [The Story of the Teacher Sukhomlinsky]*, Moscow, Molodaia gvardiia, 1972, pp. 151/155.

CHAPTER 3

A Foundation in Health and Values

Physical Education and Health

Sukhomlinsky adopted a holistic approach to physical education and health. He felt that the whole education process must be health-oriented. One should not expect physical education lessons by themselves to provide the foundation for good health:

> Physical education and sports activities play a definite role in the all-round development of the pupils only when all scholastic and educational work is permeated with a concern for health.[1]

Sukhomlinsky was less interested in achieving excellence in competitive sport than in building up positive health and vitality, so as to sustain all the children's work and study activities and enable them to find joy in them:

> Good health — a sense of abundant, inexhaustible physical energy — is an important source of a joyful outlook on life, of optimism, of a readiness to overcome any difficulties.[2]

There is a hint here of a link between physical and moral education — of the influence of health on attitudes. For Sukhomlinsky health meant the abundance of energy which can sustain positive attitudes, rather than a mere absence of disease. He was also particularly interested in the effect of health on intellectual achievement. He considered that attenuated forms of disease — mild, chronic conditions, which pass unnoticed—were responsible for most cases of failure to cope with studies:

> Research into the physical and intellectual development of children who failed or fell behind led me to the conclusion that in 85% of cases the reason for falling behind ... was a poor state of health, some sort of illness or indisposition, more often than not imperceptible to a doctor, and able to be diagnosed only as a result of the combined efforts of mother, father, doctor and teacher. We uncovered conditions which were imperceptible at first glance, masked by the child's lively and active nature—conditions affecting the circulatory system, the respiratory and digestive systems. With each year we saw more and more clearly the dependence of a child's inner life—of intellectual development, thought, attention, memory, assiduity—on the 'play' of his physical energy.[3]

As a consequence of these observations, Sukhomlinsky and his staff decided to give children detailed health checks as they entered the school. Any children found to have health problems were singled out for special therapeutic measures. Many of these measures were merely extensions of prophylactic measures which applied to all children at the school, so we shall commence by looking at these.

Sukhomlinsky felt that a lop-sided emphasis on study could have a detrimental effect on children's health. He discouraged children from sitting too long over their books and tried to incorporate as many elements of a healthy lifestyle as possible into the life of the school. Central to his idea of a healthy lifestyle was a daily routine which involved early retiring and rising, allocation of the first hours of the day to study, maximum time spent in the open air, and the avoidance of evening hours for intense intellectual work.

He considered sleep habits to be very important and, as well as asking parents to encourage early rising and retiring, he taught children from an early age to become independent in this respect. In order to make it easier for children to observe the school's recommendations in this area, parents were requested to accustom their children to early rising during the two years before they entered school. Sukhomlinsky believed that the quality of sleep was best if 40–45% of it took place before midnight. Recommended hours of sleep for young children (aged approximately 7–11) were 8 pm to 6 am, and for older children 9 pm to 5.30 am.

Early rising enabled students to observe another recommendation — to do homework in the early morning hours before school commenced, rather than in the evening. Sukhomlinsky was convinced that one and a half or two hours work in the morning was twice as effective as the same time spent in the evening. (One and a half to two hours was the time it was recommended that children spend on homework in the senior classes. Children in years 1–2 were expected to do 20–25 minutes homework and children in years 3–5, 40–45 minutes.)[4] He felt that doing homework in the evenings was quite detrimental. In his view, study should be conducted in the first five to ten hours after waking (depending on age and health) and the rest of the day spent in creative recreational pursuits. Breakfast and the walk to school provided a break between homework and school lessons. If children lived very close to school, they were encouraged to take a walk in the forest before lessons commenced.

Lessons at school were organised so that those demanding the most intense intellectual effort (mathematics, physics, chemistry, biology, grammar) were held early in the day. Subjects such as literature and history, involving reading and discussion, were held in the middle of the day and the final lessons were reserved for subjects such as drawing, singing, physical education and work practice. As in all Soviet schools, a meal was provided in the middle of the day.

After lessons the children had a considerable amount of free time which was generally spent in the open air. It was during this time that children participated in the many clubs and interest groups to which we have already referred.

As far as possible, children's routines were maintained during holidays, with the exception that nearly all day was spent in the open air:

> Just as excessive intellectual work is inadmissible during term time, an absence of intellectual life is inadmissible during holiday time. The intellectual work of our pupils during holiday time is connected with experimentation in nature — on the plots, in the collective farm fields, in the orchard, in the apiary, on the [animal] farm — with construction and modelling, with the operation of machines.[5]

During the summer, working in the fields and sleeping outside were especially recommended:

> If a pupil has spent the whole summer breathing air saturated with the phytoncides of grains and pastures he will never catch colds.[6]

Dress was another area of concern. Sukhomlinsky encouraged parents not to overprotect their children and to let them go barefoot from spring to autumn until they were thirteen or fourteen years of age. He thought this practice particularly helpful in developing resistance to illness and claimed to have records for 980 children who had always gone barefoot in summer and not one of whom had ever fallen sick. During the 'eighties this practice was also recommended by the controversial Russian writer on family education, B.P. Nikitin[7], who claimed that going barefoot stimulated receptors in the ankles, activating temperature regulating mechanisms in the body.

Sukhomlinsky thought outdoor work was the best form of physical education, and we have already quoted his comparison between some work activities and gymnastics. In both work and sport he tried to develop the children's appreciation of beauty in movement. In sport activities he tried to reduce aggressive competitiveness, drawing the focus away from a quest for speed towards the development of grace and harmony.

> When performing such exercise as running, skiing and swimming, we attach great significance to aesthetic satisfaction. In these and other sports it has become our custom to conduct competitions on the criteria of beauty, elegance, harmony of movement, while speed is considered secondary ... One must not turn sport from a means of education for all children into a means of struggling for personal success ...[8]

Work activities, such as helping care for plants in the orchard and vineyard, collecting and sorting seeds, or growing seedlings, were commenced during a child's first days at school. Middle and senior school students generally spent two or three hours daily working outside.

Posture was considered important and various measures were taken to try and ensure that children's posture did not suffer from long hours of study. Periodic checks were carried out to ensure that each pupil had a desk of suitable dimensions, and in the case of some individuals with poor posture, modifications were made to desks in an attempt to correct the fault. Limits were recommended on the number of hours per day children spent sitting at desks (home and school combined), ranging from two hours per day for grade one students to five and a half hours per day for grades eight to ten.

Another feature of school life at Pavlysh was the number of lessons which were held outdoors. Special "green classrooms" — grassed areas enclosed by trellised grapevines — were used for some school lessons and after-school activities. During their first two years at school children spent no more than three hours per day on classroom lessons. At home, parents, brothers and sisters constructed green shelters for the young children, where they could read, write, draw and pursue their interests in the fresh air. Cuttings and seedlings were propagated at the school specifically to supply families with plants for this purpose.

As mentioned earlier, special measures were taken to help students whose studies were hampered by weak health.[9] Diets were improved by the inclusion of vitamin-rich foods such as honey, milk, butter, eggs, meat and fresh and dried fruits (presumably in greater quantities than were commonly available at that time). In some cases families were encouraged to undertake programs such as fruit drying to ensure the supply of nutritious foods over the winter. Many families took up bee-keeping.

Other recommended measures to strengthen children's health included swimming, sunbathing and sleeping outdoors during spring, summer and autumn. Sukhomlinsky claims these measures were completely effective in overcoming susceptibility to colds, lack of vitality and disorders of a constitutional nature. Children's eyesight was regularly tested and in the case of any abnormality dietary supplements and special reading regimes were recommended. Sometimes such children were given breaks in the middle of lessons.

Work in the open air was found to be the most effective treatment for emotional disorders. Activities requiring care and concentration, such as pruning fruit trees or basket weaving, conducted in a quiet setting, helped in overcoming nervousness and irritability.

Throughout his writing Sukhomlinsky puts health considerations above concerns for academic achievement, health being seen as a necessary precondition for success in studies and for all-round development.

He criticises attempts to increase the tempo of learning through intensive methods which may undermine the child's health:

> The child is a living creature, his brain is a most delicate and tender organ, which must be treated with care and concern. It is possible to give primary education in three years, but only on the condition that there is a constant concern for the children's health, and for the normal development of the child's organism. The basis for effective intellectual work is not to be found in its tempo and intensity, but in the due attention being given to its organisation, in carrying out multifaceted physical, intellectual and aesthetic education.[10]

Moral Education

> There is no person in whom, given skilled educational work, a unique talent will not unfold. There is no sphere of activity in which the individual will not flourish, if only we, the educators, are able to entice a person with that most noble of creative endeavours—the creation of joy for other people.[11]

These words sum up Sukhomlinsky's view of the essence of moral education and its central role in the all-round development of the personality. He believed that the greatest force for releasing the child's creativity and talent, for stimulating all-round development, was the urge to bring happiness to others, and that this in turn was the essence of morality. In his discussion of moral education he constantly returns to the idea of teaching children to find happiness through giving joy to others. When a whole group of people lives in this spirit, the essence of communism has been realised. For Sukhomlinsky, communism meant a collective search for happiness through mutual service.

> For what and in the name of what are we struggling? For people's happiness. Communism for us is above all happiness and joy for all people. We are striving to see that each will not try to drag happiness into his own little corner, will not surround it with a high fence and guard it with chained dogs, but will create it together with others, will seek it among his comrades and find it in common work.[12]

This reference to "common work" indicates another key tenet in Sukhomlinsky's ethical stance—the central role of labour in sustaining life and happiness and the consequent need to educate pupils to express themselves through work.

The idea of a collective search for happiness through work is for Sukhomlinsky symbolised by a communal vineyard in which each gives freely a little of their time and the whole community enjoys the fruits. He regrets that in his village the community as a whole is not yet ready to create such a vineyard, but welcomes signs that some families are moving in this direction, tearing down the fences between their houses and cultivating their land together. Sukhomlinsky clearly felt that the greatest promise for realising this ideal lay in education.

For Sukhomlinsky the role of education in social development was critical. He rejected the notion that moral ills were merely the result of the "remnants of capitalism" in peoples' consciousness, seeing the causes rather in poor upbringing. Virtue would not come about of its own accord or because of the removal of gross forms of exploitation. It required a positive program of education.

Though not suggesting that there are two clearly distinguishable stages in moral development, he does discuss separately moral education in early childhood, when elementary notions of goodness, honesty and justice are formed, and in adolescence and youth when moral autonomy is attained and conscious moral convictions are developed. He also suggests that effective moral education in adolescence requires that a proper foundation has been laid in childhood.

It has been widely acknowledged that early childhood is the most critical period in character formation. The Jesuits boasted that if they had control of a child's upbringing till the age of seven he would be a Catholic for life. Tolstoy suggested that a child learnt more in its first five years than in the remainder of its life. Makarenko expressed a similar view, and Sukhomlinsky concurred with him and with Tolstoy. He felt that early childhood was the time to impart what he called the "ABC of morality" or "universal human norms of morality".

What are these universal human norms? In *Pavlysh School* Sukhomlinsky suggests five basic principles which young children need to understand. We might summarise them as follows:

1. Never forget that you are living with other people. Act in such a way that others benefit. Not all your desires may be satisfied.

2. Be grateful for all the good things you enjoy as a result of others' efforts. Repay kindness with kindness.

3. One cannot live honestly without working.

4. Be kind-hearted and help those in need. Respect and honour your mother and father.

5. Do not be indifferent to evil. Actively oppose it.[13]

There is a traditional, at times almost biblical ring to his moral exhortations, which are written in the form of direct appeals to children accompanied by explanations and illustrations. Consider the language of the following example, which is an exhortation to follow the fourth principle outlined above:

> Be kind and sensitive to people. Help the weak and defenceless. Help a comrade in trouble. Do not cause people harm. Respect and honour your mother and father — they have given you life, they are educating you to become an honest citizen, a person with a kind heart and a pure soul.[14]

Sukhomlinsky considered such moral formulations to be very important. He thought that the teacher's word, if the child was receptive to it, was at once the most potent and the most subtle instrument in the education process. The child's receptivity or, as Sukhomlinsky called it, "educability" was another key concept in his approach. In *How to Educate a True Human Being*, a book devoted to moral exhortations and explanations, or what Sukhomlinsky called "education through the word", he writes:

> I consider the teacher's word to be the most necessary and most subtle contact between a person, convinced of the truth and beauty of his views, of his philosophy of life, and the heart of a person *thirsting to be good* … Education through the word becomes possible only when you have before you *an educable person*.[15]

He goes on to list four factors which contribute to a child's "educability":

1. Happiness

Every effort should be made to protect the child's happiness. The teacher should remember that a child may experience real grief over what, to an adult, appears a trivial matter. Adults should always be ready to share a child's grief and to find ways to alleviate it. A child who is deeply unhappy is unable to appreciate moral beauty. (Perhaps this last statement reflects Sukhomlinsky's experience with children traumatised by the war, as well as with children who came from disturbed families.)

2. Sensitivity to others' feelings

Children's hearts should be open to the joys and sorrows of other people. Sensitivity can be cultivated by opening children's eyes to the beauty in Nature, by using words to awaken a child to another person's inner state, and by involving children in a communal life in which mutual service becomes a habit. Another interesting technique Sukhomlinsky used to develop sensitivity in older children was to study portraits painted by masters such as Rembrandt and to try and read the inner state of those portrayed, paying particular attention to the eyes.

3. Faith in another person

Children will only appreciate moral values if they see them exemplified in someone who inspires their respect and trust, who awakens in them a sense of the beauty of human virtue. If positive examples are lacking in the child's life the teacher should endeavour to fill this role.

4. Beauty

If the preceding three factors are present, exposure to beauty in nature, art or human relationships makes the child more educable. In seeing beauty in the world around them, children see, as in a mirror, their own beauty. If the teacher can awaken the child's sense of beauty, he will also awaken the child's urge to become a better person.

The operation of the above four factors in the child's moral education is most clearly illustrated in Sukhomlinsky's best known book — *My Heart I Give to Children*. The words from this book which every Soviet schoolteacher associated with Sukhomlinsky's name were "the school of joy". Sukhomlinsky invited the children he was to teach to come to school a year early. During their preschool year they did not enter the school buildings. Like Rousseau's Emile, they wandered through the forests and by rivers and lakes, or sat in the shade of a grapevine to listen to the teacher's stories. Their first lessons were in observation of nature, in exploring the richness of their native language and in acts of human kindness. Fairy stories played an important role in developing the children's minds, and as well as listening to the teacher's they composed many of their own.

Later, stories would play a key role in moral education, whether fairy stories, fables or accounts of the lives of famous people. Sukhomlinsky and his staff compiled an anthology of such moral tales, which, as well as containing traditional folk values, featured stories about social reformers and scholars from past centuries, revolutionaries and "heroes of socialist labour". This anthology reflected the Party line on social development and educational policy:

> The pages of this anthology describe the lives of outstanding people who fought for the interests of working people, displaying loyalty to their nation, devotion to the motherland, heroism, fortitude, courage, loyalty to their convictions, a readiness to face any trials, and even death, for the sake of noble ideals — freedom, the triumph of reason, friendship between nations ... The anthology presents the lives and the struggle for socialism and communism of the founders of marxism-leninism ...
>
> ... there are also materials about the great utopian socialists, enlightenment humanists, revolutionary democrats, great scholars, writers, poets, artists and composers.[16]

As is apparent from the above quotation, education in basic norms of traditional morality was, as the children grew older, combined with what Sukhomlinsky called "social orientation", for which some might read "political indoctrination". Sukhomlinsky's approach with younger children, however, was, from the perspective of most Soviet teachers, relatively free from overt political indoctrination, his emphasis being on the family and the immediate community. He liked to repeat the Ukrainian philosopher Skovoroda's maxim that it is easier to love humanity at large than to love one person in a practical way.

In order for the moral concepts imparted through stories, explanations and exhortations to be transformed into moral convictions, the children needed to acquire what Sukhomlinsky called "moral habit" and "moral consciousness".[17] By "moral habit" he meant habituation to moral actions — particularly those of industriousness, of looking after the environment and of caring for other people. By "moral consciousness" he meant the experiencing of positive emotions in association with "moral habit" and the acts of will involved in sustaining it. For Sukhomlinsky, "moral habit" preceded "moral consciousness". From their first days at school, children were trained, for example, to observe the condition of the hundreds of fruit and nut trees in the school grounds. If they noticed a broken branch they were to mend it themselves or to call on someone older to help them. They were helped to plant an apple tree at home for their mother. It did not matter to Sukhomlinsky that this did not initially spring from any inner urge to be helpful, or that the small children needed to be constantly reminded to tend the trees they had planted. The important thing was that a habit was formed, and when the time came to pick the first fruit and present it to their mother, they experienced strong feelings of satisfaction that their consistent efforts had brought joy to someone they loved. The cumulative experience made a deep impression on their minds. When many such acts merged to constitute a creative lifestyle, associated with good health and positive emotions, the foundation of the child's character had been laid. The child had a conscience:

> Gradually these actions become habitual. The adolescent, young man or woman, no longer thinks about whether it is necessary to bind a broken branch, to cover with soil the exposed roots of a tree after heavy rain, to help an old woman carrying a heavy suitcase; they simply cannot remain unconcerned and walk past without paying attention. They cannot help making an effort when it concerns another human being or society at large. The repeated experience of joy accompanying good deeds in childhood is transformed over time into that voice of conscience which bears witness to a high level of moral consciousness.[18]

This is not an original, but on the contrary an old-fashioned or traditional approach to teaching moral values. Sukhomlinsky's daughter commented in conversation that her father was greatly influenced by traditional Ukrainian values and educational practices—particularly in the family. Similar approaches to moral upbringing may be observed in many traditional societies, where the emphasis is more on practical training than on literacy-based learning. What Sukhomlinsky did was to combine classroom schooling, which by itself has a tendency to withdraw a child from the practical processes of living, with traditional moral training through practical activities. The fact that Khrushchev during the late 'fifties was calling for a closer link between the school and life no doubt encouraged Sukhomlinsky, but one suspects that he would have pursued the same path in any case, and indeed he commenced doing so before Khrushchev's directives.

The role of the emotions in developing "moral consciousness" is considered crucial, and Sukhomlinsky devotes considerable attention to this question. Sensitivity and empathy are key qualities to be developed. He narrates a number of incidents where his pupils have shown care and concern to those in need of it, and suggests that people who have acquired a sensitivity to others' feelings will gravitate to those in need of comfort:

> The years of friendship, filled with the mutual creation of joy for each other, educated in the children a sensitivity to a person's inner world, an urge for human fellowship. One who has this urge is led by some sixth sense to people in need of kindness.[19]

In one such encounter his pupils befriended an old man who had recently moved to Pavlysh from a neighbouring village, following the death of his wife. The old man liked to grow flowers, which he took each Sunday to his wife's grave. The children began to help him tend the flowers, and in consequence came to learn a great deal from him. The experience contributed to their aesthetic development as a whole. In Sukhomlinsky's understanding there is a close link between aesthetic and moral development, as both involve a refining of the emotions and a heightening of sensitivity and empathy.

Not only are moral impulses essentially emotional. Rational thought about moral issues also relies on these emotions for its motivating force. Sukhomlinsky cites Pavlov's studies of the brain to support this idea, explaining that it is the emotional centres of the sub-cortex which are responsible for stimulating the rational activity which takes place in the cortex. As we shall see later, this same concept influenced his ideas on intellectual development, as he sought to stimulate children's thought processes through emotions of wonder and delight in beauty.

Intellectual processes play an increasing role in the moral education of older children. Adolescents and senior students are interested in consciously rationalising their values, in finding a philosophy of life and affirming their moral autonomy. Sukhomlinsky encouraged older students to conduct discussions and debates on moral issues. He approved of the striving for self-affirmation which is natural to adolescents, and tried to direct it towards a quest for personal development and service to the community. By the time children reached adolescence, "moral habit" should have been established, but work projects continued to play an important role in moral development and were designed to be challenging:

> As the blade of a plough is cleaned of rust and becomes mirror clean when it daily turns the soil, so a human soul shines when it labours and overcomes difficulties, courageously meeting failure and not being deluded by success.[20]

One area in which Sukhomlinsky sought to find challenges for adolescent and senior students was in the conservation and development of the natural resources of their rural environment. Through tree planting, soil conservation and soil improvement projects children developed a sense of their power to improve the world in which they lived. In one instance a group of adolescents was involved in a project to rehabilitate one tenth of a hectare of infertile ground, on which they planned to grow a crop yielding two and a half times as much as the same area of the most fertile soil on the collective farm. Sukhomlinsky describes in detail how the work proceeded and how after four years the goal was achieved. A year later they far exceeded their initial target. The aim of such exercises was not so much to achieve a material result as to awaken in the children an awareness of what they could achieve through their own efforts. The issue of environmental education is one we shall deal with separately later on, as it is one which permeated a great deal of Sukhomlinsky's work and in which he was ahead of his times.

Another area of moral education addressed by Sukhomlinsky was sex education. This he considered in the context of education for family life and of moral and aesthetic education in general. What was of most interest to him was not the relatively simple task of imparting information on human reproduction and sexual hygiene—a task entrusted to senior staff members—but the much more complex task of educating attitudes to sex, of educating human sympathy, empathy, and respect for those moral qualities which impart beauty and dignity to human conduct. All those aspects of moral education which we have already mentioned were considered important in elevating and refining the sexual instinct, so that it would be channelled into a loving relationship, capable of sustaining the growth of a family:

> Love is, figuratively speaking, the flower which crowns all that is noble in a human being, and one must think about the beauty of this flower long before a person spontaneously experiences sexual attraction, their feelings must be ennobled …
>
> … The whole of a child's life, everything that he sees, does and feels, should instil the conviction that the dearest thing in life is a human being; that the highest honour, the greatest moral distinction, is to bring happiness to another person, to create beauty for them and at the same time to be kind and beautiful oneself … True love, especially the love of a man for a woman, of a boy for a girl, is an enormous expenditure of one's inner resources, a creative act giving rise to happiness.[21]

The education of kindly feelings, of empathy and sensitivity, to which we referred earlier, was considered by Sukhomlinsky to be the most essential element in moral relations between the sexes.[22] This could be part of the upbringing of children from their earliest years. He illustrates his point with the example of two seven-year-old children at a new year's party:

> Kolia and Galia, seven-year-old children, were enthusiastically preparing for the new year celebrations: learning songs, making costumes. Galia's mother sewed her a beautiful head-dress and starched it. The little girl brought it to the new year party carefully packed in a cardboard box. Just before the dancing began someone sat on the box and squashed it all. We adults would consider it a minor episode not worthy of attention, but for the child it was a grievous matter. Kolia noticed that Galia was standing to one side with her head lowered, and the squashed box beside her, and before we had time to intervene he approached her. Without saying a word—he didn't know how to express his sympathy in words, but tears appeared in his eyes—he took Galia by the hand and took up position. A second later the pair were dancing as if nothing had happened.

> No words are necessary when there is a living, palpitating feeling. For the little girl the boys sympathy was a bright ray, giving light to her soul: so there is a person in the world who experiences my grief as his own. And now, instead of tears, Galia's eyes sparkle with joy. The little girl plays and dances and nobody notices that she is without her beautiful head-dress.
>
> There are so many events in a child's life when sincere feeling turns out to be that fabulous water of life which drives away sorrow, lightens grief, returns joy. To give a person the warmth of one's feeling, to share their anxiety, to take their concerns to heart, this is the prime source of that noble feeling of love, which makes a youth a man and a faithful husband, and a girl affectionate, devoted and at the same time firm, strict and unassailable.[23]

The above passage illustrates several key characteristics of Sukhomlinsky's approach: keen observation of children and their fleeting changes of consciousness, an attempt to see events from the child's perspective rather than judging them according to adult standards, and the concern with simple human sympathy which is a leitmotif in all his writing. The language is also typical.

Sukhomlinsky also considered the awakening of creative interests to play an important role in providing a foundation for sexual morality:

> The heartfelt love between two people remains pure for many years only when they are able to share throughout their life the inner beauty which was created in youth. We strive to impart to each pupil in their youth a multifaceted inner wealth sufficient to last a lifetime of giving.
>
> Before the awakening of a mutual sexual attraction, each finds life's happiness in their favourite work, and is not seeking love merely to fill an emptiness of soul. In the flowering of abilities, talents and gifts, in the fact that each one feels a poet in some endeavour, we see a preparation for a morally pure family life. When the fire of creativity is kindled in a person, its light illuminates from within the face, eyes and movements, and the beauty of the external features is animated and ennobled by an inner beauty.[24]

It is this beauty which Sukhomlinsky feels should inspire human love, and which should be cultivated before sexual maturity is reached.

> Before falling in love with the woman in a girl, a boy experiences a feeling of reverence for the beauty of the girl as a human being.[25]

All the various cultural and work activities conducted at the school were considered to play a role in this process. All were aimed at creating the "inner wealth", which could sustain a loving relationship for a lifetime. This was seen as necessary not only for personal happiness, but also for the upbringing of the future generation and for the evolution of society.

Sukhomlinsky saw the family as an arena where intimate and civic concerns converged, where the school had a role to play, but where the greatest tact was needed so as not to offend parents' sensitivities. During the last years of his life he devoted considerable attention to the issue of parent education, and wrote a series of essays which were later published under the title "Parental Pedagogy".

These essays are thematically very simple, being aimed more at the heart than at the head. They amount to an attempt to illumine the ideal of love in the family—love of a husband and wife for each other and for their offspring. This love is considered by Sukhomlinsky to be the greatest educating force:

> The education of children requires a special effort, a spiritual effort. We create a human being through love—the love of father for mother and mother for father, through a deep faith in the beauty and dignity of a human being. Beautiful children grow up in families where the mother and father truly love each other and at the same time love and respect other people. I can immediately recognise a child whose parents share a deep, heartfelt, beautiful and devoted love for each other. Such a child has an inner peace and calm, robust psychological health, a sincere faith in human beauty, faith in the teacher's word, and a sensitivity to the subtle means of influencing the human soul—to a kind word and to beauty.[26]

As always, Sukhomlinsky illustrates his ideas with examples from his own experience, describing the life of families he knew. It is usually these examples which bring home his message most forcefully. One such example concerned the family of a doctor who lived in a nearby village:

> A bright star in the evening sky of my memory—such will always be my recollection of the life of Nikolai Filippovich, a fine doctor and a sensitive human being. For forty-two years he worked in a large settlement on the Dnieper. His wife Maria bore him six children—three

sons and three daughters. When, after a complex operation, Nikolai Filippovich used to come home weak from fatigue, Maria would say: "Lie down here in the grape bower, have a rest, there is no work more exhausting than yours." He, smiling, would reply: "No, the hardest work in the world is a mother's. The hardest, the most exhausting and the most honourable. I help people in trouble. You create humanity's happiness, you create humanity."

Recalling Nikolai Filippovich's life, I see in it an expression of the richness of the human spirit, of human love. A summer's dawn. Maria is sleeping, tired out by the daily round of caring for the children. Her sons and daughters are asleep. Nikolai Filippovich gets up quietly, so as not disturb his wife and children. He goes into the garden, cuts a rose, brings it into the bedroom and places it in a wooden vase on his wife's bedside table. Nikolai Filippovich had carved that vase during the first year of their marriage, had carved it for several months, and now it stands there in the shape of a maple leaf... Maria is sleeping and yet not asleep, she hears through her slumber her husband's cautious steps and is unable to go back to sleep from the strong scent of the rose. She lies happily with eyes closed for half an hour or so.

Thus it was every morning for years, for tens of years. Nikolai Filippovich built a small glass house especially for flowers. He would come to the glass house at dawn in fierce frosts, in bad autumn weather, in early spring, take a delicate flower and carry it to his wife. One by one the children grew up. And as they grew they rose with their father at dawn, and there were now two, then three, four, five, six, seven flowers in the vase ... [27]

Sukhomlinsky cites Tolstoy's statement that the essence of educating children consists in educating oneself, and suggests that an important part of self education is developing the qualities of sensitivity and empathy, which he so often stressed. Sukhomlinsky's ideal of "human love" involves something akin to Tolstoy's ideal of "self-perfection", the mutual spiritual enrichment to which we have already referred involving constant effort, continual self-enrichment:

... Human love is a union of body and soul, of the intellect with the ideal, of happiness and duty.
And through it all runs the thread of effort, effort and more effort — constant and unrelenting effort which creates the wealth of the human spirit within you, father and mother.[28]

66 Each One Must Shine

Sukhomlinsky considered that a man's moral integrity was reflected in the way he related to women. He was particularly concerned that husbands take a share of the home duties and not allow their wives to become exhausted by taking on the double load of a full-time job combined with all domestic and child-raising duties.

No examination of moral education in a Soviet School would be complete without some consideration of the teaching of atheism. John Dunstan has identified two approaches to the teaching of atheism:

> There is the 'pro-atheistic' approach and the 'anti-religious' approach. The pro-atheistic approach is essentially positive and exhortatory; the anti-religious approach, rather, is negative and admonitory. The pro-atheistic approach involves creating an optimistic and progressive environment, bringing about social change that will make people better educated and healthier and happier, so that they will not want a substitute ideology. It also entails setting up holidays and rituals for people to enjoy in place of religious ones. The anti-religious approach stresses criticism of religious beliefs and practices, exposing believers as fools or hypocrites, and going sometimes as far as harassment. The two approaches are combined in an enormous propaganda campaign, devised and supervised by the Propaganda Department of the Central Committee of the CPSU and implemented at the usual administrative levels, usually with the assistance of 'councils of scientific atheism'.[29]

In Sukhomlinsky's approach the "pro-atheistic" element far outweighs the "anti-religious". While he accepted Lenin's view that it is necessary for communists to oppose religion (defining a religious outlook as one which sees the world as split into real and supernatural realms), he did recommend tact and restraint in this area. He considered that the vast majority of believers were good citizens, and that atheistic education should not be conducted in a way that undermined children's respect for and obedience to their parents.

Indeed, it often seems that Sukhomlinsky, despite his attempts to be a good materialist, was an idealist at heart, and that this led him to hold contradictory views. For instance, he asserts that history is governed by objective laws independent of man's will, and in one and the same sentence writes that man is the active creator of history.[30] His attitude to the role of the individual in history is made more explicit in a passage in *Letters to My Son*.

> ... I want to finish this letter with the ancient physicians' motto: "Giving light to others, burn". Ponder these words, son. If it were not for countless examples of self-sacrifice in the name of the common good, there would be no human history and our whole life would be transformed into a dark dungeon. From Mucius Scaevola to Mikhail Panikako, to Zoia Kosmodemianskaia and Aleksandr Matrosov — the firmament of human history is strewn with the eternally burning stars of service to humanity, with dreams of its splendid future. May the radiance of these stars light up your way, son. Giving light to others, burn.[31]

His tendency to give priority to moral development as the core of education, and to see ideological commitment as an extension of simple moral values, was not the norm, and attracted criticism from many quarters, including from members of the Academy of Pedagogical Sciences.

Sukhomlinsky's atheism was further tempered by recognition and acceptance of people's need to believe in their own immortal spirit and in their capacity to transcend the animal level of existence. In *Letters to my son* he writes:

> I am staggered by the primitive nature, by the utter lack of culture of that illiterate atheism which is forcefully promoted by many lecturers, teachers and writers, and which is more likely to drive people into the embrace of religion than to free them from faith in god. The most wretched aspect of this illiterate atheism is that as its trump card, as its main proof that god does not exist, the thesis is put forward that a person has no immortal soul, that he disappears without a trace, just like any animal. It would be hard to find anything more degrading to a human being.[32]

While denying the existence of God, he does affirm the existence of an immortal soul, albeit in a non-religious interpretation:

> Who said that a human being has no soul? A human being has a soul, and it is incomparably richer than the soul of which religion speaks. A human's soul is his mighty spirit, his thought, his bold impulse to know, to tame the forces of nature. It is this soul which a human being may make immortal.[33]

In his view, a person becomes immortal by leaving "a trace upon the earth", something he considered it was possible for anyone to do:

> I am firmly convinced that the human personality is inexhaustible; each may become a creator, leaving behind a trace upon the earth. This is really what we are building communism for. There should not be any nobodies—specks of dust cast upon the wind. Each one must shine, just as billions upon billions of galaxies shine in the heavens.[34]

The essence of atheistic education, in Sukhomlinsky's view, was the quest for happiness in this world, rather than the next. Sukhomlinsky's objection to religion (in line with Party doctrine) was that it encouraged indifference to worldly issues. The key thrust of his efforts at atheistic education was to give children confidence in their ability to achieve happiness in this world, through self-mastery and through collective mastery over their environment. The fostering of an optimistic and creative atmosphere in the school community was thus seen as the most effective means of countering religious and quietistic views in the family. Open attacks on the religious views of family members by teachers were considered counter-productive.

As Dunstan has noted, it is difficult to assess the effectiveness of Soviet attempts to promote atheism, as there is a tendency for religious views to be eroded in any industrialised society. It would appear that Sukhomlinsky, through encouraging scientific and technological clubs and activities, was hoping to utilise these factors in promoting atheism. Dunstan has also identified some inherent shortcomings of a materialistic and secular belief system—principally an inability to comfort in the face of unavoidable suffering, and of death. Sukhomlinsky has gone further than most Soviet educators in addressing this issue, by suggesting that it is possible to transcend human mortality, through creativity and service.

Notes

1 Sukhomlinsky, V.A., "Pavlyshskaia sredniaia shkola", *Izbrannye proizvedeniia v piati tomakh [Collected Works in Five Volumes]*, Kiev, Radianska shkola, 1979–80, Vol. 4, p. 147.
2 Ibid., p. 131.
3 Ibid.
4 Ibid., p. 140.

5 Ibid., p. 141.
6 Ibid.
7 Nikitin, B.P., Nikitina, L.A., *My i nashi deti [We and our Children]*, 3rd edition, Moscow, Moskovskii rabochii, 1988.
8 Sukhomlinsky, V.A., "Pavlyshskaia sredniaia shkola", *Izbrannye proizvedeniia v piati tomakh [Collected Works in Five Volumes]*, Kiev, Radianska shkola, 1979–80, Vol. 4, p. 148.
9 Ibid., pp. 132–146.
10 Ibid., p. 133.
11 Ibid., p. 178.
12 Ibid., p. 175.
13 Ibid., pp. 153–158.
14 Ibid., p. 156.
15 Sukhomlinsky, V.A., "Kak vospitat' nastoiashchego cheloveka", *Izbrannye proizvedeniia v piati tomakh [Collected Works in Five Volumes]*, Kiev, Radianska shkola, 1979–80, Vol. 2, p. 162.
16 Sukhomlinsky, V.A., "Pavlyshskaia sredniaia shkola", *Izbrannye proizvedeniia v piati tomakh [Collected Works in Five Volumes]*, Kiev, Radianska shkola, 1979–80, Vol. 4, p. 183.
17 Ibid., p. 163.
18 Ibid., p. 164.
19 Ibid., p. 199.
20 Ibid., p. 179.
21 Ibid., p. 208.
22 Ibid., pp. 201–209.
23 Ibid., p. 210.
24 Ibid., p. 213.
25 Ibid., p. 212.
26 Sukhomlinsky, V.A., "Roditel'skaia pedagogika [Parental pedagogy]", *Izbrannye pedagogicheskie sochineniia v trekh tomakh [Selected pedagogical works in three volumes]*, Moscow, Pedagogika, 1979–81, Vol. 3, p. 405.
27 Ibid., p. 411.
28 Ibid.
29 from Dunstan's article in Avis, G., ed., *The Making of the Soviet Citizen*, London: Croom Helm, 1987, p. 67.
30 Sukhomlinsky, V.A., "Pavlyshskaia sredniaia shkola [Pavlysh School]", *Izbrannye proizvedeniia v piati tomakh [Collected Works in Five Volumes]*, Kiev, Radianska shkola, 1979–80, Vol. 4, p. 306.
31 Sukhomlinsky, V.A., *Pis'ma k synu [Letters to My Son]*, 2nd edition, Moscow, Prosveshchenie, 1987, p. 116.
32 Ibid., p. 52.
33 Ibid., p. 53.
34 Ibid.

CHAPTER 4

Intellectual, Vocational and Aesthetic Development

Intellectual Education

> One must not see the aim of instruction as being to ensure by any means that pupils master the material in the programme. One must not assess the effectiveness of the means and methods of instruction only on the basis of the quantity of knowledge acquired by the pupils. The aim of instruction is to ensure that the process of acquiring knowledge contributes to the optimum level of general development, and that the general development achieved through the process of instruction should facilitate greater success in the acquisition of knowledge. In our school we assess the effectiveness of the methods of instruction by the extent to which they facilitate the process of the child's general intellectual development, by the extent to which the process of instruction is at the same time a process of intellectual, moral, ideological and aesthetic education.[1]

AS WITH ALL other aspects of "all-round development of the personality", intellectual education, in Sukhomlinsky's approach, is to be governed by moral and ideological considerations. Its aim should be not so much to acquire a given volume of knowledge as to develop a philosophy of life. Knowledge acquired should contribute to the formation of personal convictions which direct the course of a person's life. Sukhomlinsky considered that, as learning is a life-long process, it was more important to develop a creative, questioning mind than to absorb a set amount of information, though these two aspects of intellectual education were not mutually exclusive. They needed to be combined, and the process of instruction was one of the vehicles for intellectual education:

> Intellectual education takes place during the process of instruction only when the accumulation of knowledge—an increase in the volume of knowledge—is seen by the teacher not as the ultimate aim of the process of instruction, but only as one of the means of developing the cognitive and creative powers, of developing flexible, investigative thought. In the lessons of such a teacher the knowledge acquired by the pupils is used as an instrument with the help of which a pupil consciously takes new steps in discovering the world around them. The transfer of acquired methods of cognition to new objects then becomes a regular feature of the pupils' thinking activity: they continue in future to independently investigate the cause and effect relationships of new phenomena, processes and events. In this connection important elements in intellectual education become, for subjects in the natural science cycle—productive work, research and experimentation, and for humanities subjects—the independent study of life phenomena and literary sources, and attempts at creative writing.[2]

For knowledge to contribute to a philosophy of life it needs to be applied in an attempt to transform the world, to harness the forces of nature. Sukhomlinsky cites Marx's assertion that:

> The actual spiritual wealth of an individual is entirely dependent on the wealth of their actual relationships.[3]

A philosophy of life informed by knowledge (*nauchnoe mirovozzrenie*), writes Sukhomlinsky, is a blend of thought, feeling and will. For intellectual activities to result in such a philosophy of life they need to be combined with work activities which transform the environment:

> In our system of intellectual education there are work assignments whose principal aim is the formation of a philosophy of life. For example when working on an experimental plot a pupil may demonstrate that soil is a particular medium for the activity of microorganisms. The demonstration of this truth is only the first step towards autonomous activity leading to the formation of a philosophy of life. The next step is the creation of a soil which will yield a rich harvest. It is in this work that there unfolds that wealth of actual relationships of which Marx wrote.[4]

Through efforts to transform their world, children come to know not only external reality, but also themselves and their creative capacities. Through investigative and experimental approaches to learning children discover themselves as truth-seekers. Sukhomlinsky considered investigative approaches to learning very important, not only in training an inquiring mind, but also in motivating a student to learn. He often returned to the theme of the emotional bases of learning, to the idea that the student needs to experience positive feelings of wonder and discovery during the learning process. Wherever possible he advocated a "hands-on" approach to learning, and considered that there was a direct link between manual skills and intellectual capacities. In all of these areas Sukhomlinsky was generally faithful to Marx's ideas on education, as they have been elucidated by Price.[5] However, as Price has shown, practical attempts to apply Marx's ideas in the USSR were marred by an excessive dogmatism and rigidity which was contrary to the spirit of Marx's ideas. Sukhomlinsky's work in education also suffered from the constraints imposed by adherence to narrow ideological concepts, a factor we cannot ignore in a discussion of his approach to education of the intellect.

Sukhomlinsky was working within the framework of a centrally controlled school system with a centrally determined curriculum. Children throughout the Soviet Union used essentially the same textbooks, which reflected Soviet ideology. The content of courses was often tailored to fit narrow ideological stereotypes. The influence of ideology was particularly pronounced in the case of subjects such as history, literature, and social studies. Sukhomlinsky accepted as a matter of course that these subjects would have an ideological component:

> The chief aim in studying humanities subjects in schools is to educate a citizen, a staunch and courageous patriot, a campaigner for the ideals of communism. Studying history, social studies, literature, a person must come to an understanding of the laws of social development in the past, present and future, come to know and love the spiritual riches created by humanity.[6]

The distortion of the past which took place in history lessons in Soviet schools is well known, and was openly acknowledged. Indeed, on two occasions after the death of Stalin, history textbooks were discarded and final year history exams cancelled. (The first occasion, in the late 'fifties, followed Khrushchev's denunciation of Stalin, and the second, in 1988, was a consequence of Gorbachev's policy of *glasnost'*.) It is also extremely doubtful whether the "laws of social development" enshrined in Soviet textbooks of the time could have foreseen the demise of the Soviet Union.

To do Sukhomlinsky justice, however, we should note that the "spiritual riches" which he endeavoured to pass on to his pupils did include a rich selection from the classics of world literature. He writes that the majority of students at his school succeeded in reading through a selection of some 250 works of Russian, Soviet and world literature, which all students at Pavlysh were exhorted to read before they completed year 10. The list contained classics of Greek and Indian literature, epics from Finland and Iceland, Irish sagas and classics of Western literature from Dante through to Steinbeck. While the selection of modern literature may be tendentious, and the inclusion of some Soviet works questionable, most of the works listed are undisputed classics. It would seem that Sukhomlinsky's pupils were indeed widely read, and that Sukhomlinsky went to great lengths to obtain multiple copies of the works in question for the school library.

Any ideological distortion of the intellectual content of education at Pavlysh was due principally, then, to the national curriculum framework within which Sukhomlinsky was working. As other studies of Soviet education have amply shown[7], even matters seemingly totally divorced from ideological issues were, in the Soviet Union, frequently made the subject of ideological interpretation. The Soviet press in general was subject to the same gross ideological influences. Lyndall Morgan, in her doctoral dissertation on the language of Soviet newspapers, has demonstrated the way in which ideological constraints lead to a distortion of truth, to the interpretation of complex realities in a way that owed more to myth than to fact. The Soviet reader was, in her words:

> … presented with a political picture drawn in black and white which grossly oversimplifies reality. Moreover he has no legitimate access to any alternative view. All this, combined with harsh penalties for mental deviance, means that the Soviet citizen is forced to tailor his official political expressions to the level of formulae described in this work. Such a restraint cannot fail to colour to some extent his inner world

Intellectual, Vocational and Aesthetic Development 75

and for many Soviet citizens it is obvious that the official view is totally assimilated in spite of abundant life experience running in direct contradiction to the official platform.[8]

Morgan was writing before the age of *glasnost'* and the press did change dramatically after the advent of *perestroika* (though many of the formulae she identified still lingered), but her comments apply fully to the period during which Sukhomlinsky was working.

All this means that, as far as the content of intellectual education was concerned, Sukhomlinsky was working with severe limitations, which were in stark contradiction to the progressive, investigative methods he advocated. He had no choice in determining the content of standard courses or in the selection of textbooks. What he could and did do, was to encourage students to go beyond the curriculum through extra reading and through interest groups. Even in this, however, he was limited by central control of the Soviet press and by the widespread perpetuation of myth to which Morgan has drawn attention. One of Sukhomlinsky's greatest admirers, Simon Soloveichik, who had access to his archives and personal library, candidly suggested to the writer of this study that the educator's huge personal library consisted of "17,000 second rate books". While this comment may be an example of the hyperbole of a "publicist", it also must reflect the limitations which a Soviet country school principal faced, working as he did in what was essentially a closed system. (Soloveichik also considered that Sukhomlinsky was a genius who owed his best ideas not to Soviet pedagogical science, but to his love for children and his own natural talent as a teacher, working as he did in relative isolation.)

As far as can be ascertained, Sukhomlinsky was not conscious of any contradiction between open, investigative approaches to learning and ideological constraints. He seems to have believed that objective investigation would confirm the validity of Soviet Marxism, though considerable direction of such investigation by teachers was envisaged, as the following quotation shows:

> One of the main tasks of a process of instruction which truly educates is to guard against apathy and indifference on the part of the pupil towards the knowledge acquired, where he feels that the content has nothing to do with him. The formation of a philosophy of life informed by knowledge involves the educator's reflective insight into

the soul of the child and skilful pedagogic management of his thinking, of the process of getting to know the surrounding world, of his work activity.[9]

This may seem excessively intrusive, not only from a western point of view, but also from the point of view of many Soviet intellectuals. One Soviet teacher, in a personal conversion, cautioned against accepting Sukhomlinsky too uncritically and accused him of "emotional despotism". This is a serious criticism, as it goes to the heart of Sukhomlinsky's methodology: the deliberate stimulation of emotion as part of the education process. As we shall be devoting a separate chapter to considering the education of the emotions, we shall not go into this issue in depth now. Readers may judge for themselves, as the account proceeds, how despotic Sukhomlinsky was. In the context of common practices in Soviet schools of the time, Sukhomlinsky's approach is generally regarded as non-authoritarian, and many contemporary observers commented on his ability to motivate students to find joy in learning.

Let us look at Sukhomlinsky's work in teaching literacy skills. The influence of ideology at this level of instruction was far less pronounced, and in this area of his work we see Sukhomlinsky at his most creative. We have already noted that in the immediate post-war years Sukhomlinsky was concerned to help children overcome the traumas of the war and rediscover the joys of childhood. His work as a class teacher during the early 'fifties is described in *My Heart I Give to Children*. Dissatisfied with the fact that his duties were mainly administrative, he took charge of a group of six-year-olds in 1951 and remained their class teacher until they completed their schooling. During their first year he concentrated on teaching the children to read "the living book of nature", an expression he seems to have adopted from Comenius. The children did not enter the school buildings during this year, nor have a regular timetable. One day they might assemble in the morning under the shelter of a grape vine in the school grounds, the next day gather in the evening to view the sunset by the banks of a pond. Always, though, they would be observing natural phenomena, and always they would be involved in listening to and composing stories about what they saw.

The freedom to conduct such a loosely structured program was won by persuading parents to send their children to school a year early. (Their official schooling would not commence till the following year, when they turned seven.) The reasoning behind this unorthodox approach was that education must be tailored to the child's nature — to children's keen interest in exploring the world of the senses and in making sense of their perceptions. In this, Sukhomlinsky was following Rousseau. He maintained that reading and writing should not be taught until children's interest in words had been heightened through emotional experiences mediated by the senses:

> I strove to ensure that for a child a word was not merely the designation of an object or phenomenon, but carried within it an emotional colouring — its own fragrance, its own subtle shades. It was important … that the beauty of the word, and the beauty of that little part of the world which the word reflected, should awaken interest towards those drawings which convey the music of the sounds of human speech, towards letters. Until a child senses the fragrance of a word, until he sees its subtle shades, one should not begin instruction in literacy, and if a teacher does, he condemns the child to hard labour. (The child will in the end overcome the difficulty, but at what cost!)[10]

Such an approach was partly due, no doubt, to Sukhomlinsky following his natural inclination to organise pleasurable activities for children outdoors, as he had been doing since he was a teenager. It was also a response to observation of the difficulties encountered with more traditional, "book-based" approaches to teaching literacy:

> For many a year I had thought: what a difficult, exhausting, uninteresting business reading and writing become during a child's first days of school life, how many failures children meet on the thorny path to knowledge — and all because study turns into a purely bookish affair. I saw how children struggled during the lesson to differentiate the letters, how the letters danced before their eyes, melting into a pattern which was impossible to decipher. And at the same time I saw how easily children memorise letters and make words with them, when the activity is lit by some interest, is connected with a game, and — most importantly — when no-one demands: you must definitely remember this, if you don't know it — it will be the worse for you.[11]

By utilising to the full the spell which nature was able to cast over his young charges, he was tapping into what he called "the emotional well-springs of thought". He referred to nature as "the source of living thought", and to his excursions with the children as "journeys to the well-springs of words". The following passage gives some idea of how this approach worked in practice:

> We went on 'journeys' to the sources of words with albums and pencils. Here is one of our first 'journeys'. My aim was to show the children the beauty and the subtle nuances of the word *meadow*. [In Ukrainian this is a three-letter word which may be transliterated as 'LUH' or 'LUG'.] We seated ourselves under a weeping willow which leant over a pond. In the distance a meadow, lit up by the sun, showed green. I said to the children: "Look at the beauty in front of us. Above the grass butterflies are flying, bees are buzzing. In the distance is a herd of cattle that look like toys. It seems as if the meadow is a light green river and the trees are its dark green banks. The herd is bathing in the river. Look how many beautiful flowers early autumn has sprinkled around. And as we listen to the music of the meadow can you hear the soft buzzing of the flies and the song of a grasshopper?"
>
> I draw the meadow in my album. I draw the cows, and the geese, scattered about like white fluff, and a barely perceptible puff of smoke, and a white cloud on the horizon. The children are spellbound by the beauty of the quiet morning and they are also drawing. I write underneath the drawing 'LUH'. For the majority of children, letters are drawings. And each drawing reminds them of something. Of what? Of a blade of grass. Bend the blade over and you have an 'L'. Put two blades together and you have a new drawing, an 'U'. The children write the word 'LUH' below their drawings. Then we read the word. Sensitivity to the music of nature helps the children to sense the meaning of the word. The outline of each letter is memorised. The children impart to each letter a living sound, and each letter is easily memorised. The drawing of the word is perceived as a whole. The word is read, and this reading is not the result of lengthy exercises in phonic analysis and synthesis, but a conscious reproduction of a phonic, musical image, which corresponds to the visual image of the word which has just been drawn by the children. When there is such a unity of visual and auditory perception, infused with a wealth of emotional nuances, which have been imparted to the word, the letter and the small word are memorised simultaneously. Dear reader, this is not a discovery of some new method for teaching literacy. It is the practical realisation of that which has been proven by science: that it is easier to memorise that which one is not obliged to memorise and

that the emotional colouring of perceived images plays a crucial role in memorisation.[12]

It was through many such "journeys" over a period of some eight months that Sukhomlinsky's charges learnt the fundamentals of reading and writing:

> The days and weeks passes and we continually made new 'journeys' to the sources of living words. Especially interesting was our acquaintance with the words *village, coniferous forest* [in Ukrainian a word of one syllable — 'BOR'], *willow, forest, smoke, ice, mountain, ear of grain, sky, hay, grove, lime-tree, ash-tree, apple-tree, cloud, burial mound, acorn, autumn leaf-fall*. In spring we devoted our 'journeys' to the words *flowers, lilac, lily, acacia, grape, pond, river, lake, forest edge, mist, rain, thunder storm, dawn, doves, poplar, cherry-tree*. On each occasion a picture was drawn in an album entitled "Our native tongue" by the child in whom the word awakened the most striking images, feelings and recollections. Nobody remained indifferent to the beauty of their native language ... About eight months after we began our work the children knew all the letters, wrote words and read.[13]

He did have reservations, however, about how easy it would be to duplicate his experience:

> One must issue a word of caution here about attempts to mechanically duplicate someone else's experience. Teaching reading and writing by this method is a creative process, and creativity cannot be produced with a template. To borrow something new one must be creative.[14]

It is evident from the above passages that there was considerable overlap between intellectual and aesthetic education in this approach, and that Sukhomlinsky's concern for children's feelings led him to attach great importance to the emotional bases of learning, to motivation. However critical one may be of any political, indoctrinational element which was present in Sukhomlinsky's teaching, one should also give him credit for recognising that the intellect exists only as part of a total personality, and that it is this total personality which needs to be educated. Even the attempt to educate the intellect must, especially where young children are concerned, address the child's total personality and awaken an emotional response, in order to be effective.

A western parallel to Sukhomlinsky's experiments with infant literacy teaching may be found in the work of the New Zealand teacher and writer, Sylvia Ashton-Warner. Like Sukhomlinsky, she believed that the first words which children learnt to read must be of personal significance to them, must relate to their experience:

> First words must have intense meaning for a child. They must be part of his being … Pleasant words won't do. Respectable words won't do. They must be words organically tied up, organically born from the dynamic life itself.[15]

The comparison should not be stretched too far. Ashton-Warner was more inclined to rely on the child's experiences at home and outside the school, while Sukhomlinsky had a greater tendency to try and structure the children's learning by organising experiences for them. Both, however, considered it important to relate to the child's inner world, and both adopted what may be broadly termed an 'experience-based' approach to teaching literacy. Ashton-Warner herself considered that her method, which she called 'organic reading', had been foreshadowed in the work of Tolstoy and of Helen Keller.[16]

Having mastered the rudiments of reading and writing through making their own experience-based booklets, Sukhomlinsky's pupils were ready for further reading material. Sukhomlinsky did not want to offer them "the clumsy poems that proliferate in some readers", fearing that "dry poems written in bureaucratic language are more likely to kill any feeling for poetry than to educate a love of language." He could not find any material he considered suitable in the book shops, so, like Ashton-Warner, he wrote and illustrated stories himself. The reading of this material prepared his pupils to tackle children's literature by Tolstoy, Ushinsky, Pushkin, Lermontov, Nekrasov, Shevchenko, Lesia Ukrainka and Ivan Franko.

The same concern to base learning on the children's first-hand experience and to make learning joyful, influenced the teaching of Sukhomlinsky and his staff at various levels throughout the school. Sukhomlinsky had called his experimental work with six-year-olds "the school of joy", and a candidate thesis (roughly equivalent to a Ph.D) written in the Soviet Union in the 'eighties examined the role of joy in learning in Sukhomlinsky's system.[17] The writer of that thesis, M.V.

Boguslavsky, conducted experimental lessons in Moscow schools in an attempt to demonstrate the effectiveness of principles elucidated by Sukhomlinsky. He was conducting his research at one of the institutes of the Academy of Pedagogical Sciences, and his experimental lessons were indicative of attempts by the Academy's institutes to counter criticism by Soviet teachers, that they were too far removed from the realities of teaching, and that their research had little relevance to practice.

As far as "using joy to motivate learning" at Pavlysh is concerned, nature continued to be a key source of inspiration for children's work throughout the school. Children of all ages were encouraged to write "miniature essays" — short descriptions of natural scenes which attempted to capture nature's fleeting moods. These were exercises aimed at developing observational skills as well as the sensitive use of language. Sukhomlinsky boasted that on one autumn walk in the forest his pupils identified and found names for seventy different autumn colours.[18] Nature was the background against which all the children's intellectual activity took place, and the concrete foundation upon which experience and thinking were based. Difficulties in intellectual development could often be remedied by returning to nature:

> I advised teachers: if a pupil does not understand something, if his thought beats helplessly like a bird in a cage, look carefully at your work. Has the consciousness of your child become a little dried up pond, cut off from the eternal and life giving source of thought — the world of objects, of natural phenomena? Connect this pond with the ocean of nature, of objects, of the surrounding world, and you will see how a spring of living thought will begin to flow.[19]

In Sukhomlinsky's view the development of a child's brain, and correspondingly of its thought processes, was greatly stimulated by exposure to the colourful and complex phenomena of the natural world. In *My Heart I Give to Children* he reflects on the "infancy of the nervous system" and the role of exposure to nature in a child's intellectual development:

> Here, in the midst of nature, it was particularly clear that we teachers are dealing with the tenderest, the most delicate and sensitive thing in nature, — with a child's brain ...

A child thinks in images. This means that if, for instance, he is listening to a teacher's description of the journey of a drop of water, he is picturing in his mind's eye the silver waves of morning mist, the dark storm cloud, the claps of thunder and the spring rain. The brighter these pictures are in his mind's eye, the more deeply he comprehends the laws of nature. The tender, sensitive neurons of his brain have not yet become strengthened, they need to be developed and strengthened.[20]

Sukhomlinsky goes on to describe the operation of the brain cells in receiving and processing sense impressions and ideas, and to explain the child's need for concrete images in order to think:

The nature of a child's brain requires that its intellect should be educated at the source of thought—amongst visual images, and first and foremost, in the midst of nature, so that thought may switch from the visual image to the processing of information about that image. If children are cut off from nature, if from his first days of schooling a child perceives only words, the brain cells quickly become exhausted and cannot cope with the work presented by the teacher.[21]

Children's intellectual and emotional development are linked, and this is clearly seen in their love of fairy tales. Sukhomlinsky not only told the children fairy tales, he encouraged them to compose their own, based on the phenomena they observed in the natural world. By composing fairy tales about their natural surroundings, children were laying foundations for the future development of their thought processes:

Children experience an elemental joy when they perceive the images of the surrounding world and add to them something of their fantasy. The emotional richness of perception is the inner charge which sparks children's creativity. I am deeply convinced that without emotional uplift the normal development of the child's brain cells is impossible. Physiological processes, too, are connected with the emotions: at moments of intensity, of uplift, of enthusiasm, the cells of the cerebral cortex experience increased levels of nutrition. At this time the cells expend much energy, but at the same time they receive much from the organism. Observing the intellectual work of pupils in the beginning classes over a period of many years, I have become convinced that at times of great emotional uplift a child's thinking becomes particularly clear, and memorisation takes place more intensively.[22]

The above passage shows the link, figuratively speaking, between education of the heart and education of the brain. It contains in seminal form one of the ideas central to intensive teaching methods developed by Russian scholars such as Kitaigorodskaia and Akishina—that emotional uplift can accelerate learning.

Excursions into nature continued to form an integral part of Sukhomlinsky's teaching methodology throughout the primary school, and he developed a series of some 300 outdoor lessons aimed at developing keen observation and a capacity for independent thought. He asked questions of the children which stimulated them to try and understand the relationships between the various phenomena of nature. In this way the children were led to reflect on the difference between the living and the non-living and the relationship between them, on the constant change evident in the natural world, the cycles of growth and decay, on the role of the sun in sustaining life, and on many other themes arising from observation of nature. Sukhomlinsky considered observational skills to play a key role in intellectual development:

> The most important feature of a developed intellect is the power of observation, "the ability to see, with the eye of intellect, an object in the centre of all its relationships ... ". Closely connected with the power of observation are other features of intellectual development: curiosity, i.e. an active relationship to the phenomena of the surrounding world, a striving to learn and to know; a systematic approach, i.e. the purposeful selection of the objects of cognition, of concepts and inferences; capacity, i.e. the ability to retain knowledge in one's memory and to find one's way amongst intellectual riches; discipline, flexibility, independence and critical sense.[23]

Other elements in Sukhomlinsky's approach to educating the intellect were the use of riddles and folk puzzles, and of chess. Sukhomlinsky felt that many of the difficulties which children experienced at school resulted from not having sufficiently developed the capacity to think, the capacity to hold two or more ideas simultaneously and relate them to each other. This undeveloped capacity for thought was the consequence of both hereditary and environmental factors. Biochemical conditions inhibiting the formation of neural pathways in the brain played a role, as did the circumstances in which children were raised in early childhood.

Sukhomlinsky sought to stimulate the capacity for thought by posing riddles and number problems (many of which he drew from folk culture) which required children to correlate several variables. He cites several examples of such problems, including the well known puzzle of how to ferry a wolf, a goat and a cabbage across a river, taking no more than two at a time, and without any of them being eaten by another. Chess likewise required the children to hold several moves in their heads at once. Such problems and games were an invaluable supplement to the school curriculum, especially for those children whose memory and capacity for thought were poorly developed. For those with special difficulties he devised simple problems which acted as stepping stones to the solution of more complex ones.

We have already referred to the many clubs and activity groups which functioned after school and which were aimed at providing a milieu in which children could identify and pursue some special interest. In these areas of special interest the children could experience the joy of exploring some area in depth, without the pressure or limitations imposed by a set curriculum. We have also noted that class marks were never used as a punishment, but only as a reward for constructive effort. If children had not reached the necessary standard, they were given more time to master the material. Every effort was made to ensure that nothing soured the children's attitude to study or diminished their natural urge to learn.

An example of investigative approaches to learning in the senior classes may be found in what Sukhomlinsky called the "lecture-laboratory system of lessons"—a system reminiscent of the "project method", which was developed by Kilpatrick on the basis of Dewey's ideas, and extensively used in Soviet educational experiments in the 'twenties. This system was introduced at Pavlysh during the early 'fifties, and aimed at maximising the time students spent on independent study, experiments and reading a variety of sources. "Lectures" were used to explain the goals and methods of the next stage of study, to demonstrate experimental techniques, or, in the case of literature, to review an area of study already covered. In this latter case, the "lecture" might be conducted by one of the students and involve a good deal of discussion. While the methods of study naturally varied from one discipline to another, the aim was to encourage students to seek knowledge for themselves:

> The lecture-laboratory system facilitates the pupil's active participation in the acquisition of knowledge. Under this system the pupil and his inner world are not merely the object of the method of instruction, they are the prime motivating force in the methodology.[24]

Observers who visited Pavlysh were struck by the attitudes of students and staff. Soloveichik reported that students in year 10 participated in lessons with the same enthusiasm as children in year 1, and that staff appeared to really enjoy their work, despite the high expectations placed on them. Soloveichik thought the school's success was due to the following factors:

- an overriding concern for the child's happiness and well-being,
- a methodology for teaching young children observational, investigative and reasoning skills during nature study outings by means of intensive questioning,
- a strong emphasis by teachers in all disciplines on the development of language skills,
- reduction of the quantity of material which children were expected to commit to memory (limiting it to those essential orthograms, formulae, etc., which formed a basis for all further study), and a greater emphasis on reasoning and interpretation, most memorisation taking place unconsciously in the process of applying knowledge,
- removal of emotional obstacles to learning, and especially, in the early years, of the experience of "failure",
- the encouragement of extra-curricular interests and the creation of a rich background of intellectual activity against which formal classes were conducted.[25]

Work Education

According to Sukhomlinsky, work education (*trudovoe vospitanie*) is more than vocational guidance and training. It also refers to the development of a creative orientation and a positive attitude to work in general:

Work education is the practical preparation of the younger generation for participation in social production and at the same time an extremely important element in moral, intellectual and aesthetic education. Our teaching staff are working to create a system of work education in which work gives shape to the moral and intellectual temper of the personality. We see our educational task as being to ensure that work should become part of the spiritual life of the person we are educating, of the life of the collective, that enthusiasm for work should already have become an important interest during the years of adolescence and early youth.[26]

Work education is a key element in the constellation of "all-round development". It was enshrined in Soviet educational policy from the time that Lenin and Krupskaia defined the nature of the Soviet school as "polytechnic". In developing the notion of "polytechnical education" they were influenced by Marx, who in turn had been influenced by Robert Owen.

Price has suggested that work education is one of the areas in which Western educators would do well to look at the experience of their Soviet counterparts. As Price notes, in both socialist and capitalist societies attempts to combine education with productive labour have met with difficulties, though for different reasons. In capitalist countries such attempts have been dogged by complaints of "unfair competition" or "child labour". In socialist countries "they have run into other equally difficult problems, both of definition and purpose and of administration."[27]

Price has explained the priority Marx gave to work in the education process.[28] For Marx, work was the most essentially human of all activities. The ability to imagine the fruits of one's actions and to work towards a goal was, in his view, what distinguished people from animals. Much of Marx's critique of capitalist society focussed on the alienation of people not only from the fruits of their labour, but from work as a creative process. People were made the appendages of machines, rather than the initiators and masters of creative activity. One of Marx's goals was the abolition of the antithesis between mental and physical labour.

Marx's assertion, that labour is a prime necessity of life, and not merely a means to life, became part of Soviet educational doctrine, and is central to Sukhomlinsky's views on work education. Sukhomlinsky's

Intellectual, Vocational and Aesthetic Development

work was exceptional in the degree to which he managed to give creative expression to this idea, compared with the majority of Soviet schools.

As stated earlier, one of the aims at Pavlysh was to help all children to uncover their unique talents and develop a vocation in life. It was not enough for pupils merely to have acquired some practical skills which would enable them to find employment. They should have found joy in excelling in some area of work. Moreover, pupils should have a moral basis for their future work involvements. They should feel motivated to serve society and have already experienced joy in combining creativity and service. This is another instance of the presence of moral education in all areas of the curriculum.

In order to achieve these aims Sukhomlinsky thought it necessary to adhere to certain principles. These included the following:

a) Early involvement in productive work

Sukhomlinsky took a radical stand on this point, insisting that even seven-year-olds in their first year at school should be involved in genuine service to the community. He came under attack at a session of the Academy of Pedagogical Sciences for this stance[29], but defended his views and insisted that his experience refuted the criticisms levelled at him. The following passage provides an example of the sort of work which was carried out by the youngest children at the school:

> At our school children of seven and eight years already carry out interesting and engaging work of considerable social significance. By established tradition, certain types of work are performed only by children. For instance, two months before they commence grade one, the little ones collect seeds from trees. In the spring they perform their first work of major social significance: sowing the seeds of trees on the slopes of ravines and gullies. Then they look after the trees, thus creating defensive wooded belts preventing soil erosion in the fields. The work of the smallest pupils in the fields of the local collective farm has created several major defensive forest belts which, during the course of ten years, have stopped soil erosion on an area of 160 hectares. It would be hard to place too high a value on the public wealth saved due to this action, and multiplied by the subsequent work of the very same pupils in their middle and senior years: each hectare of fertile soil returned to productive use will give a harvest for many years.[30]

Sukhomlinsky acknowledged that work should be appropriate to age-level and never overtax children. He maintained, however, that children commencing work activities at an early age showed great enthusiasm, especially if the work resembled that undertaken by adults.

Not only did Sukhomlinsky endeavour to see that children's work resembled adults' in being socially significant; he also encouraged the creation of miniature tools and machines, resembling adult ones, but with additional safety features. In the many clubs where children participated in extracurricular work activities it was not uncommon for primary school children to be working alongside senior children, using miniature lathes and power tools. These replicas of adult tools had often been made by senior students and teachers. They were very attractive to young children and were used as an incentive to encourage them to master manual skills. Before using an electric fret saw, for instance, they had to master the use of a hand one. It followed that access to such power tools depended on the level of interest and competence.

b) Diversity of work activities

A diversity of work activities was necessary to give pupils a sufficient range of experience on which to base their choice of vocation. Only by trying many activities could they discover where their unique talents lay:

> The diversity of types of work which surround a child from the time he sets foot in our school, are, figuratively speaking, so many magnets of varying strength, which attract the sensitive needle of the compass guiding the child on his path. The stronger the magnet, the more interesting the work in which the child becomes involved, the more clearly he develops abilities, inclination and vocation for that work.[31]

This diversity also catered to children's natural urge to change activities frequently, to their thirst for new and varied experiences. With some 45 clubs operating at the school, children often attended two or more.

c) Continuity of work activities over an extended period of time

This was another tenet questioned by members of the Academy of Pedagogical Sciences and vigorously defended by Sukhomlinsky. He felt that

Intellectual, Vocational and Aesthetic Development

it was essential that work activities were part of a child's daily life, and not relegated to a particular time of the week, month or year. He held that working on projects which spanned several years (such as caring for fruit trees planted in the first year of schooling) had a far greater effect on children's characters than intermittent bursts of activity. Prolonged application to a single area of work was also a precondition for developing the high degree of skill which might lead to a future vocation. Sukhomlinsky was concerned to see that children achieved what he called 'significant success' in at least one area of work:

> We strive to ensure that a pupil achieves significant success in his favourite activity. The path to success usually lies through prolonged experimentation. The pupil tries his strength in a variety of activities, acquires many skills, but if his success in some activity does not extend far beyond the bounds of what is normal for his age it means he has still not found his path. Significant success is not merely the satisfactory, good or excellent execution of what is achievable by anyone. Anyone may do an excellent job of making a ruler, or assembling a model generator — some just need more practice, others less. But for work to become a favourite activity, a passion, requires success which exceeds the highest standards achievable by all pupils of a given age. It is such success which we call significant.[32]

Students who appeared to be missing out on such 'significant success' were encouraged to focus their attention on some interest they had:

> Deeply believing that each person can become a poet, an artist in some pursuit, we aspire to see that these pupils, figuratively speaking, should concentrate all their energies on a single point — should go deeply into the details and subtleties of some particular pursuit. If success is not achieved at first, we help to make a fresh start; if there is failure at the second attempt, we help to approach the matter from a different direction.[33]

d) Ensuring all work had a creative and intellectual dimension

This principle relates to Marx's view of work as creative activity and to the idea that work should contribute to all-round development. Sukhomlinsky wanted his students to see any work — even the most mundane agricultural activities — as a field of creative endeavour. In one passage he describes how pupils involved in cleaning manure from cow sheds devised a labour saving device to simplify the task, and incidentally improved the quality of the animals' bedding straw. In most cases pupils involved in agricultural activities were doing so as part of some research project:

> One of the strongest motivating factors in physical work is the significance of the idea behind the work, the combining of the efforts of intellect and hands. The more significant the idea behind it, the greater the interest with which even the simplest work is performed. Mastering a trade, research, experimentation, utilising scientific data in work, all of this is recognised and experienced by the child as [an expression of] moral dignity.
>
> It is especially important to ensure the coordination of physical effort and intellect in agricultural work, where there are many monotonous work processes … For example in growing sugar beet there are many monotonous, uninteresting work processes. But even this work can become creative if it has a research aim. (Our children are researching ways of increasing the sugar content in the roots of the beet.)[34]

Finding an intellectual dimension to work activities had a beneficial effect on other studies. Quite often work activities reinforced knowledge acquired in the classroom. In some instances work activities paved the way for the introduction of theoretical material in class. This particularly applied to such subjects as physics, chemistry, biology and mathematics.

e) Productive work should be undertaken by all without exception

This principle reflects the philosophy of the workers' state and relates to the moral dimension of work education. Sukhomlinsky considered that all pupils should be involved in such activities as keeping classrooms and other areas clean and tidy (referred to in Russian as 'self-service') and in collective projects such as tree planting, preparing fertiliser, and other large-scale agricultural work. 'Self-service', although the simplest form of work, was considered important in developing discipline, a sense of duty, and aesthetic sensitivity to daily surroundings. Again children were involved at an early age:

Intellectual, Vocational and Aesthetic Development 91

A conscious attitude to work — to self-service — is only possible when a person has acquired in childhood a habitual, internalised intolerance of dirtiness and untidiness, when this habit has become an emotional and aesthetic sensitivity to the surrounding environment.[35]

f) Work should not be pursued to the exclusion of other interests

This principle acknowledges the existence of intrinsically valuable pursuits other than work, which are needed to give work greater significance. Cultural and recreational activities were particularly encouraged during times when work demands were great:

> The more sources of human culture to which the mind and heart are exposed in adolescence and early youth, the more work ennobles a person. So we try to ensure that a diverse spiritual life continues uninterrupted in the collective. In summer in particular, when our pupils are hard at work in the fields for several weeks, we conduct literary and musical evenings at the school, evenings of science and technology, collective readings.[36]

Having considered some of the principles upon which work education was based at Pavlysh, let us look more closely at the methods adopted to implement these principles. Work lessons were conducted as part of the curriculum of all Soviet schools, but in the light of frequent complaints in the Soviet press of inadequate provision of work education in schools, and allegations that for some senior students work lessons consist of sweeping factory floors, it becomes clear how exceptional the work program at Pavlysh was. O'Dell, in an essay on "Forming Socialist Attitudes Towards Work Among Soviet School Children"[37] has highlighted some of the difficulties in implementing educational policy in this area. These included the reluctance of young people to accept certain jobs, due to differentials in status and remuneration, disparities between theory and practice, family pressure, bureaucratic and organisational failures and the existence of the black economy. She also suggests that 'unlike patriotism, love of work does not have such firm roots in the Russian tradition.'

Crucial to the success at Pavlysh was the very extensive extracurricular program which supplemented regular work lessons. The regular work lessons involved gardening and hand crafts in years one to four, the cultivation of experimental plots and the use of machine tools in years five to seven, and the basic principles and practice of industrial and agricultural production in years eight to ten. The further the children advanced through the school, the greater was the intellectual and experimental or inventive component of these lessons. High levels of technical competence were achieved, in large part due to the extracurricular program.

Sukhomlinsky obviously took great pride in the extent of extracurricular activities, and in *Pavlysh school* he goes so far as to list all the clubs at the school and describes their mode of operation and the equipment they used. A key feature of these clubs was the way younger children worked alongside older children and learnt from them:

> The first thing that catches the eye of a child who enters our school in grade one is the array of interesting things that all, without exception, are busy with. Each pupil has a favourite workplace, a favourite hobby, and an older friend whose work serves as a model. The overwhelming majority of pupils are not only learning something, mastering something, but passing on their acquired skills and knowledge to their friends. A person is being truly educated only when they pass their knowledge, experience and mastery on to someone else. One only begins to sense one's creative powers and abilities when one enters into moral relations with another person, becomes concerned about increasing their spiritual wealth. This is how a vocation is born and how self-education occurs. In the work process moral relations between personalities arise from the moment when one begins to see in another their own virtues, when the other person becomes as a mirror to them. It is on these moral relationships in the collective that vocational self-education is built.[38]

The above passage captures the spirit of education through the collective, as understood by Sukhomlinsky. Soviet views of education through the collective (and Western interpretations of Soviet practice) have been formed principally under the influence of Makarenko's ideas. Makarenko of course worked under very different conditions from Sukhomlinsky—in institutions for homeless children. Many of his charges had been roaming the countryside in gangs before coming to live in his colonies. It is understandable, therefore, that the organisation

Intellectual, Vocational and Aesthetic Development   93

of his communes took on a military character, and that the collective frequently took on a disciplinary role. Strong discipline was necessary to give the children basic security, physical as well as emotional. It is regrettable, though, that practices developed by Makarenko to cope with exceptional circumstances became enshrined in teacher training manuals for decades, and were even twisted to become instruments of suppression. In consequence children were often encouraged to condemn their peers as a way of extending the teacher's authority. Sukhomlinsky had great admiration for Makarenko and numbered him amongst his mentors. He condemned, however, the use of the children's collective to discipline pupils, holding that the trauma of being condemned by one's peers was always counterproductive.[39]

For Sukhomlinsky, the power of the collective lay in its ability to nurture the development of each of its members, to kindle interests, stimulate creativity and support in times of trouble. This seemingly reasonable stand caused quite a deal of controversy, and following the publication of "Essays on communist education" Sukhomlinsky was accused of being an opponent of Makarenko's ideas. This led to a popular perception that Makarenko was a proponent of collective education and Sukhomlinsky of education for the individual. Such a view is not entirely supported by a closer study of the work of the two men. Makarenko took a keen interest in each individual child in his care, and Sukhomlinsky wrote volumes on the power of the collective. Sukhomlinsky's views on collective education did, however, mark a significant departure from Makarenko's ideas. They offered a much needed critique of the mindless orthodoxy which was a legacy of the Stalin years.

There is much in Sukhomlinsky's ideas on the educative power of the collective which is relevant to teachers in the West. The recognition that children's influence on each other rivals the influence of the teacher, together with the awareness that this influence can be very positive, opens up new possibilities for a practising teacher. One child's enthusiasm for literature, electronics or astronomy, can be a spark which kindles the interest of other children. Sukhomlinsky saw it thus:

> One of the most important objectives of our educational endeavours is to ensure that, figuratively speaking, no child's heart should remain unkindled, that all talents and abilities should fully unfold, that the

most talented and gifted children should become educators—only then will they be educated themselves ...

... Around each talented, gifted pupil gather several youngsters —boys and girls—in love with the same pursuit—often simply interested in what the older ones are doing. The talented pupil more often than not has no thought of guiding the others, he is immersed in his work and at first does not know those who work beside him. Conscious guidance appears later. At first children and adolescents with varying degrees of preparedness for work, with varying abilities and skills, appear to come together chaotically: a year two pupil is working with a year eight pupil, a year five pupil is learning from a year ten pupil. But later this apparent chaos becomes genuinely self-directed: the children are united by their enthusiasm for the work.[40]

The work clubs which operated after normal classes, then, were an integral part of the educational experience at Pavlysh, having a great influence on the general atmosphere of the school and on children's interest in and success at their studies. They also provided a key avenue for pastoral care.

How was it possible for Sukhomlinsky to develop a successful work program when so many Soviet schools failed to do so? Sukhomlinsky's position in the Party and his status may have helped in obtaining necessary resources, especially after he became well-known, but these would seem not to have been the main factors. Enthusiasm was the main force which drove the work program at Pavlysh, and the teachers and students themselves created most of the material resources needed, even supplying other schools with some equipment. The main factor contributing to success was the priority given to productive work. One of Sukhomlinsky's main criteria in selecting teachers for the school was their ability to impart some work skill. The creative orientation of the whole school program, its emphasis on health and the inculcation of moral values, was significant, as was the practice of doing homework in the morning which created a large reserve of free time after classes, much of which was devoted to participation in the various clubs.

Aesthetic Education

If work activities were the most characteristic vehicle for Sukhomlinsky's educational methods, the quest for beauty was the most characteristic goal. Sukhomlinsky saw aesthetic appreciation as a blend of thought and feeling, influenced by the pupil's activity:

> In aesthetic perception, as a cognitive and emotional process, there is a close connection between concepts, notions, judgments—thought in general—on the one hand, and feelings and emotions on the other. The success of aesthetic education depends on the extent to which the pupil apprehends the nature of the beautiful. But the influence of the beauty of nature, of works of art, of the surrounding environment, on his inner world, depends not only on the objective existence of beauty, but also on the character of the pupil's activity, on the way in which beauty is incorporated in his relationships with those around him.[41]

The link between appreciation and activity is the basis for incorporating aesthetic education into all other aspects of the education process. We have already described the aesthetic considerations in Sukhomlinsky's approach to physical education, the emphasis on grace in movement. There was an aesthetic component in all work activities, some of which, such as cultivating flowers, had a primarily aesthetic motivation. Conversely, Sukhomlinsky considered that work activities were a necessary component of aesthetic education:

> Beauty only ennobles a person when he labours to create beauty. We seek to ensure that a person labours not only for his daily bread, but also for joy.[42]

As noted in the discussion on moral education, Sukhomlinsky had great faith in the power of beauty to instil sensitivity and compassion:

> In the places of beauty which each class creates in the school grounds are roses, lilacs, grapes, pears. A concern for beauty is experienced as a concern for a tender, delicate, defenceless being, who would perish if people did not care for it.[43]

As with other aspects of all-round development, Sukhomlinsky considered the preschool and early school years to be crucial.[44] He considered the appreciation of moral beauty to be an important aspect of aesthetic education, the ultimate aim of which was to affirm beauty in one's own character.[45]

Acknowledging an intellectual component to aesthetic appreciation, Sukhomlinsky also considered there to be an aesthetic component in the urge to gain knowledge:

> The aspiration to do investigative, experimental work is at the same time a satisfaction of the aesthetic need for beautiful, intellectually fulfilling work.[46]

Sukhomlinsky wrote that the happiest moments of his life had been moments of liberated thought following upon the bliss of contemplation. We have already noted the extent to which he tried to stimulate his pupils' sense of wonder as a first step towards gaining knowledge.

Sukhomlinsky was a romantic, and for him the appreciation of beauty always began with the contemplation of Nature:

> We teach the children: man was singled out from the world of the animals and became a gifted being not only because he made the first tools with his hands, but also because he saw the depth of the dark blue sky, the twinkling of the stars, the overflowing rosiness of sunset and dawn … [47]

We earlier quoted a lengthy passage describing how Sukhomlinsky took his six-year-old pupils on nature outings to teach them how to read. Such outings were used to stimulate language activities throughout the school, and poems were selected for each age group to be read on such outings. Creative writing was encouraged:

> The ability to use words creatively, to embody one's thoughts, feelings and inner experiences in an artistic image, is necessary not only for a writer, but for any cultured person. The more this ability is developed, the higher a person's aesthetic and general level of culture is, the more refined his feelings, the deeper his experiences, the more clear his aesthetic perception of new artistic values.[48]

Music was seen as an expressive medium which complemented language:

> The ability to listen to and appreciate music is one of the elementary marks of aesthetic culture, and a complete education is inconceivable without it. Music's domain begins where speech ends. That which it

is impossible to express in words may be expressed with a musical melody, because music directly conveys moods and feelings.[49]

One of the most creative music educators in the Soviet Union, the composer D.B. Kabalevsky, wrote a glowing tribute in defence of Sukhomlinsky shortly after an attack had been made on him in the press. In it he cited several instances where he had used Sukhomlinsky's words as epigraphs for his books, including the dictum that "Music education is not the education of a musician, but first and foremost the education of a human being". He claimed that reading Sukhomlinsky had helped him to formulate his own ideas on teaching music in schools.[50]

As with the teaching of language, Sukhomlinsky frequently used nature outings as an introduction to musical appreciation. He might, for instance, take a junior class to listen to the sounds of a meadow in early autumn as an introduction to Rimsky-Korsakov's "The Flight of a Bumble Bee".[51]

He adopted a similar approach to teaching an appreciation of painting. Though not included in the state curriculum, lessons in art appreciation were integrated into language classes and nature excursions. As noted earlier, the study of portraits was one technique for making children more sensitive to others' feelings.

Sukhomlinsky tried to ensure that the school grounds and classrooms also contributed to the aesthetic education of the pupils. Here the pupils' own activity enhanced the surroundings:

> We seek to ensure that everywhere in the school grounds pupils should see the beauty of nature, which becomes even more beautiful because they, the children, are caring for it.[52]

We have already described the school grounds at some length, but the following passage illustrates the care that was taken in the classrooms themselves:

> We give considerable attention to the creation of the aesthetic environment in the classrooms and working rooms, in the workshops. Each class group seeks to ensure that their room is distinguished by something special. The uniqueness of the aesthetic environment is created by a plant placed next to the blackboard. In one class it may be a lemon tree, in another a rose, in a third a little pine tree. This plant determines the style of the aesthetic environment of the whole

room. On one of the window sills is a small flower or piece of greenery reminding one of the beauty of the school grounds. The important thing here is not the quantity of greenery (windows are for light), but the striking shape of the stem and leaves silhouetted against the sky.[53]

The following passage develops this idea further and throws some light on Sukhomlinsky's own aesthetic sensibilities:

> The harmony between the objects which surround a child imparts a common aesthetic spirit to the environment only when individual objects do not cry out for attention, when one seems not to notice them. If, for example, in a broad, well lit window, looking out on an orchard, one places several large flowers, the harmony will be destroyed, the flowers will extinguish the aesthetic qualities of the other objects — of the orchard itself. If, however, in the window there is a single cutting, harmonious in form with the trees in the orchard, with the time of year (harmony may also consist in contrast), then the cutting, the orchard and the expanses of the distant fields will all be perceived quite differently.[54]

It is indicative of Sukhomlinsky's approach, and his concern for the individual, that he was opposed to having a school uniform. While the school did set down guidelines for dress, these were in the nature of aesthetic principles rather than strict rules:

> We are against having a single uniform for all pupils. (The current uniform is no good at all, especially for the girls. It is hideous, and it is no wonder that the young pioneers in their newspaper recently requested the Ministry of Education to give them a new form of dress.) We try to see that clothing emphasises and draws attention to the aesthetic features of the child's individuality.[55]

In the matter of hairstyles a similar approach was adopted, students being advised to adopt a hairstyle that suited their individual features.

Holistic Education at Pavlysh Secondary School

We are now in a position to review Sukhomlinsky's model of holistic education. It may be seen to incorporate five elements: health education, moral education, intellectual education, work education and aesthetic education.

Central to the whole system is the moral core which motivated all other aspects of education at Pavlysh. The essence of this moral core is the collective quest for happiness and personal growth through knowledge and work. The ultimate value is enshrined in individual human beings, as each person is a whole world in themselves.

How rich that world is depends on the 'spiritual wealth' accumulated through all the other aspects of education. Health provides the foundation for all personal growth, and was Sukhomlinsky's chief preoccupation when dealing with children during the first years at school, so health education may be regarded as the foundation stone. It incorporates the establishment of a daily regime capable of sustaining study and work activities. Intellectual education and work education were conducted simultaneously, each relating to the central moral concerns.

Crowning all is the aesthetic component of education, aiming at the creation and appreciation of beauty in all aspects of daily life, including human relationships. In practice, of course these various aspects were integrated into a single approach and did not exist separately. They do not correspond to separate subjects in the curriculum, but reflect the preoccupations of teachers and students in all their activities.

On the basis of Sukhomlinsky's description of his aims and experience at Pavlysh, (and as confirmed by observers who visited the school), we have to conclude that Sukhomlinsky's approach was indeed a holistic one, to some intrusively so. How one responds to Sukhomlinsky's work depends to a large extent on whether one accepts the moral values at the heart of his endeavours. If one accepts (or disregards) the elements of political indoctrination, and responds to his idealistic vision of a society in which kindness and empathy are the norm and all work for the common good, then one may indeed draw inspiration from his educational legacy.

Notes

1 Sukhomlinsky, V.A., "Pavlyshskaia sredniaia shkola [Pavlysh School]", *Izbrannye proizvedeniia v piati tomakh [Collected Works in Five Volumes]*, Kiev, Radianska shkola, 1979–80, Vol. 4, p. 247.
2 Ibid., p. 215.
3 Ibid., p. 214.
4 Ibid., p. 217.

5   See Price, R.F., *Marx and Education in Russia and China*, London: Croom Helm, 1977, and his *Marx and Education in Late Capitalism*, London: Croom Helm, 1986.
6   Sukhomlinsky, V.A., "Pavlyshskaia sredniaia shkola [Pavlysh School]", *Izbrannye proizvedeniia v piati tomakh [Collected Works in Five Volumes]*, Kiev, Radianska shkola, 1979–80, Vol. 4, p. 230.
7   See, for instance, Shneidman, N.N., *Literature and Ideology in Soviet Education*, Lexington: Lexington Books, 1973.
8   Morgan, L., *The Socializing Function of Myth in the Soviet Press*, Ph.D., University of Queensland, 1981, pp. iv–v.
9   Sukhomlinsky, V.A., "Pavlyshskaia sredniaia shkola [Pavlysh School]", *Izbrannye proizvedeniia v piati tomakh [Collected Works in Five Volumes]*, Kiev, Radianska shkola, 1979–80, Vol. 4, p. 222.
10 Sukhomlinsky, V.A., "Serdtse otdaiu detiam [My Heart I Give to Children]", *Izbrannye proizvedeniia v piati tomakh [Collected Works in Five Volumes]*, Kiev, Radianska shkola, 1979–80,, Vol. 3, p. 84.
11 Ibid., pp. 81/82.
12 Ibid., pp. 84/85.
13 Ibid., pp. 86/87.
14 Ibid.
15 Ashton-Warner, S., *Teacher*, Harmondsworth, Middlesex: Penguin, 1966, p. 27.
16 Ibid., pp. 23/24.
17 Boguslavsky, M.V., *Ideia stimulirovania radosti poznaniia u shkol'nikov v pedagogicheskikh trudakh i opyte V.A. Sukhomlinskogo, Dissertatsiia … kand. ped. nauk [The idea of stimulating pupil's joy in learning in the works and experience of V.A. Sukhomlinsky, Dissertation …]*, Moscow, 1986.
18 See Sukhomlinsky, V.A., "Rozhdenie grazhdanina [The Birth of a Citizen]", *Izbrannye pedagogicheskie sochineniia v trekh tomakh [Selected pedagogical works in three volumes]*, Moscow, Pedagogika, 1979–81, Vol. 1, p. 468.
19 Sukhomlinsky, V.A., "Serdtse otdaiu detiam [My Heart I Give to Children]", *Izbrannye proizvedeniia v piati tomakh [Collected Works in Five Volumes]*, Kiev, Radianska shkola, 1979–80, Vol. 3, p. 181.
20 Sukhomlinsky, V.A., "Serdtse otdaiu detiam [My Heart I Give to Children]", *Izbrannye pedagogicheskie sochineniia v trekh tomakh*, Moscow, Pedagogika, 1979–81, Vol. 1, p. 49.
21 Ibid., p. 50.
22 Ibid., p. 60.
23 Sukhomlinsky, V.A., "Pavlyshskaia sredniaia shkola [Pavlysh School]", *Izbrannye proizvedeniia v piati tomakh [Collected Works in Five Volumes]*, Kiev, Radianska shkola, 1979–80, Vol. 4, p. 256.
24 Ibid., p. 299.
25 See Soloveichik's comments in Sukhomlinsky, V.A., *O vospitanii [On Education]*, 6th edition, Moscow, Pedagogika, 1988, pp. 66–73.
26 Sukhomlinsky, V.A., "Pavlyshskaia sredniaia shkola [Pavlysh School]", *Izbrannye proizvedeniia v piati tomakh [Collected Works in Five Volumes]*, Kiev, Radianska shkola, 1979–80, Vol. 4, p. 315.

Intellectual, Vocational and Aesthetic Development 101

27 Price, R.F., "How is the Study of the USSR and China Relevant to Australia?", in *Problems and Prospects for Comparative and International Studies in Education in Australia*, LaTrobe University, Melbourne, 1977, pp.56-57. See also Price, R.F., *Marx and Education in Russia and China*, London, Croom Helm, 1977, pp. 184-203.
28 *Marx and Education in Russia and China*, pp. 11-22.
29 See *Sovetskaia pedagogika [Soviet Pedagogy]*, 1962, No. 6, pp. 156-160.
30 Sukhomlinsky, V.A., "Pavlyshskaia sredniaia shkola [Pavlysh School]", *Izbrannye proizvedeniia v piati tomakh [Collected Works in Five Volumes]*, Kiev, Radianska shkola, 1979-80, Vol. 4, p. 317/318.
31 Ibid., p. 364.
32 Ibid., p. 365.
33 Ibid., p. 368.
34 Ibid., p. 321.
35 Ibid., p. 377.
36 Ibid., p. 324.
37 In Avis, G. ed., *The Making of the Soviet Citizen*, London: Croom Helm, 1987, pp. 80-106.
38 Sukhomlinsky, V.A., "Pavlyshskaia sredniaia shkola [Pavlysh School]", *Izbrannye proizvedeniia v piati tomakh [Collected Works in Five Volumes]*, Kiev, Radianska shkola, 1979-80, Vol. 4, p. 358/359.
39 Sukhomlinsky, V.A., "Sto sovetov uchiteliu [100 pieces of advice for teachers]", *Izbrannye proizvedeniia v piati tomakh [Collected Works in Five Volumes]*, Kiev, Radianska shkola, 1979-80, Vol. 2, pp. 665-668.
40 Sukhomlinsky, V.A., "Pavlyshskaia sredniaia shkola [Pavlysh School]", *Izbrannye proizvedeniia v piati tomakh [Collected Works in Five Volumes]*, Kiev, Radianska shkola, 1979-80, Vol. 4, p. 360,362.
41 Ibid., p. 396.
42 Ibid., p. 405.
43 Ibid., p. 406.
44 Ibid., p. 392.
45 Ibid., p. 387.
46 Ibid., p. 394.
47 Ibid., p. 387.
48 Ibid., p. 403.
49 Ibid., p. 401.
50 Kabalevsky, Dm., "Bol'shoi rezerv v pedagogicheskom arsenale [A great reserve in the pedagogical arsenal]", *Kommunist*, 1977, No. 13, p. 91.
51 Sukhomlinsky, V.A., "Serdtse otdaiu detiam [My Heart I Give to Children]", *Izbrannye pedagogicheskie sochineniia v trekh tomakh [Selected pedagogical works in three volumes]*, Moscow, Pedagogika, 1979-81, Vol. 1, p. 76.
52 Sukhomlinsky, V.A., "Pavlyshskaia sredniaia shkola [Pavlysh School]", *Izbrannye proizvedeniia v piati tomakh [Collected Works in Five Volumes]*, Kiev, Radianska shkola, 1979-80, Vol. 4, p. 405.
53 Ibid., p. 408.

54 Ibid., p. 405.
55 Ibid., p. 408.

CHAPTER 5

Education of the Heart

> In childhood a person must pass through an emotional school—a school which educates kindly feelings.[1]
>
> A wise love for children is the pinnacle of our educational culture, of our thought and feelings. Cordiality, warmth, goodwill towards the child—that which in a word may be called *kindness*, is the result of the teacher's prolonged efforts at educating his own feelings.[2]

IN THIS chapter we shall focus on the central concern of all of Sukhomlinsky's work—the education of the subjective factors in the human personality. It was the psychological bases of human behaviour—perceptions, emotions and attitudes—that Sukhomlinsky saw as being crucial in the shaping of human relations and human society at large. He was always more concerned to influence the individual psyche than to exact conformity to a particular standard of behaviour. He considered it most unwise to mistake obedience and submissiveness for virtue.[3]

He believed that virtue was something that needed to be consciously nurtured and could not be left to nature. The means for educating virtue needed to be deeply personal:

> Our work addresses subtle aspects of the spiritual life of the developing personality—the intelligence, feeling, will, conviction, self-consciousness. One may influence these spheres only through like action, through intelligence, feeling, will, conviction, self-consciousness. The most important means for influencing the spiritual world of the pupil are the teacher's word, the beauty of the surrounding world and of art, the creation of circumstances in which feelings find their most striking expression—human relationships covering the whole emotional gamut.[4]

In educating the heart, the use of force was inappropriate and indeed counterproductive. Sukhomlinsky cites Dostoevsky's view that punishment releases a person from the judgment of their own conscience.[5] The appropriate, albeit far more difficult, approach was to awaken an individual's conscience, so that their moral development became autonomous.

Dostoevsky was undoubtably one of the formative influences on Sukhomlinsky's thought. In his youth his grandfather had left him a collection of Dostoevsky's works which he treasured.[6] Like Dostoevsky, Sukhomlinsky took an interest in criminal proceedings and tried to understand the origins of anti-social behaviour. In *The Birth of a Citizen* he describes how he made a detailed study of 460 cases of juvenile crime. He interviewed the young people involved, visited their families and made enquiries at the schools where they had studied. He writes of his conclusions:

> I studied the lives of those 460 families in which adolescents committing offences and crimes had been brought up, and saw the following picture. The more serious the crime, the greater its inhumanity, cruelty and mindlessness, the poorer the intellectual, aesthetic and moral interests and impulses in the family. Not a single one of the families of these adolescents who had committed a crime or offence had a family library, even a small one.
>
> … None of [the adolescents] … could name a single work of symphonic, operatic or chamber music. Not one could name a single composer of classical or contemporary music.[7]

Here we see Sukhomlinsky's belief in the role of intellectual and aesthetic development in developing character. He saw a clear link between holistic development, as discussed in the previous chapters, and the development of humaneness.

A second line of enquiry which Sukhomlinsky pursued in studying adolescent crime was to explore the network of human relationships which had sustained the growth of the young people concerned:

> I analysed the relationships which these difficult adolescents (or, more correctly, people with a spiritually impoverished childhood and adolescence) had experienced, at the schools where they studied. Had they experienced relationships, the essence and content of which were

the gift of one's inner resources, the creation of happiness by one person for another. Had they experienced concern for the fate of another, the attainment by the mind and especially by the heart of the highest human joy—the joy of giving happiness to another human being? And it became clear that this, the most important thing of all, was absent both at home and at school.[8]

In examining Sukhomlinsky's approach to the education of the heart, then, we shall be focussing on the approach to aesthetic development, and on the network of human relationships which can nurture (or erode) a young person's humane qualities. We shall devote the greater part of our attention to the relationship between teacher and student, as being the archetypal educational relationship, and the one with which Sukhomlinsky was principally concerned. We shall consider specific techniques Sukhomlinsky used to educate the hearts of his students, techniques aimed at awakening an appreciation of beauty and at developing empathy.

We shall also consider the other relationships which nurtured the children's development: relationships within the family, children's peer relationships, and teachers' relationships with each other. We shall look at the methods Sukhomlinsky evolved for influencing the nature of these relationships, at his involvement in parent education, his contribution to developing an *esprit de corps* among the staff, and his method of educating through the collective. We shall take the opportunity to discuss how Sukhomlinsky's approach to education through the collective differed from Makarenko's—an issue which generated some controversy in Soviet educational circles. We shall conclude the chapter with a brief summary of how children's educational experience at Pavlysh was structured to bring out their humane qualities.

The most vivid account of Sukhomlinsky's relationship with his students is to be found in his most popular work, *My Heart I Give to Children*. In it he describes his work with a particular class of children for whom he was responsible throughout their primary schooling. The sequel to that book, *The Birth of a Citizen*, describes his work with the same group of children during the first four years of their secondary education—their adolescent years. Both books have been referred to extensively in preparing this chapter.

While trying not to idealise a child's nature, Sukhomlinsky valued a child's perception of the world and saw qualities in children to which adults could often only aspire:

> The eminent Polish educator, Janusz Korczak, in one of his letters, refers to the need to ascend to the level of the child's spiritual world rather than condescend to it. This is a very subtle thought, the essence of which we teachers would do well to ponder deeply. Without idealising children, without ascribing to them some miraculous qualities, a true teacher cannot fail to note that children's perception of the world, children's emotional and moral response to the reality which surrounds them, is distinguished by a particular clarity, subtlety and spontaneity. Janusz Korczak's summons to ascend to the spiritual world of the child should be understood as a sensitive understanding and appreciation of the child's way of knowing the world—knowing with mind and heart.[9]

Much of Sukhomlinsky's work can be seen as an attempt to foster certain qualities already inherent in children. His frequent departures from common school practices were due to his perception that such practices often destroyed the virtues he wished to preserve in children. Hence his wish not to confine young children in classrooms for long hours and his avoidance of language divorced from experience.[10] Hence his approbation of teenagers independently taking action against poachers rather than simply reporting matters to the authorities.[11]

The first section of *My Heart I Give to Children* is entitled "The School of Joy", and describes his pioneering work with six-year-old children. Something of Sukhomlinsky's approach with these children has been outlined in the previous chapter—particularly his approach to the teaching of literacy in natural surroundings. As already stated, the children did not enter the classroom during this first year. All of Sukhomlinsky's efforts were aimed at developing the children's imaginative faculties, their sensitivity to beauty, and their relationships with each other and with their families.

At the first lesson the children had with him, Sukhomlinsky asked the children to remove their shoes (they were not used to wearing shoes at that time of year) and follow him to a bower covered with grape vines. As they sat in the shade and watched the the sun's rays filtering through the leaves, Sukhomlinsky (prompted by the children) composed a fairy story into which he wove the children's own observations of the natural beauty around them. It was a story of giant blacksmiths toiling each day to forge a new crown for the sun, the sparks from their blows showering down in rays of light. The children suggested new twists to his tale, and as he spoke he drew an illustration to match the words. It was his way of heightening the children's awareness of their surroundings and their sense of joy in them, of stimulating their imaginations and of establishing his relationship with them as a joyful one. He finished the lesson by giving each child two bunches of grapes — one to eat themselves and one to give to their mothers. It was his plan for each child, when they were strong enough, to plant their own grape vine and tend it.[12]

We can discern here key elements in Sukhomlinsky's approach: the selection of beautiful natural surroundings in which to conduct lessons, the composition of stories (by both teacher and pupils) about those surroundings, attention to children's diet and health, and concern that children should learn to bring joy to family and friends. Sukhomlinsky did not have a detailed plan of activities for the year. He saw himself as simply facilitating children's discovery of the world and creative response to it:

> The life of our school [for six-year-olds] developed from an idea which inspired me: a child is by its nature a keen researcher, an explorer of the world. So let there open before it a wonderful world in living colours, in bright and thrilling sounds, in fairy tale and play, in its own creativity, in beauty which inspires the heart, in the urge to do good to others. Through fairy tale, fantasy, play, through the unique creativity of children, is the true way to the child's heart.[13]

Sukhomlinsky frequently includes in the text of his books fairy tales and poems composed by his pupils, as well as some composed by himself. The children's first attempts were generally responses to his own stories, but before long they were composing stories in response to each other. Stories helped children to form notions of good and evil, and allowed them to give expression to their hopes and fears, as well as encouraging observation and appreciation of nature. The composition of stories took place orally and collectively, and provided an opportunity for Sukhomlinsky to observe the thought processes of each child:

The fairy tale is, figuratively speaking, a fresh wind which fans the fire of a child's thought and speech. Children not only love to hear fairy stories. They create them. Looking out at the world through the grape vine, I knew that I would tell them a story, but did not imagine exactly which. My flight of fantasy was triggered by Katia's words: "the sun is scattering little sparks" … What truthful, precise, artistically expressive images children create. How striking and colourful their language is![14]

Similar sentiments were expressed by Tolstoy in his account of how he wrote stories with village children at Yasnaia Poliana.[15] Tolstoy found the best way to encourage children's writing was to compose stories with them, allowing them gradually to take charge of the process. He was stunned by the children's artistic sense, which he considered superior to his own and to that of other recognised writers. He concluded that children's sense of truth, beauty and goodness was inherent and became corrupted as they grew older, and were subjected to adult expectations and all the pressures inherent in human development and socialisation.

In *My Heart I Give to Children* Sukhomlinsky describes many of the beautiful settings in which the children spent their first year with him. He would take them at sunset to sit by weeping willows at water's edge. They found a cave in a ravine which they dubbed their "place of dreams", lighting campfires there at dusk, and composing fantastic stories in the flickering light. They climbed the ancient burial mounds of the Scythians and took in the sweeping views of rolling steppes, and the distant Dnieper. They went for long walks in the forest, coming home with flushed cheeks and voracious appetites. The children's health improved markedly.

Sukhomlinsky considered that during the early childhood years emotional education was linked with the education of the senses and with language development:

> Experience confirms that the roots of kindly feelings reach back into childhood, and that humanity, kindness, affection and good will are born in labour, in care and concern for the beauty of the surrounding world. Kindly feelings are a concentration of humanity. If kindly feelings are not educated in childhood you will never educate them, because that which is truly human gains a foothold in the soul along with the awareness of the first and most important truths, along

with the experience and feeling of the subtlest shades of one's native tongue.[16]

Awakening children to the beauty in nature was seen as an integral step in children's emotional education that provided a foundation for humane feelings. Beauty was to be found not only in nature and in language. Music and art were also invaluable media through which to educate the heart. On music, Sukhomlinsky writes:

> Music, melody, the beauty of musical sounds—are an important means for educating a person morally and intellectually, for ennobling the heart and purifying the soul. Music opens people's eyes to the beauty in nature, in moral relations, in work. Thanks to music a person wakens to a consciousness of that which is sublime, majestic and beautiful, not only in the surrounding world, but within himself. Music is a powerful means for self-education.
>
> Many years of observation of the spiritual development of one and the same students, from their early years until maturity, has convinced me that the uncontrolled, unorganised influence on children of cinema, radio and television hinders rather than assists a proper aesthetic education. A surfeit of chaotic musical impressions is particularly harmful. I saw one of the main tasks of children's education as being to ensure that listening to musical works should alternate with listening to the background against which a person may understand and feel the beauty of the music—with listening to the quiet of the fields and meadows, the rustling of the oak trees, the song of the lark in the azure sky, the whisper of the ripening ears of wheat, the buzzing of the bees. This is the music of nature, the source from which people draw inspiration when creating a musical melody.
>
> In aesthetic education in general, and musical education in particular, the psychological aims of a teacher who is acquainting children with the world of the beautiful are important. For me the most important aim was to educate an *ability* to relate emotionally to beauty and a *thirst* for impressions of an aesthetic nature. I saw the main aim of the whole system of education as being to ensure that the school taught people to live in the world of the beautiful, so that they could not live without beauty, so that the beauty of the world created beauty in themselves.[17]

Sukhomlinsky's approach to the musical education of young children included outdoor excursions to heighten sensitivity to natural sounds, carefully prepared exposure to a limited number of folk songs and evocative works of classical music, and teaching the children how to make and play a simple folk pipe.

Sukhomlinsky considered that in developing sensitivity to music children could gain an emotional enrichment which was not achievable through any other means. They could be exposed to a range of human feelings to which they would otherwise have no access. Music was capable of uplifting their perception of human nature and of themselves. It was in this context that he made the oft-quoted statement that "music education is not the education of a musician, but first and foremost the education of a human being."[18]

Sukhomlinsky did not wish to bombard the children with a surfeit of musical images, fearing that this might blunt their sensitivity. He offered them about two pieces per month, and always in association with nature outings which provided a suitable background for presentation of the music. In early autumn, when the meadows were covered in wildflowers, and the bees were especially active, the children listened to Rimsky-Korsakov's *The Flight of the Bumble Bee*. When the trees were decked in autumn colours, and the geese were migrating south for the winter, they listened to Tchaikovsky's *Autumn Song*. The music would conjure up many associations, and after sharing these the children would listen to the music a second time. Evocative works such as Grieg's *Peer Gynt* or Tchaikovsky's *Baba Yaga* were powerful stimuli for the children's creative writing, the favoured genre being fairy tales in which good and evil did battle. Music was especially useful as a stimulus for the children in the winter months, when they were more often confined indoors. In spring the children spent much time outdoors, and were encouraged to listen to the sounds of the forests and meadows, a highlight being the sound of the lark ascending. In each case they listened to corresponding musical compositions.

On one occasion Sukhomlinsky took the children to an elder grove and showed them how to fashion a folk pipe. He played a tune for them and soon all the children were keen to make their own pipes. Several of them displayed a particular gift for playing these, and as well as learning to play folk songs they developed a capacity for improvisation. Even those without any particular musical gift were infected with the enthusiasm generated by the group.

Sukhomlinsky worked hard to extend the musical resources of the school. It was no simple task, in a village school, to build up a record collection or to acquire musical instruments. When the children were in grade three the school obtained two bayans and three violins for them. Initially, nine of the children started learning these instruments. By the time they completed grade four, nineteen of the thirty-one class members had their own violins or bayans at home.

In some cases music was the key which opened the door to a child's heart. One boy with a difficult family background, whose father had been imprisoned for receiving stolen goods, turned out to be a gifted musician. It was through music that Sukhomlinsky was able to relate to him.

As the children grew older they practised choral singing of Ukrainian folk songs and of songs by classical and modern composers. Sukhomlinsky wrote:

> Song instils a poetic vision of the world. I remember how one day, after singing a song in which our people had expressed deep feelings, we went out into the steppes. Before us spread an endless sea of wheat, on the horizon some ancient burial mounds showed blue, between the yellow fields the road wound in a narrow ribbon, a lark was singing in the sky. The children stopped as if seeing for the first time this part of their native land. "It's like the song about the reapers", said sensitive, impressionable Varia. I felt at that moment that in each child's soul the words of this favourite song were sounding out.[19]

Songs heightened the children's sensitivity both to the natural beauty of the countryside and to the subtleties of language. Sukhomlinsky thought that there was also a link between musical appreciation and moral sense, which deserved more attention from educators:

> There is a human quality — sensitivity, emotionality. It is expressed in the fact that one's surroundings sharpen one's capacity for feeling. A person with a sensitive, emotional nature cannot ignore the grief, suffering or misfortune of another human being; his conscience obliges him to help. This quality is educated by music and song.[20]

This sensitivity, which could be developed through music, was also expressed in a person's responsiveness to a kind word or to some heartfelt advice. In *The Birth of a Citizen* Sukhomlinsky goes so far as to recommend music therapy for adolescents showing tendencies towards coarseness and insensitivity. Sukhomlinsky's own attempts in this direction were not overt, but took the form of musical appreciation groups. Where children had already learnt to appreciate music in childhood, listening to music as adolescents served to reawaken childhood feelings, to stimulate their "emotional memory". This concept of "emotional memory" is an important one to grasp in order to understand Sukhomlinsky's overall approach to education of the heart. On the education of adolescents he writes:

> It is in the development and enrichment of the emotional memory that we find the union of emotional and aesthetic education. Our pupils during their childhood had discovered several places of striking beauty. These were the weeping willows, leaning over a pond, the quiet twilight of the oak grove, an old cherry tree in a ravine, a lilac garden. The beauty of these places had awakened a sense of wonder in the children. They had looked at the world with wide open eyes and experienced the happiness of appreciating beauty. These childhood memories, linked with images of nature, sharpened their sensitivity and openness to the surrounding world. As adolescents they saw the beauty of nature because they had discovered it in childhood and it had left an impression in their emotional memory.
>
> Music is a source of enrichment of the emotional memory. I strove to link listening to musical melodies in childhood with pure, noble, lofty feelings and (most importantly) impulses. Listening to works by Tchaikovsky, Grieg, Beethoven and Bach in the midst of nature, the children created in their imagination pictures of a battle between good and evil; in their minds and hearts they were on the side of good, of beauty, of justice. It was at just such times that the urge to do something good awoke in the children. This ennobling effect of music carried on into adolescence.[21]

We find here a simple explanation of the role of stories and music in moral education. All cultures have traditional stories and songs which form part of the upbringing of children. In some cultures the moral and spiritual significance of these stories is greater, in some less, but in all societies they have formed a part of the cultural heritage and have contributed to the development of children's moral perceptions. Plato considered that it was of no small consequence what stories were told to young people and what music they listened to, that these were matters of great significance for the health of the society.[22]

It may be salutary to consider the cultural experience of many of today's young people in the light of such traditional attitudes. The processes of industrialisation and commercialisation have, in the space of a mere couple of centuries, done much to dehumanise society and cast its members adrift from their ethical moorings. What impressions are being stored in the "emotional memory" of a child who grows up with computer games rather than fairy stories? Perhaps it is possible to make a computer game with the moral content of a traditional story, but this will not happen unless the inventors of such games are motivated by the same concerns as moved an Aesop or an Andersen.[23]

Sukhomlinsky generally gave a verbal introduction to any musical compositions he presented to his pupils:

> I tried to make sure that the words used to explain music created a type of emotional stimulus which awakened sensitivity to music as the direct language of the soul (A.Serov) ... An explanation of music should really carry within it something poetic, something which brings words close to music. I sought this poetic quality in the emotional memory of my pupils: with the help of words I created pictures which wakened memories of past experience, and these words, dug from the depths of the emotional memory, tuned the heart-strings to respond to the music.[24]

Sukhomlinsky cites as an example his introduction to the Ukrainian folk song "A mountain stands tall", which became a favourite with the children. It is a song about the beauty and transience of all living creatures:

> I say to the adolescents: "Do you remember a sunny day in early autumn, when we were hiking along the bank of a river and discovered a beautiful spot: the mirror-like surface of a quiet inlet, two weeping willows right on the river—one old and hollow, dying, and the other shapely, young, 'melodious' as Liuda said at the time. We experienced mixed feelings—melancholy and joy. A tree or a flower is not immortal, but life is immortal. And the crown of immortality is humankind. The song 'A mountain stands tall' is about the very feelings that we experienced at that time."[25]

This passage illustrates the interconnection of all educational activities in Sukhomlinsky's educational system, the "harmony of educational influences" discussed in a previous chapter. In particular, it shows the progression from nature outings, through language, to music, which Sukhomlinsky made use of in order to elicit a heart-felt response to beauty.

A similar progression was followed in teaching an appreciation of visual art. The first reproductions to be shown to the children were generally depictions of natural scenes such as Shishkin's *Rye*, Savrasov's *The Rooks have Come*, Levitan's *Golden Autumn*, and *Birch Forest*, Yuon's *Russian Winter* and Plastov's First Snow. The children progressed from works such as these to paintings on historic and patriotic themes, and ultimately to paintings by the great masters. Paintings such as Leonardo's *Last Supper* and Raphael's Sistine Madonna were studied with a view to exploring the psychological depth of the human portrayal.

Viewing of portraits might also be associated with the reading of literature. When studying *Anna Karenina*, for instance, a large reproduction of Kramskoy's portrait of Tolstoy was displayed in the classroom. This portrait had been painted while the author was working on the novel, and Sukhomlinsky maintained that the presence of the portrait in the classroom helped pupils to sense the presence of the author behind the text, and to gauge the extent to which the characters' utterances reflected the author's views.

Teaching an appreciation of the beauty in Nature, in art and music, was only the first step in education of the heart. Sukhomlinsky considered it essential that an emotional response to beauty be followed by actions which created and sustained beauty. This should preferably arise from the pupil's own awareness and impulse, rather than merely in obedience to a teacher's instructions. Sukhomlinsky was prepared to wait for this awareness to arise, even if it meant initially allowing the children to behave in a destructive manner.

On one occasion he took a group of six-year-olds to a quiet corner of the school grounds where some older children had planted chrysanthemums. The children were delighted by the spectacle of so many flowers showing off their colours in the autumn sun. Some of the children began picking the flowers, and before long only half remained standing. At this point one of the girls questioned whether it was all right to pick them. Sukhomlinsky deliberately remained silent, wishing to make his point when the experience had ripened:

> The children picked a few more flowers and the beauty of the spot disappeared, the clearing appeared orphaned. The surge of delight at beauty, which had blazed for an instant in the children's hearts, went out. The little children didn't know what to do with the flowers.[26]

The time was now right to draw the children's attention to the consequences of their actions, to the fact that the flowers had been planted by other children for all to enjoy, to the value of creating beauty rather than destroying it. Sukhomlinsky made plans with the children to transplant the chrysanthemums to a greenhouse before the winter frosts set in. In order to pick one flower, he taught them, one should plant ten. When, several days later, they visited another part of the school grounds where chrysanthemums had been planted, it was not necessary to remind the children of the appropriate behaviour. The lesson had been learnt.

Care for plants and animals was one of the key methods Sukhomlinsky utilised in his attempt to develop the children's humane qualities. The growing of flowers, fruit trees and grape vines was an activity pursued enthusiastically throughout the school by both pupils and staff. Sukhomlinsky wrote:

> … if a child has nursed a weak plant with his own hands, has warmed it with his breath, has lived through concern, worry and suffering for its sake, if his inner resources have been spent ensuring that a tender and defenceless shoot grows to become a strong and mighty tree, he will become a kind, sincere, cordial and responsive human being.[27]

Left to their own devices, though, young children frequently displayed senseless cruelty. Spending time outdoors with the children, in an informal atmosphere, gave Sukhomlinsky the opportunity to observe the children's tendencies and to respond appropriately. On one of their walks the children happened upon an injured lark. Its wing had been lacerated and it was unable to fly. One of the boys picked up the terrified bird and squeezed it, causing it to cry out pitifully. The children laughed. Sukhomlinsky studied their eyes to see if any of them felt compassion for the bird. Five of the children were distressed by the bird's suffering and one of them took charge of it.

Sukhomlinsky sat down with the children and told them about the life of the migratory birds. This one, he suggested, had probably been left behind after escaping from the claws of a predator. He reminded them how beautifully the lark sings in spring, and painted a vivid picture of its fate if left to endure the winter. He drew on the children's own experience of bitterly cold weather:

> And who among you does not know how painful it is, when in a strong frost your fingers are growing stiff and numb, when the searing wind chokes your breath. You hurry home, to a warm hearth, to a friendly fire … But where can the bird go? Who will shelter it? It will turn into a frozen little ball.[28]

This is an instance of what Sukhomlinsky calls *education through the word*. He considered heartfelt words to be the most subtle instrument at the teacher's command, and his books contain many examples of how he tried to touch the children's hearts with carefully chosen words.

In this case the response was immediate. A place was found at the school where the bird could be cared for, and soon the children were running a "hospital" for injured birds and animals. Eventually all the children were drawn into this activity. One little boy, who had been accustomed to trapping birds and tormenting them, was able to put his hunting knowledge to a different use. When an injured woodpecker was brought in, he was the only one who knew what food it would eat, and where to find it. While initially he agreed to gather food for the bird in order to impress the other children with his superior knowledge, the experience of caring for the injured creature eventually led to an awakening of a powerful new emotion which made it impossible for him to continue with his previous practices.

Caring for animals helped to develop the qualities needed in caring for people. Sukhomlinsky was particularly concerned to teach children ways of giving joy to members of their immediate family, and to enlist the support of parents and other family members in educating the young children:

> It is impossible to educate humaneness, if affection for a close, dear person is not already established in the heart. Words about love for people do not constitute love. The true school for educating warmth,

sincerity and empathy is the family. The relationship with mother, father, grandfather, grandmother, brothers and sisters is the true test of humanity.[29]

One of the principles governing Sukhomlinsky's work, was that the school should always enhance the child's relationships with family members. The idea of a child taking home a report expressing a teacher's dissatisfaction and urging parents to "take measures" horrified him.[30] In *How to Educate a Real Human Being* he writes:

> We invite mothers and fathers to the school very often. We invite them to Mothers' Day and Fathers' Day, to Book Day and Creative Work Day. On these occasions — and this is our intention — mothers and fathers come in contact with their children's intelligence, abilities and talents. Parents see the intellectual work and progress of their sons and daughters. Each mother, each father, comes with the secret hope that today their son's or daughter's progress will bring them joy. These hopes may not always be realised today, but not one mother or father has hopes which are never realised. Without that it would be impossible to imagine educating children correctly. To me it seems strange, astonishing, completely incomprehensible, that in the overwhelming majority of schools the most important stimulus which motivates a child to study well and indeed to be a good person — the desire to bring joy, happiness and peace to their family — is ignored. This desire is the most delicate and at the same time the strongest thread binding the school and family together. If there is no such thread, or it has broken, parent education is no more than hollow words, and no good will come of turning to the family for help. The united efforts of school and family become possible only if the son strives to bring and in fact brings home joy to his family ...
>
> I know many families in which deep cracks in the relationship between the mother and father disappeared because a child brought joy and peace into the family. The nature of the human spirit is such that a mother and father see their son's or daughter's happiness as their common creation, and the deeper that happiness is, the more it strengthens the psychological harmony and mutual devotion of the mother and father. The school's role in strengthening the family is very subtle and delicate: a child should bring joy home from school. I will never agree with possible objections: but what can you do if a child is studying badly, where is his joy going to come from? The

whole point is that not one child should feel or have the experience: I am a failure, I can't do anything, nothing good will come of me. If these thoughts arise in a child's head, that child is no longer being educated by you, and his family, his mother and father, have fallen out of the sphere of your educational influence. The humane calling of the educator is to ensure that even the weakest pupil experiences the joy of success—only then is he being educated by you, and in his family his little joys constitute a powerful spiritual force strengthening the psychological harmony between mother and father.[31]

The incident with the chrysanthemums cited earlier had a sequel, which provides an example of the way in which Sukhomlinsky attempted to enhance family relationships through school-based activities. In autumn the children transplanted the chrysanthemums to a greenhouse. Each day they watered them and impatiently waited for the first flowers. Their efforts were ultimately rewarded with a fine display of flowers.

Sukhomlinsky suggested that the children invite some guests to enjoy the spectacle. Many of them had younger brothers and sisters, whom they brought to see the flowers. Then Sukhomlinsky suggested that if they could grow enough flowers they could each present their mother with one on 8th March (International Women's Day). The mothers were duly invited and presented with flowers. In some instances children's relationships with step-parents or guardians were improved as a result of such activities.

Sukhomlinsky had direct discussions with parents about measures to strengthen the children's health—an issue he considered the most important of all when working with primary school children:

> I am not afraid of repeating again and again: concern for health is the educator's most important task. Children's spiritual life, their outlook, their intellectual development, the soundness of their knowledge, their faith in themselves, all depend on their joy in life and their energy. If I were to measure all my cares and concerns for children during their first four years of study, a good half of them would be about health.
>
> Caring for the children's health is impossible without constant contact with the family. The overwhelming majority of conversations with

parents, especially during the first two years of the children's schooling, are conversations about the little ones' health.[32]

Sukhomlinsky's recommendations to parents regarding their children's health included: spending as much time as possible outdoors, early retiring and rising, good ventilation in bedrooms, and sleeping outside during the warmer months. Parents were encouraged to construct gazebos for outdoor reading, drawing and recreation, and sometimes senior pupils at the school helped in doing this. The children became habituated to rising at the same time each morning and doing exercises, which were followed by a swim, shower or wash, depending on the time of year.

On the question of diet, Sukhomlinsky was particularly concerned that the children should have an adequate intake of minerals and vitamins, and that they should have a good breakfast. His research had shown that 25% of children came to school without breakfast, and that only 22% had a breakfast that met established norms for adequate nutrition.[33] Parents were encouraged to preserve fruit for the winter months. The school kept a number of bee colonies and assisted parents who wished to start keeping a hive at home.[34]

Reference has already been made to twice-monthly meetings for parents, which strengthened ties between the school and the home and facilitated cooperation between parents and teachers. Through lectures, discussions and articles Sukhomlinsky made a more overt attempt to foster strong family relations, with an orientation towards health and personal growth.

If all the above seems intrusive, one needs to take into account the social and cultural context within which Sukhomlinsky was working. His was a rural school at which most of the teachers had been working for many years. A high proportion of the parents and even some of the grandparents had been taught by teachers still working at the school. Traditional family values were widely respected, as were the teachers. The official ideology was communist, and it was expected that individualism would be subordinated to community interests. All of these factors magnified the personal authority which Sukhomlinsky evidently enjoyed.

Family relations were a daily testing ground for children's characters and the most important in their emotional development, but relations with other people could be highly significant. Sukhomlinsky was very concerned to develop the children's sensitivity and responsiveness towards others' suffering. It would appear that he was on the lookout for people who could benefit from contact with the children in his care. In several of his major works we find descriptions of relationships which his pupils struck up with old people who had suffered some loss, or with sick children. Such relationships were frequently of mutual benefit. Reference was made in the previous chapter to the friendship between the children and an old doctor who passed on to them his knowledge and love of flowers. Other friends included an old beekeeper who had no family of his own, a widow who had lost all her family during the war, and a young boy bed-ridden with a long-term illness. These were all relationships which endured over several years, and through which the children developed such qualities as empathy and tactfulness. In the case of the sick boy, the children, through their interest and practical help, contributed significantly to his recovery, which was experienced by them as a personal joy.

Sukhomlinsky expects his readers to be sceptical about the level of emotional maturity displayed by his young pupils, but insists that the best time for educating sensitivity towards others is during the primary school years.[35] It is natural, he suggests, for young children to respond to suffering from the heart. That response simply needs to be refined by the teacher's more mature perspective.

As well as special relationships such as those we just described, children formed friendships within the class group or "collective". Here, too, Sukhomlinsky attempted to heighten the children's sensitivity towards each other, and particularly to each other's suffering. One did not have to look far to find suffering. Several children in Sukhomlinsky's class experienced deep family grief: serious illnesses, accidents, deaths and, in one case, a father's imprisonment. In each case Sukhomlinsky tried to help the rest of the class to find a tactful and thoughtful response, a way to show their concern and sympathy without causing additional pain. Where parents were ill, practical help around the home might be the most appropriate response. In another case, it might be better not to mention the problem at all, but simply to make allowances for changes in mood and behaviour, or to distract the person through some pleasurable or interesting activity.

In all of this Sukhomlinsky tried to avoid the use of rewards or punishment. He did not want children to act virtuously in order to attract praise, but rather because of the inner rewards it brought. This was the characteristic feature of his approach to educating through the collective — the priority he gave to the individual within the collective, and to the individual psyche or consciousness. Following prolonged thought and discussion with other experienced teachers, he came to the following view:

> ... the children's collective only becomes an educating force when it elevates each person, when it affirms each one's feeling of self-worth, their self-respect. After all, the essence of true maternal or paternal love is that sons or daughters, feeling respect for themselves, experience the urge to be good people.
>
> The sincerity and warmth of relationships in the collective became the subject of my constant concern. The diverse life of the children's collective began to be seen by me not only as an association of like-minded people, united by common goals and common work, but also as an expression of mutual sympathy for each other, of an inner capacity to experience with mind and heart another's joy and grief. It is in this warmth and sincerity of relationships within the collective that one finds a noble expression of the urge to be good: not for show, not in order to be praised, but out of an organic need to feel one's own worth.
>
> All the subsequent years of my educational work were, in essence, years of concern to elevate the human worth of the child, adolescent, young man or woman.[36]

All of the approaches to all-round development described in the previous chapters were aimed at achieving this heightened self-respect and sense of worth. Most central to the development of self-respect, though, was the child's perception of himself or herself as a benevolent person, as one who brought joy to others.

Sukhomlinsky's views on education through the collective were a significant departure from the accepted canon, and in particular from the common practices associated with Makarenko's theories. It was common practice, for instance, for the collective to be enlisted in a disciplinary capacity, and not at all uncommon for children to be publicly censured by their classmates. We have already noted Sukhomlinsky's abhorrence of this practice, which he considered unjustified in any circumstances.

Sukhomlinsky always expressed great admiration for Makarenko, for the spirit which inspired his work, and for his faith in the goodness within each child. He took issue, however, with some aspects of Makarenko's theoretical position. In 1967 Sukhomlinsky wrote an article on Makarenko which contained devastating criticism of some of his ideas. He was unable to get the article published at that time, but it did appear in 1989, at the height of the period of *glasnost'*.[37] In the article Sukhomlinsky suggests that Makarenko's educational views were excessively influenced by the sociopolitical notion that an individual can only develop in a social or "collective" setting:

> A mechanical transfer of the functions of the collective from the sociopolitical sphere, to the educational sphere, turned the collective into a threatening force standing over the individual, [who was perceived as] a mere cog in the machine. Makarenko considered that in the case of a conflict between an individual and the collective "deference to the interests of the collective must be followed through to the end, even to a merciless end, and only then can there be a genuine education of the collective and of the individual personality". This recommendation, when applied to a children's collective, is fraught with danger, and is in its very essence deeply misguided, I would say unpedagogical. This recommendation gives rise to the tendency to break the will of the individual, to cut a human being down. Experienced educators never follow this recommendation. A merciless end is no means for resolving a conflict between the individual and the collective. [We should rather look to] the educator's ability to enter intelligently, tactfully, wisely into the inner spiritual world of a person, to understand the slightest movements of his soul, to the ability to calm a conflict without allowing it to reach a merciless end. But Makarenko in theory did not allow that, he was firmly against one-on-one education, in essence he belittled the role of the educator.[38]

The elevation of Makarenko's theories to the status of dogma had, in Sukhomlinsky's view, had disastrous consequences for Soviet education as a whole:

The educational function of the collective, in Makarenko's view, consisted in the fact that "the collective has its organs, it has authority, responsibility, a relationship between its members, interdependence, and if it does not have these things, then it is no collective, but simply a crowd or mob". Dependence, subordination, direction — it is these features of the collective which Makarenko considers to be the main source of the educational power of the collective. A reliance on the organisational structure, on the ability to give directions and to obey, on the decisive role of the most active members as the driving force of the collective, all of these elements gradually hypertrophied in the works of many Makarenko commentators. The ability to direct and to obey, the ability to be active, began to be perceived as ends in themselves and in practice had and continue to have grotesque consequences: the collective is divided between the leading gas-bags with their empty words, on the one hand, and the faceless 'masses' on the other. Some are constant leaders, others only follow.[39]

Sukhomlinsky turned Makarenko's dictum on its head: from an educational perspective, the individual was the end, the collective was the means. In a school there were many collectives (or groups), and the most educationally significant were those based on common interests. None of them, however, was an end in itself:

> Education will be degraded if these collectives become the aim of education. The aim of education is a human being, a personality with all-round development. The collective is a means of educating. Each pupil actively participates in several collectives, and somewhere his activity must blossom, somewhere he will achieve the highest level of creativity which his age permits.[40]

Nor was the collective the only means through which the individual was educated:

> Makarenko categorically stated that "in the Soviet Union there can be no personality outside the collective, and therefore there can be no personal fate, personal way or happiness in opposition to the fate and happiness of the collective." In this statement I was always amazed by the abstract posing of the question about the "happiness of the collective" and the opposition between the collective life and the life of the individual. It flies in the face of reality to say that the personality is formed only in the collective and that there can be no personality outside the collective. The spiritual life of the collective and

the spiritual life of the individual are formed due to mutual interaction. The collective exerts an enormous influence on the individual, but there is no collective without the rich, diverse spiritual life of the individuals within it. What is "the happiness of the collective"? It is unthinkable unless each person within it is happy. And personal happiness is an extremely complex thing, and is created not only in the collective. The richness of the individual's world, the fullness of their personal, spiritual life, the discovery and blossoming of abilities and talent, of a vocation, personal success in creative work, the satisfaction of a deep-seated and insatiable need for human fellowship, love, friendship, repeating oneself in one's children, these are what happiness consists of, and if these are not present, there can be no collective happiness.[41]

Sukhomlinsky shared Makarenko's belief in the power of the collective. Within it resided a mighty educational force, capable of nurturing, enthusing and uplifting the individual. Such a force would only come into being, however, if the teacher succeeded in the preparatory education of the individuals within the collective, along the lines already described in this chapter. This was the responsibility of the primary school teacher:

There is a whole period in the spiritual life of school children — when they are being taught in grades one and two — when there is still no collective, it is just being created, and here the artistry of the teacher's direct influence on each personality plays a decisive role. During this period, while creating the collective, the teacher must be concerned first and foremost with the education of heart-felt sensitivity towards the spiritual world of another person — from this quality there gradually grows a collective sensitivity to the individual, an intolerance of 'washing someone else's dirty linen in public'. My own experience has convinced me of the great importance of individual chats with pupils in the six to eight age group, with the purpose of educating a heart-felt sensitivity to the people around them.

How important this is — to teach small children to recognise, from the eyes, movements and speech of the people around them, grief and joy, disappointment and concern, anxiety and confusion. If we do not carry out this work a person may grow up to be an insensitive blockhead. Collect thirty such blockheads together and you will have a 'collective', but what sort? It will be a blind, soulless force, prepared to trample an individual into the ground. Unfortunately such collectives do exist in our schools. Blunt indifference, heartlessness, emotional insensitivity — these provide a fertile soil for hypocrisy and demagogy.[42]

Sukhomlinsky's emphasis on educating the individual psyche made the personal role of the teacher central. Intelligence could only by educated by intelligence, feeling by feeling, will through will, consciousness through consciousness. If the teacher was to awaken the pupils' sensitivity to each other, he himself needed to be sensitive to each pupil:

> I am firmly convinced that there are qualities of soul without which a person cannot become a genuine educator, and amongst these the ability to enter into the inner world of a child takes pride of place.[43]

It was the teacher's awareness of the inner world of each child which determined the character of the teacher-pupil relationship, and dictated the means for educating children, individually and collectively. Without that awareness, and the intimacy which was born of it, teachers might find their relationship with pupils degenerating into one of open hostility. It was for this reason that Sukhomlinsky felt it so important for teachers to spend time with their pupils outside class, and placed such emphasis on the many extracurricular clubs and activities at the school. The character of the teachers, their level of emotional refinement, was the key to the whole process of character education.

Any reflections on character education must eventually lead back to this central issue. Teachers educate the heart not so much by what they do as by what they are, through their personalities. Conformity to a standard of behaviour can be exacted by force, but this does not educate strength of character. In order to truly educate, teachers have to win the respect of their pupils, and to awaken in them an impulse towards personal growth. Pupils need to feel drawn towards their teachers and to see qualities in them worthy of emulation.

Sukhomlinsky's teaching style was related to his personality and depended on a range of personal qualities and artistic skills which he had developed throughout his life.

Each of the teachers at his school had particular talents, skills and interests, which determined the methods they used. What they all shared in common was an attempt to understand each individual child and to bring out the best in them. On educating humane qualities, one of the primary teachers at Pavlysh, Ekaterina Markovna Zhalenko, had the following to say:

> There are no special techniques and methods for educating kindness, sensitivity and humanity. One simply needs to see each child as one's own. One needs to think: it hurts a mother when something is going badly for her child. And this thought in itself will give birth to a kindly feeling. And if a child feels kindness, he will become kind to his friends, to his elders and to his parents.[44]

Sukhomlinsky wrote an essay on the importance of teachers' love for their pupils, entitled "How to Love Children". In it he writes:

> … love for a child in our profession is the flesh and blood of the educator as a force, capable of influencing the inner world of another person. A teacher without love for the child is like a singer without a voice, a musician with no ear, an artist without a sense of colour.
>
> One cannot understand a child without loving him. All the outstanding educators of the past became torch-bearers for educational culture, for humanity, primarily because they loved children. Comenius, Pestalozzi, Ushinsky, Diesterweg, Rousseau, Tolstoy, Krupskaia, Shatsky, Makarenko, Korczak — these names will always shine for us as eternal flames of wise human love.[45]

Sukhomlinsky is aware that the ideal represented by such educators is a far cry from the reality experienced by many teachers:

> And what if I don't love them? … What if their racket gives me a headache? If I only experience unclouded moments when I cannot hear or see them?[46]

In his view, teachers who feel like this have two options — either find another job or reeducate themselves. Most of the article is devoted to describing the psychology of love, and how feelings of love for children may be cultivated. Sukhomlinsky suggests that one aspect of this psychology of love is an awareness of the uniqueness of each child:

> When the little six-year-olds start being educated by me, a year before they commence their schooling, I am struck by the dissimilarities in the children's perception of the world. I look into the black, the deep blue, the light blue and the grey eyes, and it seems that each child has

just opened their own little window on the world and is looking out, enchanted, at the sky and the earth, the sun and the moon, at a flower or a bird. And each little window is unique, with its own peculiarities. One child apprehends the world through the music of nature — listens attentively to the song of the birds and the buzzing of the bumble-bee, to the whispering grass and the rustle of the leaves. Another discovers the world through its colours and shades. One experiences phenomena as a single whole, another concentrates on the details ...

The more one discovers these subtleties in children's perception of the world, the more one loves each child.[47]

Some children are easier to love than others, and Sukhomlinsky devotes some attention to the issue of how to love difficult children, or, as he preferred to call them, children with difficult fates. The essence of his approach appears to be one of faith in the goodness within each child, and a conscious effort to disregard any evil masking that goodness:

> In my educational practice there is a rule: however horrible the evil in a child's soul may be, one must see in this disfigured soul first and foremost a person who is waiting for someone to help him, to cure him of evil. I address myself not to the voice of evil, but to the voice of human beauty, which is always present in a child, which cannot be stifled by anything.[48]

Sukhomlinsky found that the contemplation of natural beauty, which figures so much in his teaching methods, was an effective way of developing a rapport with children whose experience of life had caused them to close their hearts to people. When the teacher was able to respond to beauty with child-like enthusiasm, bonds of friendship were formed with the pupils. When the teacher experienced the same feelings of wonder as the pupils, he was able to enter into their world and developed love for them:

> To love children means to love childhood, and for childhood optimism is the same as the play of colours is for a rainbow: if there is no optimism, there is no childhood.
>
> But here we encounter a common woe in school life: the educator, without realising what he is doing, hews at the root of optimism, hews methodically, mercilessly. Optimism is a magic coloured lens,

through which the surrounding world appears to the child as a great miracle. The child not only sees and understands, he evaluates emotionally, he loves, is enthused, wonders, hates, seeks to come to the defence of good against evil. We must not take this magic lens away from a child. We must not turn him into a cold, calculating rationalist ...

In children themselves, in their optimistic perception of the world, is the source of my love for them.[49]

Sukhomlinsky has some interesting observations on the role of memory in developing love for children. He explains that during the course of his work with a group of pupils, extending over many years, he retains in his memory the record of certain critical moments, when children's intrinsic qualities have shone through. Such moments have endeared children to him, and the memory of them sustains his love:

These recollections, forever impressed in my heart's memory, are the well-springs, the little streams, from which a strong love for each child grows and is fed. The time spent in our work passes swiftly, the hours spent with the children are fleeting, but they do not pass without a trace: they leave moving recollections in our memories, in our hearts. And the more vivid these recollections, the more of them have been impressed upon my heart, the more strongly I am drawn to children, the deeper the joy which fresh contact with them brings, the more uniqueness I discover in each new generation of little ones commencing school.[50]

The cultivation of such memories builds up a reserve of good will, capable of withstanding the disappointments and failures which are the lot of any teacher:

Creating wealth in his emotional sphere, the teacher guards himself against an uncontrolled emotional state, such as may beset him at times of failure or disappointment.[51]

Finally, Sukhomlinsky suggests that a teacher's love for children, and their love for the teacher, is a product of the teacher's "wealth of spirit", of his knowledge and creativity:

That which we understand by the concept *the teacher's love for the children, the children's love for the teacher*, begins, in my view, with one person's sense of wonder and reverence at another's wealth of spirit, and especially at the wealth of their thought.[52]

The absence of such "wealth of spirit", on the other hand, leads to a barren relationship between teacher and pupils:

> An emptiness of spirit never inspired or fed a genuine love. You have probably observed more than one case of cold indifference, a kind of strange alienation in the relations between teacher and pupils. The pupils could not say whether they like or dislike the teacher: he comes to the lesson merely to retell the next section from the text book, to set questions and award marks. He does not reveal himself to them as a living embodiment of human culture. It is one of the most annoying phenomena which one still, unfortunately, encounters in our schools. Such a teacher causes harm by his facelessness, by the fact that he sows emptiness in the souls of his pupils.[53]

Earlier we cited four main attributes which Sukhomlinsky looked for in teachers: love of children, love of their subject, knowledge of educational thought, and a work skill. Clearly expectations of teachers at Pavlysh were high, but so was the level of support. There was an unusual degree of cooperation and like-mindedness among the staff. How was this *esprit de corps* achieved?

One critical factor was the fact that Sukhomlinsky himself selected teachers for the school. He considered it essential for principals to have this right if schools were to have a coherent philosophy. One gets the impression that Sukhomlinsky scoured the countryside looking for teachers. He describes several instances where he persuaded people working in other fields to undertake teacher training and come to his school. These were people with a great love for some area of knowledge such as mechanics or plant breeding, and who also loved sharing their interest with children. Sukhomlinsky would invite them to the school to visit lessons given by experienced teachers, and offer them support in undertaking part-time teacher training. George Bernard Shaw caustically suggested that "Those who can, do. Those who can't, teach." Sukhomlinsky tried to ensure that it was those who could *do*, who taught at his school.

In *Pavlysh School* he describes all the members of his staff individually, giving a brief outline of their particular interests and teaching styles. One gains the impression that the educational methodology which evolved at Pavlysh was indeed the fruit of collective efforts, and that educational convictions were arrived at through an exchange of experience and ideas. Each teacher's particular interests and talents left their mark on the life of the school community. It frequently happened that one teacher's hobby was taken up by other teachers, as well as by many of the children.

Sukhomlinsky's individual orientation when educating children through the collective was paralleled by his approach to leading the school staff. His focus was on the personal growth of each staff member:

> Collective wealth is composed of individual, personal wealth. The foundation on which the school stands, and on which everything that happens in the school is built, is the diversity of knowledge, the richness of intellectual life, the breadth of vision, the continual intellectual growth of each teacher.[54]

Every effort was made to ensure that teachers were free to focus on the central issues of education and to remove the pressures so often endured by Soviet teachers in rural areas: endless meetings, excessive demands to participate in non-school activities, poor wages and inadequate housing. At Pavlysh teachers were remunerated for extra-curricular work and generally allotted sufficient teaching hours to ensure they received about one and a half times a regular teacher's salary. They were guaranteed adequate holidays and rest days. Staff meetings were limited to one day of the week and were generally devoted to educational discussions rather than administrative matters, though important decisions, such as the allocation of teaching responsibilities, were taken by the school council, which included all the teachers:

> We strive to combine management of the school by the principal with collegiality in the discussion and resolution of important matters concerning the instructional and educational work.
>
> The effectiveness of collegiality depends on holding common views on those matters of principle which determine the direction and essence of education. This common ground regarding educational views and convictions permits our teachers to make collective decisions — at school council meetings — on practical issues concerning

the life and work of the school (the school council meets seven or eight times a year).⁵⁵

One of the important means for fostering cooperation between staff was a twice-monthly seminar held on Monday afternoons.⁵⁶ This was divided into two parts. The first part consisted of a presentation by one of the staff, evaluating their experience with a particular group of children. After discussing his or her work with the class group as a whole, the teacher would narrow the focus to one or two children who were felt to merit particular attention. A detailed profile of their character and behaviour would be given, after which other teachers would offer additional perspectives based on their observations and experience. Collectively the staff would seek ways to meet the needs of these children.

The second half of a Monday seminar was usually a lecture of a more theoretical nature on some educational or methodological issue. This was generally given by the principal or one of the more experienced teachers. The lecture would typically be followed by a lively discussion involving all the staff. Such talks and discussions helped to keep teachers informed about experience in other schools and the latest developments in educational thought. Considerable interest was aroused, for instance, by the research of the Soviet psychologist A.N. Leontiev on the development of musical abilities in children who appeared to be lacking in aptitude for it.⁵⁷ Lectures by staff members were accompanied by displays of literature.

Each staff member had a personal library of some magnitude and subscribed to several journals, and there was considerable exchange of these. New books of interest were displayed on a stand in the staff room and sometimes discussions were devoted to new publications.

The more experienced teachers frequently lent support to their younger colleagues. Their knowledge of children's families gave them insights which were valuable to new teachers.⁵⁸ Of particular importance for new teachers was the practice of visiting other teachers' lessons. A regular part of Sukhomlinsky's own duties was the visiting of teachers' lessons and the presentation of demonstration lessons. In *Pavlysh School* he gives a detailed description of his work with one teacher who had just commenced duties at the school. Sukhomlinsky and the new teacher visited each other's lessons and the lessons of other experienced teachers. Together they analysed the lessons, paying particular attention to the individual work of the students. This went on for several years. At the end of each year they set an agenda for the year to come, and made up a program for visiting lessons in order to study specific issues. Simultaneously they studied relevant educational theory.

For Sukhomlinsky, as well as for the new teacher, the classroom was a laboratory where one studied the processes of learning and refined the practice of teaching. After several years of this joint activity the new teacher was able to present talks to the rest of the staff on the issues which had arisen during his teaching experience and the practices he had developed.

Sukhomlinsky thus encouraged an unusual degree of cooperation between the various staff members. He broke down the isolation in which most teachers work, and established practices which gave an extraordinary degree of support to inexperienced teachers.

We are now in a position to review the practice of "education of the heart" as it occurred at Pavlysh. Children attending the school found themselves in a very stable environment in which a well-established and close-knit staff worked, together with families, in pursuit of common goals. Every effort was made to ensure the children enjoyed excellent health and to avoid damaging their self-esteem. Attention was given to refining the senses and to cultivating an appreciation of beauty in nature, music, art and human relations. Exhaustive attempts were made to discover each child's unique talents (their "golden vein"), and the children were surrounded by others involved in a variety of interesting hobbies. From their first days at school, all children were taught to care for plants and animals, and to find joy in giving joy to others.

In all this the emotional and imaginative faculties inherent in children were nurtured and refined. The preadolescent years were used as a period of active training in good works, so that values, attitudes and habits were well established before the onset of adolescence, with its inevitable trials. Sukhomlinsky aimed for a refinement of individual consciousness which would make vulgar or cruel behaviour unthinkable. His method was in principle simple: to share with young children his joy in beauty and his compassion for suffering, and to give them the opportunity to create beauty and to bring joy to others. Sustaining all his efforts was faith in the goodness within every child.

Notes

1 Sukhomlinsky, V.A., "Serdtse otdaiu detiam [My Heart I Give to Children]", *Izbrannye pedagogicheskie sochineniia v trekh tomakh*, Moscow, Pedagogika, 1979–81, Vol. 1, p. 73.
2 Sukhomlinsky, V.A., "Kak liubit' detei [How to Love Children]", *Izbrannye proizvedeniia v piati tomakh*, Kiev, Radianska shkola, 1979–80, Vol. 5, p. 316.
3 See Sukhomlinsky, V.A., "Rozhdenie grazhdanina [The Birth of a Citizen]", *Izbrannye pedagogicheskie sochineniia v trekh tomakh*, Moscow, Pedagogika, 1979–81, Vol. 1, p. 274.
4 Sukhomlinsky, V.A., "Sto sovetov uchiteliu [100 pieces of advice for teachers]", *Izbrannye proizvedeniia v piati tomakh*, Kiev, Radianska shkola, 1979–80, Vol. 2, p. 450.
5 See Sukhomlinsky, V.A., "Rozhdenie grazhdanina [The Birth of a Citizen]", *Izbrannye pedagogicheskie sochineniia v trekh tomakh*, Moscow, Pedagogika, 1979–81, Vol. 1, p. 427.
6 See Tartakovsky, B.S., *Povest' ob uchitele Sukhomlinskom [The Story of the Teacher Sukhomlinsky]*, Moscow, Molodaia gvardiia, 1972, p. 15.
7 See Sukhomlinsky, V.A., "Rozhdenie grazhdanina [The Birth of a Citizen]", *Izbrannye pedagogicheskie sochineniia v trekh tomakh*, Moscow, Pedagogika, 1979–81, Vol. 1, p. 273.
8 Ibid., pp. 273/4.
9 Sukhomlinsky, V.A., "Serdtse otdaiu detiam [My Heart I Give to Children]", *Izbrannye pedagogicheskie sochineniia v trekh tomakh*, Moscow, Pedagogika, 1979–81, Vol. 1, p. 30.
10 Ibid., p. 79.
11 Sukhomlinsky, V.A., "Rozhdenie grazhdanina [The Birth of a Citizen]", *Izbrannye pedagogicheskie sochineniia v trekh tomakh*, Moscow, Pedagogika, 1979–81, Vol. 1, p. 493.
12 See "Serdtse otdaiu detiam [My Heart I Give to Children]", *Izbrannye pedagogicheskie sochineniia v trekh tomakh*, Moscow, Pedagogika, 1979–81, Vol. 1, pp. 46–48 for Sukhomlinsky's account of the lesson.
13 Ibid., p. 48.
14 Ibid., p. 49.
15 Tolstoy, L.N., "Komu i kogo uchit'sia pisat', krestianskim rebiatam u nas ili nam u krestianskikh rebiat? [Who should learn to write from whom, peasant children from us or we from peasant children?]", Sobranie sochinenii v dvatsati dvukh tomakh [Collected works in 22 volumes], Vol. 15, pp. 10–33.
16 Sukhomlinsky, V.A., "Serdtse otdaiu detiam [My Heart I Give to Children]", *Izbrannye pedagogicheskie sochineniia v trekh tomakh*, Moscow, Pedagogika, 1979–81, Vol. 1, p. 73.
17 Ibid., pp. 74/75.
18 Ibid., p. 75.
19 Ibid., p. 188.
20 Ibid.
21 Sukhomlinsky, V.A., "Rozhdenie grazhdanina [The Birth of a Citizen]", *Izbrannye pedagogicheskie sochineniia v trekh tomakh*, Moscow, Pedagogika, 1979–81, Vol. 1, p. 487.

22 See *The Republic*, Translated by Desmond Lee, 2nd edition (revised), Penguin, 1987, pp. 129–165.
23 Note: Such stories were, in the past, often told to children by their grandparents. Another feature of modern industrial society has been the breakdown of the extended family, and the consequent weakening of the relationships between children and their grandparents. This is a further factor influencing children's emotional upbringing, which was of concern to Sukhomlinsky.
24 Sukhomlinsky, V.A., "Rozhdenie grazhdanina [The Birth of a Citizen]", *Izbrannye pedagogicheskie sochineniia v trekh tomakh*, Moscow, Pedagogika, 1979–81, Vol. 1, p. 513.
25 Ibid., p. 514.
26 Sukhomlinsky, V.A., "Serdtse otdaiu detiam [My Heart I Give to Children]", *Izbrannye pedagogicheskie sochineniia v trekh tomakh*, Moscow, Pedagogika, 1979–81, Vol. 1, p. 95.
27 Sukhomlinsky, V.A., "Pavlyshskaia sredniaia shkola [Pavlysh School]", *Izbrannye pedagogicheskie sochineniia v trekh tomakh*, Moscow, Pedagogika, 1979–81, Vol. 2, p. 70. See also p. 64.
28 Sukhomlinsky, V.A., "Serdtse otdaiu detiam [My Heart I Give to Children]", *Izbrannye pedagogicheskie sochineniia v trekh tomakh*, Moscow, Pedagogika, 1979–81, Vol. 1, pp. 69/70.
29 Ibid., p. 233.
30 Sukhomlinsky, V.A., "Rozhdenie grazhdanina [The Birth of a Citizen]", *Izbrannye pedagogicheskie sochineniia v trekh tomakh*, Moscow, Pedagogika, 1979–81, Vol. 1, p. 279.
31 Sukhomlinsky, V.A., "Kak vospitat' nastoiashchego cheloveka [How to educate a true human being]", *Izbrannye proizvedeniia v piati tomakh*, Kiev, Radianska shkola, 1979–80, Vol. 2, pp. 228/229.
32 Sukhomlinsky, V.A., "Serdtse otdaiu detiam [My Heart I Give to Children]", *Izbrannye pedagogicheskie sochineniia v trekh tomakh*, Moscow, Pedagogika, 1979–81, Vol. 1, p. 110.
33 Note: In the past, studies at some schools in Australia have produced similar figures, and have, in some cases, resulted in the provision of school breakfasts at a nominal cost.
34 Sukhomlinsky, V.A., "Serdtse otdaiu detiam [My Heart I Give to Children]", *Izbrannye pedagogicheskie sochineniia v trekh tomakh*, Moscow, Pedagogika, 1979–81, Vol. 1, p. 111.
35 Ibid., p. 98.
36 Ibid., pp. 101/102.
37 Sukhomlinsky, V.A., "Idti vpered! [Let us go forwards!]", *Narodnoe obrazovanie [National Education]*, 1989, No. 8, pp. 70–78.
38 Ibid., pp. 73/74.
39 Ibid., p. 73.
40 Ibid., p. 74.
41 Ibid., p. 76.
42 Ibid., p. 77.

43 Sukhomlinsky, V.A., "Serdtse otdaiu detiam [My Heart I Give to Children]", *Izbrannye pedagogicheskie sochineniia v trekh tomakh*, Moscow, Pedagogika, 1979–81, Vol. 1, p. 30.
44 Sukhomlinsky, V.A., "Pavlyshskaia sredniaia shkola [Pavlysh School]", *Izbrannye pedagogicheskie sochineniia v trekh tomakh*, Moscow, Pedagogika, 1979–81, Vol. 2, p. 69.
45 Sukhomlinsky, V.A., "Kak liubit' detei [How to Love Children]", *Izbrannye proizvedeniia v piati tomakh*, Kiev, Radianska shkola, 1979–80, Vol. 5, p. 309.
46 Ibid., p. 308.
47 Ibid., p. 310.
48 Ibid., p. 311.
49 Ibid., p. 313.
50 Ibid., p. 316.
51 Ibid.
52 Ibid., p. 318.
53 Ibid., p. 317.
54 Sukhomlinsky, V.A., "Pavlyshskaia sredniaia shkola [Pavlysh School]", *Izbrannye pedagogicheskie sochineniia v trekh tomakh*, Moscow, Pedagogika, 1979–81, Vol. 2, p. 47.
55 Ibid., p. 76.
56 Ibid., pp. 52–57.
57 Ibid., pp 55/56 and note.
58 Ibid., p 63.

CHAPTER 6

Civic Responsibility

> To educate young citizens as politically like-minded people — as campaigners for the communist ideal — means to gradually extend the horizons of their life beyond the framework of family interests, hearth and home, their native village. It is very important that the interests of society, of our great motherland, the USSR, of all of humanity, should find a place in the hearts and minds of children as early as possible.[1]
>
> As long as there is exploitation of one person by another in this world one cannot educate love for all of humanity, because humanity does not exist in the abstract. There are brothers by class — the exploited — and their irreconcilable enemies — the exploiters. It is very important that each child at an early age should understand and feel in their heart what it means to follow a revolutionary, communist idea.[2]

IN THIS chapter we turn to the third element of humanism as it was defined earlier in this study: to the inculcation of a sense of civic responsibility, culminating in a concern for the welfare of humanity as a whole. This is a problematic area, as Sukhomlinsky's sense of civic responsibility and concern for the welfare of humanity found expression in his devotion to the communist cause and were conditioned by the nature of the society in which he lived. The outward forms of social and political life in the USSR as it was in Sukhomlinsky's day, and those in modern pluralistic societies in the English-speaking world, are so different that we should expect to find little correspondence between Sukhomlinsky's approach to civic education and our own.

Following the Renaissance and Reformation, notions of civic responsibility in Western Europe developed in a social context that was increasingly individualistic, pluralist and secular. From the time of the Enlightenment, the concept of natural rights came to dominate political thinking. In practice such rights had to be fought for and were established through conflict, which gave rise to adversarial forms of political and judicial process.

Russian society, on the other hand, retained medieval features well into the nineteenth century. The spirit of collective unity was, in the time of Nicholas I, still upheld by the principles of autocracy, orthodoxy and national identity.[3] There were subsequently attempts at political reform, but the October revolution aborted the development of political institutions analogous to those developed in the West, and ultimately led to a new Soviet form of national orthodoxy and collective identity, in which many attitudes from the Russian past survived.

Many otherwise perplexing phenomena of the Soviet period become comprehensible when seen as a continuation of tendencies expressed in earlier Russian history. Scholars such as Billington[4] and Tucker[5] have noted this continuity between the Soviet experience and its Russian antecedents, and have drawn parallels between Stalin's Russia and that of Ivan IV and Peter I.

Tucker's analysis of the political culture of the Soviet Union is illuminating. He suggests that in order to understand a society's political culture we need to be aware of the "sustaining myth" which gives meaning to the society's existence, the resulting principles or "ideal culture" which ostensibly govern political life, and the society's actual practices or the "real culture" within which citizens operate. Where there is a discrepancy between the "ideal culture" and the "real culture", there is a likelihood that reformers will emerge who will point to this discrepancy and suggest remedies. Martin Luther King's leadership of the anti-discrimination movement in America is cited as an example of such reformist leadership, as is that of Mikhail Gorbachev. Where, on the other hand, there is an attempt to overturn the sustaining myth and ideal culture of a society, we are dealing not with reform, but with revolution, as happened in Russia in 1917 and 1991.[6]

Tucker suggests that the sustaining myth of American society might be expressed as that of "a community of free and equal self-governing citizens pursuing their individual ends in a spirit of tolerance for their religious and other forms of diversity"[7] . The sustaining myth of the Communist Manifesto is that of "a community of producers, whose basic culture pattern, real and ideal alike, will be free creativity of associated human beings producing according to their abilities and receiving according to their needs".[8] The Leninist myth, arrived at during the period of the New Economic Policy, was that of "a goal-oriented all-Russian collective of builders of socialism and communism". Such a goal was to be achieved primarily through the educative function of the Party, the need to *learn* to work cooperatively being the crux of socialism's construction in Russia:

> Far more than Marx ... Lenin was a culture-conscious revolutionary. He showed it in his concept of 'cultural revolution' as a pedagogical process of overcoming habitual ways of individualist thinking and living on the part of the vast peasant majority ...
>
> No Bolshevik was more keenly cognizant than Lenin of the fact that the revolutionary party had come to power in a land peopled largely with men and women who were comfortable in the established culture, comprising not only individual economic ways but Orthodox religiosity, the old village ethos, old modes of thought and conduct.[9]

That communism was to be achieved through teaching people to live cooperatively, is an idea that finds strong expression in Sukhomlinsky's work, and is one of the dominant themes in his approach to civic education. Sukhomlinsky's formative years, however, occurred not under Lenin, but under Stalin, and the ethos of Stalinist society also contributed to his social attitudes.

Tucker explains the emergence of Stalinism partly in terms of Stalin's character, partly in terms of Russia's past and partly in terms of the heritage bequeathed by Lenin. He suggests that Lenin's bolshevism was "a body of disparate and even conflicting elements developed over a quarter of a century". In spite of the primarily educative role defined for the Party in *What is to be done?* and reiterated during the period of the New Economic Policy, his ruthless use of violent methods during the period of "War Communism" set a precedent for Stalin's later excesses. In Tucker's assessment, though, Stalin's "revolution from above" marked a radical departure from Lenin's guidelines for gradual future development towards socialism. Stalinism was a "nationalistically and imperialistically wayward form of Bolshevism", reminiscent of the revolutions from above of Ivan IV and Peter I.

In many ways Stalinism does appear to have marked a return to Tsarist goals and methods. The doctrine of "socialism in one country" was accompanied by renewed nationalism, and the spread of Soviet influence into neighbouring countries constituted a new stage of empire-building. Stalin's mass collectivisation of agriculture amounted to a reintroduction of serfdom in a different form, especially with the revival of the internal passport system in 1932 (the farm population not being issued with passports). His program of mass industrialisation relied in part on the use of forced labour, as had Peter's state building initiatives. As under Ivan and Peter, all classes of the population were bound in service to the state, the Party hierarchy being purged into a submissive role just as Ivan's boyars had been. The purges also served to eliminate many liberally-minded intellectuals from the leadership echelons, replacing leaders of middle-class origin with ones of peasant stock.[10]

Perhaps most interestingly of all, the mood of the society changed from one of post-revolutionary experimentation and innovation to one that was deeply conservative and inquisitorial. Soviet society under Stalin, like Russian society under the Tsars, was a "community of right believers", a "political community of the faithful".[11] The massive campaign of anti-religious propaganda was necessary to ensure that the new communist faith completely supplanted the old Orthodox one. Those who had grown up under Stalin were frequently sincere believers in the new order, unconsciously reliving the cultural patterns of their forbears:

> Risen from simple, often peasant origins, these New Believers were culturally disposed to think of Russia as a new Orthodox tsardom of Marxist-Leninist-Stalinist persuasion, naturally with a new tsar, albeit an uncrowned one, at its head. They could accept the equation of a socialist Soviet Russia with an industrially developed and militarily strong one, take satisfaction in their participation in the state-building effort, and be proud of the country's emergence as a great power.[12]

The Soviet Union under Stalin, then, bore closer resemblance in its political culture to the Church States of medieval Christendom or to the Russia of the tsars, than to modern pluralistic societies in the West. There was a revival of the ideal of heroic asceticism (*podvizhnichestvo*), which had contributed to the early formation of the Russian state during the 15th century, and which has been referred to as "the cornerstone of

Russian spirituality".[13] At a more mundane level there was a return to prerevolutionary attitudes towards the family and towards education, the experimentation of the 'twenties being rejected. The values of patriotism and heroism typical of the period left their mark on Sukhomlinsky's work, though the violent use of force to implement policy was alien to his nature, and he would never have equated industrial might with human progress.

Political culture under Khrushchev changed to the extent that it removed the terror and delegated a greater part of the leadership role to the Party at large, rather than leaving it in the hands of a dictator. Khrushchev's policy of destalinisation called for a return to Leninist principles and to the educative role of the Party. As shall be shown in more detail in chapter six, it was in such a climate that Sukhomlinsky's work flourished. Under both Khrushchev and Brezhnev, however, the sustaining myth and ideal culture of the Soviet Union remained the same: that of a society of believers who were building communism.

Sukhomlinsky, then, was working in a very different social context from our own: a closed and uniform system, in which adversarial forms of political expression were not tolerated, let alone institutionalised. It was assumed that the best of all political orders had been attained. In this situation, reform could only come about through the initiative of the Party. Sukhomlinsky himself seems to have believed that the political forms of Soviet life were adequate, indeed that the Soviet Union, as the first socialist country, was the most progressive nation in the world.[14] Social ills, in his view, were due to faults in upbringing, to the failure to educate humaneness and a sense of responsibility for others. For him educating a sense of civic responsibility meant instilling a sense of duty, industry and patriotism. In line with his utopian vision of communism, he concentrated on preparing young people for a life of study and service. He had little to say about the forms of public life, but much to say about the morality which should inform them, and the relevance to the public domain of personal values.

In Sukhomlinsky's view, the prime civic responsibility of all adults was the education of their children. The quality of their efforts in this undertaking determined the quality of tomorrow's citizens. Their second responsibility was to work in their chosen profession. All also had a duty to defend the motherland should the need arise.

In Sukhomlinsky's approach, the cultivation of emotional sensitivity discussed in the previous chapter was directed in order to inculcate a love of the motherland and a readiness to defend it with one's life.[15] In *How to Educate a True Human Being*, a book on education in the spirit of communist morality, one chapter is entitled "Love for the socialist motherland, lofty ideals and civic responsibility". In this chapter one comes across passages which the majority of western readers will find totally alien. The following passage, for instance, seems to strike a dissonant note when compared with Sukhomlinsky's ideas as described in earlier chapters of this study:

> Teaching the younger generation heartfelt memories and a sense of duty towards those who saved our people and all of humanity from the plague of fascism, we must preserve, like a sacred flame, the intensity of our hatred, and pass it on from generation to generation. Fascism is an evil which is not buried in the depths of the earth or of the seas; it is not a historical term, gathering archival dust. While imperialism exists, while hundreds of millions of people on earth remain the slaves of capital, each of our pupils must be prepared for a bloody encounter on the battle field. Hatred for humanity's tyrants, for the imperialists, this sacred hatred must not grow weaker but must grow from generation to generation …
>
> … Hatred is the spiritual energy of love for that which is sacred in our fatherland. When you bring your pupils to the graves of the warriors who fell defending their motherland, prepare such words as may lead, day by day, grain by grain, to the accumulation in the young patriot's heart of a mighty charge of hatred. Remember, educator, that this is the most humane, the most noble feeling, making a human being truly beautiful, kind, affectionate, sensitive.[16]

This extraordinary passage demands some commentary. It is clear that Sukhomlinsky's own wartime experiences must have contributed to the passionate tone of these remarks. In the second chapter of this study we gave some attention to this issue. We quoted Sukhomlinsky's own account of his feelings upon returning to his native village and hearing of the atrocities which had occurred there, particularly of the inhumane killing of his wife and of their new-born child. We saw then how he channelled his anger into his work so that it emerged in a subliminal form in his love for children. This experience of his may go some way to explaining the peculiar reference here to a symbiosis between love and hatred. It may throw light on the psychological origins of the above statements.

Of more importance for the Western educator, though, is the influence here of the Soviet ideology of the time, with its uncompromisingly dualistic view of the world. In Sukhomlinsky's writing one frequently encounters this Zoroastrian-like view of the world as a battleground where good and evil are locked in conflict, with the Communist Party and the Soviet nation representing goodness and truth, and capitalist imperialists representing the forces of evil. Such a view clearly has little currency now, and must be viewed as a product of Sukhomlinsky's own Stalinist upbringing and formative experiences during the war.

One can only guess at Sukhomlinsky's view of events such as the invasions of Hungary and Czechoslovakia. Sukhomlinsky's daughter commented in a personal conversation that although her father was very approachable and mild-mannered, he never completely opened up. There was always a part of him in reserve which remained unknown. He must at times have felt torn between his loyalty to the state and his dedication to humane principles, and yet there is no suggestion of it in his writing. It would appear that Sukhomlinsky's upbringing and wartime experiences were such as to make disloyalty to the state unthinkable. It seems that for him the motherland, the fatherland was the embodiment of the highest good. In the absence of a religious faith the motherland became the object of faith and the vehicle through which transcendence of ego occurred. Consider the following passage from *How to Educate a True Human Being*:

> In our life there are values which are commensurable and those which are not. One may discuss which is better—a family or solitude, devotion to an ideal or detachment. But some things are sacred and may not be compared or contrasted with anything else. These are *the Motherland, the Socialist Fatherland*, filial loyalty, devotion to the land where you were born and found meaning, to the people who fed you and brought you up.
>
> Your true birth as a citizen, as a thinking personality inspired by noble ideas, as one who labours and struggles for the victory of truth and happiness, as a family man, occurs due to the fact that you are a son of the people. As sunlight is reflected in a drop of water, so in you is

reflected the people's long history, its greatness and glory, its love and hope, its indissoluble unity with those places which are infinitely dear to our heart, which enter our life as eternal, indestructible, inextinguishable.

Your mother gives birth to your flesh, the Fatherland gives birth to your human, civic soul. Nothing is dearer than the fatherland.[17]

There is no reference in Sukhomlinsky's writing on civic education to constitutional matters or to political or judicial process. He gives a high priority to "conversations on civic-mindedness" in which tales of heroic deeds during wartime or at work predominate. These tales, like his own astonishing capacity for work, are an expression of the ideal of heroic activity (*podvizhnichestvo*), a dominant theme in his writing on civic education. In some ways Sukhomlinsky appears typical of the true believers of peasant origin who grew up under Stalin. He appears never to have lost the enthusiasm which many felt during those years, and which was typified by the Stakhanovite movement. He continued under Khrushchev and Brezhnev to educate his pupils in the same heroic spirit, his faith no doubt sustained by the transformation he witnessed at his own school and by the recognition accorded to his work.

If his unquestioning faith in the Soviet state and its "ideal culture" is a product of growing up under Stalin, his critical attitude towards the "real culture" of Soviet life, with its alcoholism, carelessness and corruption, and his attempts to bring about change through education, are typical of the Khrushchev years. His methodology of education without punishment is the antithesis of the real political culture as it had existed under Stalin.

Sukhomlinsky attempted to educate his pupils for active participation in the life of their society, and encouraged independent thought and action. Sukhomlinsky shows clear sympathy for young people who protested against the the society's ills. In one instance he relates how a boy disrupted a teacher's remarks in praise of a record turnip harvest by protesting that his mother was in the hospital after spending a month cleaning turnips on the damp ground. In the child's view this was hardly an occasion for celebrating the victory of socialist labour. In *Letters to My Son* Sukhomlinsky urges his son not to ignore mismanagement on a collective farm, but to take a stand against it:

> In your place I would have gone straight away with my friend to the Party organisation and said: "What's going on? If you can't harvest the tomatoes yourselves we students will harvest them, but you can't allow human labour to come to nothing." If I didn't get anywhere with the Party organisation I would have gone to the District Committee and stirred the people's monitoring group into action. I can't believe that everyone is indifferent to evil, that everyone has got used to doing things the wrong way … That can't be.[18]

On major problems in Soviet society, however, Sukhomlinsky, perhaps of necessity, remained silent. He seems not to have seen a need for political reform. Rather, his efforts were directed at educating people to make the existing system work. He only occasionally hints at abuses of authority and at the existence of corruption within the Communist Party.[19]

It would appear from what has been said that there is very little in Sukhomlinsky's approach to civic education that could be relevant to a western educator. There is so little correspondence between civic life in Sukhomlinsky's Ukrainian village under state socialism, and that in our own pluralistic societies. In order to find any relevance we need to consider the essential nature of social life and the moral principles and attitudes which are fundamental to it. We need to take a simple view of social and civic life, which focuses on human relationships rather than institutional forms. To facilitate such a view, we might adopt an image used by Sukhomlinsky, which likens the relationship between society and the individual to that between a tree and its fruit:

> A human being is given a memory recording the life of many generations, a memory reaching back through the centuries. What makes him a human being is that he understands and remembers where the roots of the tree on which he grows reach, and what they feed on. Becoming conscious of his people and his fatherland, a person becomes conscious of himself, comprehends his personality as a part of the people, experiences a feeling at once tender and severe, a feeling of duty and responsibility to the people, to the Fatherland.[20]

We might modify this image slightly and suggest that just as a tree is dependent on the soil, so is a society dependent on the natural environment in which it exists. An individual's dependence on society and on nature is analogous to the fruit's dependence on the tree and the soil.

Awareness of this relationship leads to an appreciation of the individual's duty towards society and towards nature. Just as the germ of a new tree is contained in the fruit, so the individual needs to embody the principles of social living if the society is to survive. Viewed from this perspective, civic education should give individuals an understanding of themselves, of society and of nature, and also train them to live in a way that promotes the health of each level of this existential chain.

Sukhomlinsky's communism is utopian and heroic. One could say that he devoted himself to building "communism in one village", not through force, as Stalin had attempted, but through education, as Lenin had suggested in some of his later writings. All the various aspects of his system of education, described earlier in this study, were informed by his civic spirit, inspired by his vision of a communist society, and sustained by his own *podvizhnichestvo*.

In all societies there is a tension between the needs and demands of the individual and those of the society as a whole.[21] In order to find a healthy balance between satisfying individual and collective interests it is helpful to study a variety of social models. Few would wish to copy the Soviet experience, but Sukhomlinsky's suggestion that an individual may find fulfilment in the service of society and in bringing joy to others is an expression of an old ideal. Such an ideal has as much place in a pluralistic society as in a totalitarian one, and the old-fashioned notion of duty is one that may be needed to balance the individualistic ethos of capitalist societies. Western educators may thus find some meaning in Sukhomlinsky's reflections on notions such as duty and service. Consider the following homily written for children:

> A human being *has a duty*. The whole meaning of our life consists in the fact that we *have a duty*. Otherwise it would be impossible to live. Living in society, you come in contact with other people at every step. Each pleasure you experience, each joy, has cost other people something—the extending of their spiritual and physical energies, care, concern, anxiety, thought. Life would turn into chaos, you could not venture onto the street in broad daylight, if there were no human sense of duty. Clear understanding and strict observation of your duty towards other people—this is your true freedom. The more humanely, the more consciously you observe your duty to other people, the more you draw on the inexhaustible well-spring of human

happiness—*freedom*. Try to free yourself from a sense of duty—and you will become the slave of fancy ...

In following a sense of duty a person always concedes to another person in something. In life it is always easier for one person and more difficult for another, one person experiences more joy, another less, one is better off, another worse off. The wisdom of the human *sense of duty* consists in seeing and inwardly judging, where you have a duty to others and where they have a duty to you.[22]

There is an old-fashioned and universal ring about many such homilies written by Sukhomlinsky. For him there can be no rights without duty. In his eyes, children are at every step presented with lessons in duty—a fruit tree with a broken branch, a person in need—and if they are made aware of this and respond accordingly, they have learnt the most important lesson in social living: the joy of following a sense of duty.[23]

Sukhomlinsky describes how he took a class of young children to the seaside by night train. One of the girls wondered how the train could continue to travel through the night. All the children were surprised to learn that the driver would stay awake all night. Sukhomlinsky regarded this as an ideal illustration of the notion of duty.

Sukhomlinsky recommended that teachers explain notions such as duty on the basis of children's daily experience of life. He thought it important that moral concepts be clearly explained, and much of *How to Educate a True Human Being* is devoted to that end. In that work he defines a vocabulary of moral discourse which contains many traditional terms such as duty, justice, mercy, sympathy, conscience, modesty, generosity, greed, kindness, cruelty, beauty and love. He touches on universal themes such as love, death and ageing. Many of his homilies and parables are expressed in terms sufficiently general to admit of their being read to children in Western societies, as they fit into a broadly Christian humanistic tradition. In Soviet society they were a significant phenomenon. One Soviet observer expressed the feelings of his admirers:

> He spoke and wrote of the important things, the eternal things. Of a spiritual ideal, of sublime love, of harmony in human relationships, of the woman as mother, giving life and keeping the hearth fire burning, of the highest moral values and foundations, about kindness as God

in the Tolstoyan sense, justifying and giving a higher meaning to all human activity.

Did he know, did he see what was going on around him? Yes! There is indisputable evidence that he did. But he never spoke cruel words, he continued to create his theatre — the theatre of the kindly fairy story with a happy ending and a moral lesson. He said that the "so called" universal human values were not a supplement to something else which gives you place in life and a crust of bread, but the most important thing, without which people will simply perish.[24]

Perhaps the highest expression of a sense of civic responsibility is a concern for the welfare of humanity as a whole. Sukhomlinsky tried to foster such a concern among his pupils, albeit within the framework of Soviet ideology. How western readers react to his writing on this theme will depend on their own political or ideological orientation. Most will probably be sympathetic to his attempt to encourage a responsible attitude towards the whole of humanity, to extend the children's sympathies to encompass people in other countries. In one typical instance Sukhomlinsky read the children a newspaper report about Sadako Sasaki, a Japanese girl suffering from radiation sickness, who had set herself the goal of making 1000 paper cranes. The children made paper cranes, sent them to the sick child, and continued to follow news about her for years to come:

> The years passed, my pupils became young men and women. They received each bit of news about Sadako Sasaki's health with deep and heartfelt pain. The sorrowful news of the death of their distant friend entered their young hearts as a deeply personal loss.
>
> The world, whose horizons gradually extend before the child, consists not only of seas and oceans, islands and continents, unheard of plants and animals, the Arctic aurora *borealis* and the eternal summer of the tropics, — it consists first and foremost of people, their labour and their struggle for a happy future … Children should enter this world not as impassive observers, knowing what happens where and able to talk about it, but as people experiencing concern for the future of humanity.[25]

Sukhomlinsky suggests that this is less likely to be achieved if young children's sensitivities are blunted by an excessive flood of sensational information about the world, and cites Tolstoy to back up his view.[26]

This is in line with his approach to the teaching of musical appreciation, described in the previous chapter, and with his comments on "blank shots" cited in the second chapter. To awaken feelings of compassion or indignation, without at the same time providing a practical avenue for acting on such feelings, is to encourage insensitivity, apathy or hypocrisy.

Much of what Sukhomlinsky wrote about giving pupils an international orientation, however, is so much an expression of cold war ideology as to appeal to only a very small sector of western educators. It might be argued that there was some validity to the Soviet critique of capitalist imperialism, and that this justifies Sukhomlinsky's position. No attempt will be made here to address such an enormous issue, save to suggest that a study of the broader Marxist critique of capitalist society might aid an understanding of Sukhomlinsky's approach to civic education.

If such a study were undertaken, it would be necessary to distinguish between Marxist thought and Soviet ideology. As a school of thought which addresses the issues of industrial society Marxism has been very fruitful and has generated genuine insights. Marx has had an enormous influence on Western thinkers generally, not only in the socialist camp. Prominent writers such as E.F. Schumacher and Erich Fromm, who are humanists in the broad sense in which we have defined the term, have acknowledged a considerable debt to Marx's thinking. Professor C. Wright Mills has suggested something of the scope of Marx's influence:

> As is frequently remarked and often forgotten, the development of social enquiry and of political philosophy over the last century has in many ways been a more or less continual dialogue with Marx. Often this sociological dialogue has been hidden, even unrecognised, by the several generations of thinkers involved in it; unrecognised or not, it has been a major thread in the historical development of the social thought of our time.[27]

The industrial revolution has clearly had enormous impact on the social fabric and Marxism is one response to the changes which it ushered in. The question of the subordination of human beings to technology and to purely economic priorities, addressed by E.F. Schumacher[28], is one which still awaits an adequate response. There is an element in

Marxist thought which raises this issue and points to the need for ensuring that people maintain control over the means of production and are not subordinated to it. Much of Sukhomlinsky's work can be seen as fitting into such a framework, and as being compatible with broadly humanistic concerns.

Soviet ideology, on the other hand, was not so much an evolving school of thought as a rigid system of dogma, characterised by jargon, slogans and myth, which bore increasingly less resemblance to reality as time passed. Soviet society as a whole was a closed system, which nurtured an unrealistic view of itself and of the world at large. Sukhomlinsky's outlook was inevitably limited by the nature of this closed system and by the cold war mentality of the post-war period.

To pursue this line of discussion further would take us far beyond the scope of this study. Whatever injustices there are in the world, the majority of today's educators are likely to reject outright Sukhomlinsky's ideologically-bound world view and the way in which this coloured his teaching on international matters. The audience for which this study is written has moved away from such a confrontationist mentality. The nurturing of hatred and of a preparedness for war was clearly born of a cold war mentality, and may be best viewed by present-day educators as an aberration resulting from the historical circumstances in which Sukhomlinsky worked and the personal fate he suffered.

It was suggested above that civic education should involve not only a study of the individual's relationship to society, but also of the society's relationship to nature. Here Sukhomlinsky's work has undoubted relevance to western educators, as he developed a model of environmental education far in advance of his time.

One Soviet educationalist who took an interest in this aspect of Sukhomlinsky's work was E. Andreeva, who wrote two short monographs and a number of articles on his approach to ecological education.[29] In one of her articles in *Uchitel'skaia gazeta [The Teacher's Newspaper]*, she suggests that Sukhomlinsky was 20 or 30 years ahead of his time in developing a comprehensive system of ecological education. In her view, the strength of his system is that it did not merely provide information about the environment, but inculcated attitudes and practices supportive of the environment:

> To love nature means to look after it, to care for it, to perfect it, to defend it from poachers and from all who would harm it. That is how Sukhomlinsky's pupils loved nature. All kinds of activity in nature, but primarily work activity, was directed at the common good. This is the most important element in the harmony of pedagogical influences. Without superfluous words, without declarations, the children planted tree belts, cultivated vineyards, established orchards. In the course of twenty years they transformed 40 hectares of infertile ground into flourishing arable land, and saved 160 hectares from erosion. And all of this was done without ostentatious formal competitions, without struggles for leadership and first prizes.[30]

Several decades later it is not so uncommon to come across schools with an active environmental program, though they are still the exception rather than the rule. Sukhomlinsky's work is an example of the way in which environmental education can be integrated with the rest of the school program. Whether teaching literacy skills, musical appreciation, history, geography or science, he would frequently take children outside to draw inspiration from nature, the "well-spring of living thought". A large part of his education in civic responsibility involved environmental projects.

Several aspects of Sukhomlinsky's approach to environmental education may be noted. Firstly, and perhaps most importantly, was the cultivation of sensitivity to natural beauty and compassion for living creatures described in detail in chapter five. Secondly, there was an orientation towards the future, a concern for future generations, which was an integral part of the school's philosophy that found expression not only in environmental activities, but in moral education generally. Thirdly, there was an active involvement in caring for the natural environment. This included soil conservation, the improvement of soil fertility, seed collection, plant propagation, tree planting and other measures against soil erosion, caring for plants, animals and birds. Fourthly, there was the scientific study of soil fertility, biology, agriculture and animal husbandry, providing an intellectual foundation for the activities just mentioned. Finally, there was education in the creative use of technology.

In Sukhomlinsky's writing one comes across many instances where thought, feeling and action were combined in an integrated approach to environmental education. Consider the following passage:

> It is very important for young people to sense the citizen within themselves, to become aware of evil and to rise up against it. Once, when sitting on the edge of the forest we discovered in the words of Maksim Gorky some deep and instructive truths, we *suddenly* noticed something to which none of us had paid any attention till then. In a large field we saw a barely perceptible channel. It had formed recently: the field had a slight slope and the flow of rain water had 'sketched out' the first stroke of a future gully. Attention children! You are eleven years old now. You are just approaching the first step of adolescence. Have a good look at this field. Think about what it means for us. This is the greatest national wealth — fertile soil, the source of our life. This source has limits. If the fertile fields of our motherland dwindle there will be nothing to eat …
>
> I see concern in the eyes of my pupils. That is good; that is what I was seeking … In the children's eyes I see a question: what should we do? This is the first spark of that great thought of which I spoke. It will turn the child into an adolescent, filling its life with civic feelings …
>
> … We walk around the field, looking closely at the future gully from all sides, studying where water flows from, how many other rivulets combine with it. It becomes clear to us that the flow of water must be stopped. We must block the path of this destructive force and direct the water into the forest — there it will partially soak into the ground and partially enter a stream flowing into a neighbouring pond.
>
> We set to work. It is not as easy as it seemed at first glance. But we are inspired by the thought that we are combating evil, we are doing good works. Life has many times convinced me: if you want to lead your pupils from thought to conviction, find a way for thought to *live and express itself*, to grow strong and, so to speak, to *triumph* in work.[31]

Sukhomlinsky's civic-mindedness is that of one tied to the land and to the society in which he lived, rather than to institutional traditions. There are aspects of his writing which will appeal to environmentalists. His homilies on duty and other traditional values may also strike a chord with religious educators and those with more traditional leanings. His utopian vision of communism has a humanist antecedent in Thomas More's work.

Civic Responsibility 153

On the other hand, his approach to educating a sense of civic responsibility does not fit into a western humanistic framework, being too doctrinaire and nationalistic to foster a universal or pluralistic outlook. His sincere desire to see a just and happy world was expressed in terms which owed much to his Stalinist upbringing. It is not so much in his efforts to educate loyal citizens of the Soviet Union that we will find ideas applicable to civic education in the West, as in his efforts to foster those moral qualities which are a prerequisite for civic-mindedness in any society.

Notes

1. Sukhomlinsky, V.A., "Kak vospitat' nastoiashchego cheloveka [How to educate a true human being]", *Izbrannye proizvedeniia v piati tomakh*, Kiev, Radianska shkola, 1979–80, Vol. 2, p. 182.
2. Sukhomlinsky, V.A., "Serdtse otdaiu detiam [My Heart I Give to Children]",*Izbrannye pedagogicheskie sochineniia v trekh tomakh*, Moscow, Pedagogika, 1979–81, Vol. 1, p. 159.
3. For a detailed treatment of this theme, see Riasanovsky, N.V., *Nicholas I and Official Nationality in Russia, 1825–1855*, Berkeley and Los Angeles: University of California Press, 1959.
4. Billington, J.H., *The Icon and the Axe*, New York: Random House, 1970.
5. Tucker, R.C., *Political Culture and Leadership in Soviet Russia*, New York: W.W. Norton, 1987.
6. Ibid., p. 17.
7. Ibid., p. 23.
8. Ibid., pp. 28/29.
9. Ibid., p. 57.
10. Ibid., p. 95.
11. Ibid., p. 116.
12. Ibid., p. 118.
13. Graham, S., *The Way of Martha and the Way of Mary*, NY, 1916, iii ff; (quoted in Billington, J.H., *The Icon and the Axe*, NY 1970, p. 651.)
14. See, for instance, Sukhomlinsky, V.A., *Rodina v serdtse [The Motherland in one's heart]*, Moscow, Molodaia gvardiia, 1978, p. 31.
15. See Sukhomlinsky, V.A., "Kak vospitat' nastoiashchego cheloveka [How to educate a true human being]", *Izbrannye proizvedeniia v piati tomakh*, Kiev, Radianska shkola, 1979–80, Vol. 2, p. 178–181.
16. Ibid., p. 176.
17. Ibid., p. 177.
18. Sukhomlinsky, V.A., *Pis'ma k synu [Letters to my son]*, Moscow, Prosveshchenie, 1987, p. 12.

19 One occasionally comes across suggestions that people may 'get on' by pleasing their superiors rather than by looking after their fellows. See, for example, "Pis'ma k synu [Letters to my son]", *Izbrannye proizvedeniia v piati tomakh*, Kiev, Radianska shkola, 1979–80, Vol. 3, p. 706.

20 Sukhomlinsky, V.A., *Rodina v serdtse [The Motherland in one's heart]*, Moscow, Molodaia gvardiia, 1978, p. 22.

21 For a treatment of this theme, see Bertrand Russell's *Authority and the Individual*, London: Allen & Unwin, 1949.

22 Sukhomlinsky, V.A., "Kak vospitat' nastoiashchego cheloveka [How to educate a true human being]", *Izbrannye proizvedeniia v piati tomakh*, Kiev, Radianska shkola, 1979–80, Vol. 2, p. 197.

23 Ibid., p. 198.

24 Malinin, V.I., "Sukhomlinsky o Makarenko: nezavershennyi trud [Sukhomlinsky on Makarenko: an uncompleted work]", *Sovetskaia pedagogika [Soviet Pedagogy]*, 1990, No. 3, pp. 86/87.

25 Sukhomlinsky, V.A., "Serdtse otdaiu detiam [My Heart I Give to Children]",*Izbrannye pedagogicheskie sochineniia v trekh tomakh*, Moscow, Pedagogika, 1979–81, Vol. 1, p. 161.

26 Ibid.

27 C. Wright Mills, *The Marxists*, Harmondsworth, Middlesex: Penguin Books, 1977, p. 36.

28 See Schumacher, E.F., *Small is Beautiful*, London: Abacus, 1974, and his *Good Work*, London: Abacus, 1980.

29 See for example Andreeva, E.K., *Put' k noosfere. Printsipy vospitaniia cherez prirodu v shkole Sukhomlinskogo: Mladshie klassy [The Way to the Noosphere. Principles of education through nature in Sukhomlinsky's school: junior classes]*.

30 Andreeva, E.K., "Zelenyi mir [Green world]", *Uchitel'skaia gazeta [The Teacher's Newspaper]*, 1987, 5 September, p. 1.

31 Sukhomlinsky, V.A., "Kak vospitat' nastoiashchego cheloveka [How to educate a true human being]", *Izbrannye proizvedeniia v piati tomakh*, Kiev, Radianska shkola, 1979–80, Vol. 2, pp. 258/259.

CHAPTER 7

Sukhomlinsky's Influence

> My comments in 'Komsomol'skaia pravda' were in essence an expression not only of my own opinions and convictions, but the opinions and convictions of thousands and thousands of teachers. I was requested to write such a letter to 'Pravda' or 'Komsomol'skaia pravda' —and requested not in private conversations, but at meetings and conferences ...
>
> ... If these attacks continue, if they are going to hound me as they are doing now, I shall have to write a letter personally to N.S. Khrushchev ...
>
> 'Komsomol'skaia pravda' acted correctly in publishing that letter. It is written with blood, sweat and tears of our teachers. I have received more than twelve hundred letters in response to that letter ... Why do the people in the Ministry so hate criticism?[1]

IN THIS chapter we shall attempt to trace Sukhomlinsky's influence on Soviet education. We shall study how and why he came to be so widely regarded as the leading post-war educator. We shall consider the role of the periodical press, of editors and publishers, and of the Academy of Pedagogical Sciences, in promoting educational ideas. We shall see that in each of these spheres of influence there were protagonists and antagonists of Sukhomlinsky's cause. Having studied the ascendancy of Sukhomlinsky's influence during the post-Stalin "thaw" and the attacks to which he was subjected at the end of that period of relative liberalisation, we shall turn to the 'seventies, when there was a resurgence of interest in his work, and to the 'eighties. During the period of *perestroika* a new constellation of educators carried on the work which Sukhomlinsky had begun, in some cases with the very same supporters and detractors.

Western observers might be intrigued as to how a person like Sukhomlinsky, espousing a philosophy in many respects close to that of the Christian humanists, came to be enshrined as one of the icons of Soviet education. When this question was put to the educational journalist Simon Soloveichik, he suggested that Sukhomlinsky had risen to prominence on the wave of liberalisation that followed Khrushchev's revelations about the Stalin era. It was during this same period that educators such as Amonashvili and Shatalov, to whom we shall turn later, commenced their work and developed their philosophy of teaching.[2]

To outsiders, the Soviet Union may have appeared monolithic and homogeneous, and a change of the Communist Party's General Secretary sometimes seemed sufficient cause for a national turnabout. Such a view may have been justified. Within the Soviet Union, however, and particularly within the Communist Party itself, opposing ideas did contend with each other, as the forces of totalitarianism and liberalism struggled for the ascendancy. This was particularly true of the post-Stalin years, when editorial boards of newspapers and journals sometimes lined up in opposing camps. It was the courage of some editors that helped to create the "thaw". The names of dissidents such as Solzhenitsyn and Sakharov are well-known in the West, but there were also those who resisted the forces of totalitarianism while remaining in the Party. It was perhaps these people, even more than the dissidents, who paved the way for Gorbachev's reforms. Sukhomlinsky's writings may be viewed as the efforts of one such person to influence Soviet educational policy and practices, and through them, the development of Soviet society.

Sukhomlinsky's efforts to influence Soviet educational thought and practice were conscious and strenuous. He was involved in Communist Party organs and in the educational bureaucracy. He sent letters all over the country and on occasion to the highest authorities. He contributed articles to a host of newspapers and journals. He was a corresponding member of the USSR Academy of Pedagogical Sciences and participated in numerous conferences, and, of course, there were his many monographs. The volume of his personal correspondence and published work is staggering, and there still exists a considerable body of unpublished material from which new publications continue to appear.

Sukhomlinsky also exercised considerable influence though personal contacts with visitors to his school. These numbered thousands and came from the length and breadth of the Soviet Union, and from other countries. Some of these visitors recorded their impressions. Among them was V.A. Karakovsky, who later became well known in his own right as one of the "teacher-innovators" of the period of *glasnost'*. He visited Pavlysh during his period as a school principal in Cheliabinsk. He wrote:

> Pavlysh school should be renamed a university! We say this quite responsibly: here a feeling of wonder and admiration overcomes anyone with the slightest love for children and schools.
>
> ... The strongest impression of all is produced by the principal himself, Vasily Aleksandrovich Sukhomlinsky.
>
> ... We have never before had the good fortune to meet such a remarkable teacher in the highest and noblest sense of the word.[3]

Another visiting principal, M. Manukian, wrote:

> I have spent only one day in this remarkable school where so much is happening, but I have received as much as I did in four years at teachers college.[4]

Sukhomlinsky frequently refers in his writings to letters he has received from all over the country. While he attempted to reply to all letters personally, some he answered through his articles. One of his major works, 100 *Pieces of Advice for Teachers*, was written largely in response to questions from teachers who wrote to him or visited his school.

Sukhomlinsky also wrote to people in positions of authority, in the hope of influencing government policy on education. In 1988, the journal *Sovetskaia pedagogika [Soviet Education]* published a letter written by Sukhomlinsky to Khrushchev 30 years earlier. The letter was a response to policy guidelines expressed by Khrushchev in his landmark speech on the need to bring the education process closer to life. The letter is an earnest attempt to focus attention on the moral dimension of vocational education — on the methods needed to instill a love of work and an impulse to serve. He points out the pitfalls of trying to bribe school leavers into undertaking industrial or agricultural work by making two years of such work a passport to tertiary studies. In

Sukhomlinsky's view this will only corrupt young people's attitude to work, which will no longer be appreciated for its intrinsic value. While agreeing that school leavers should work for two or three years before going on to tertiary studies, Sukhomlinsky considers that this should be required of all students (with the possible exception of the most academically gifted), and that the criterion for selecting students for higher studies should be their ability:

> Work experience should be expected of everybody, entrance exams should be for everybody. Production experience should not be some sort of pass to tertiary studies, as unfortunately it sometimes is now, a pass, moreover, that is often used by lazy and ignorant people. Compulsory production experience should perhaps be waived only for people awarded a gold or silver medal, for gifted people who are of significant value to scholarship.[5]

The tone of Sukhomlinsky's letter is bold. At one point he challenges Khrushchev's views:

> One of the reasons for school-leavers inadequate preparation for work, in your view, is that in the current national education system, which has developed in the light of well-known decisions taken by the Party's Central Committee, a great deal was taken from the prerevolutionary gymnasia, with their tendency to impart abstract knowledge divorced from life ... It does not serve our cause that from time to time the idea emerges and is reinforced: a lot that was done at Comrade Stalin's instigation was wrong, therefore everything that is done at Comrade Khrushchev's instigation is right. The decisions taken by the Party's Central Committee during the 'thirties concerning work in schools, were essential at the time. They played an important role in the development not only of our country's culture, but of its whole national economy. They were directed at strengthening knowledge of the foundations of science and scholarship, they put an end to all sorts of hair-brained schemes to replace a systematic course in secondary education with 'complexes' and 'projects'. Thanks to the implementation of these decisions a cultural revolution was effected in our country. There is more good than bad in the fact that there are 2.5 million people in our country at the present time, who have completed secondary school but not embarked on tertiary studies. It is bad that a certain section of them does not immediately become involved in productive work—which is due to no fault on the part

of the young men and women, but rather to the content of the educational-instructional process, which is divorced from the needs of the workplace. But even in today's unsatisfactory situation, those with secondary education are able to acquire job skills significantly more quickly and easily, and it is from their numbers that the most cultured section of the working class and peasantry is formed.

In your memorandum you several times accuse the comprehensive school of giving students abstract knowledge. This is a bewildering and unjust accusation. Your notion of 'abstract knowledge' includes anything which is not connected with work activity after graduation from school. Such an approach to this extremely important matter is mistaken, it is too hasty. In the first place, there never has been and never will be a comprehensive school, in which all the knowledge acquired by the pupils will find direct application in their work activity after graduating from school. This is all the more so in relation to the Soviet school. Life itself offers convincing evidence that effective teaching of the humanities plays no less a role in preparation for work than the acquisition of direct work experience, of concrete skills and know-how. This is not some speculative conclusion, but a truth which has been deeply experienced and, one might say, suffered for. In the second place, even now the comprehensive school program hardly contains abstract knowledge — abstract in the sense of being divorced from the spiritual life of a Soviet person. A person does not live by work alone, he wants to live a rich spiritual life.[6]

Sukhomlinsky's letter contains detailed proposals for reforming the Soviet school system and for preparing pupils for the workplace. There should be a universal eight-year school with a program based on that of the existing seven-year school, supplemented with a more substantial vocational program. After completing the eight-year program, pupils would either continue with an academic program at an eleven-year school or undertake vocational studies. The latter would remain within the sphere of influence of a school or technical college, though they might be conducted at an industrial or agricultural workplace. All Sukhomlinsky's proposals were based on the experience at Pavlysh.

That Sukhomlinsky had the temerity to write such a letter to Khrushchev shows how far he had grown in confidence by the year 1958. It may be that such boldness was to Khrushchev's liking, as in a letter written in 1962 Sukhomlinsky suggests that Khrushchev is likely to give his views a sympathetic hearing.[7] Both men were Ukrainians of peasant origin. At the time of writing the letter to Khrushchev Sukhomlinsky was about to turn 40 and, in spite of his health problems, he was at the height of his creative powers. He had been teaching for 23 years, and for 15 years he had been a member of the Party. He had already published numerous articles. In 1955 he had been awarded his Candidate's degree and in 1956 he had published his first monograph. In 1957 he had been elected a corresponding member of the RSFSR Academy of Pedagogical Sciences. He had received several awards in recognition of his work.

He had been helped along the way by Party officials and by mentors such as G.M. Borishpolets, S.Kh. Chavdarov and A.G. Dzeverin, all from the Ukrainian Educational Research Institute at Kiev University.[8] These men had encouraged him to follow an academic path and had supervised his work on his Candidate's thesis. As the political climate became more favourable, his influence began to grow, and over the coming decades he would gain a reputation unrivalled in the Soviet Union by any post-war educator. One Soviet commentator explains his initial rise to fame thus:

> … a new name, a fresh approach, a clear voice. A village teacher, from the peasantry, a company political instructor, seriously wounded, a veteran, he understands the Party's policies and the role of the school correctly, he writes compellingly, intelligibly, based on his experience of work education in a country school …
>
> In the measured rhythms of his narrative about the daily life and festivals of Pavlysh school, which had sent its roots deep into the peasant way of life, in his Ukrainian turn of phrase and intonation, there was a special charm, an authenticity.[9]

Not everyone found him to their liking, however. There were many in the educational establishment who found his Tolstoyan emphasis on eternal moral values unpalatable. Despite his being a corresponding member of the RSFSR Academy of Pedagogical Sciences, and despite the fact that two of his books had already been published by its publishing arm, a third book was subjected to severe criticism at a session of the Academy's Presidium held on 11 April, 1962.[10] A.K. Bushlia, E.I. Monoszon, S.A. Gurevich, N.K. Goncharov and A.M. Arseniev each said a few token words in recognition of Sukhomlinsky's work and them proceeded to criticise it roundly: it was not sufficiently academic in style; the terminology was too simplistic and Sukhomlinsky was held to have confused notions such as "convictions", "world outlook" and "morality"; he did not make enough reference to works by other writers or to the experience of other schools, he was considered to be too idealistic and to negate the importance of material interest in motivating work. This was considered ideologically unsound. N.K Goncharov suggested that "the summons to 'self-conquest' as the highest form of struggle for communist principles has a quite Christian ring to it." Sukhomlinsky was also accused of placing too much emphasis on work as opposed to other interests and of promoting "some sort of communist asceticism". The idea of involving small children in productive work was considered unsound. Exception was taken to Sukhomlinsky's suggestion that the meaning of life was to be found in work's moral dimension more than in its particular vocational orientation, that it was less important what one became than what sort of person one became. A.K. Bushlia took issue with Sukhomlinsky for suggesting that there was an opposition between "conscious" pedagogical influences on the one hand and "elemental" societal influences on the other. In Bushlia's view societal influences had become ever more conscious and educational as a result of the influence of the Communist Party.

Sukhomlinsky was present at the discussion and made an attempt to defend his views. Chairing the discussion, I.A. Kairov showed some sympathy for Sukhomlinsky's position, suggesting that his book was a definite "step forward" and that it filled a vacuum in current research. In his view the discussion would have been more interesting had Sukhomlinsky's critics been able to compare his book with other major contemporary contributions in the field. Nonetheless, he recommended that the author be asked to prepare a revised edition of the work, taking into account the criticisms made. The attention of the publishers was to be drawn to the inadequate review and editing of the manuscript for the first edition. (The editor of this and of the two previous books published by the Academy had been N.I. Boldyrev.)

The "discussion" described above is an illustration of the influence of hard-liners even during the "thaw". The 'sixties were a period when a battle between progressive and conservative forces was being conducted in the media. Sukhomlinsky was promoted by the former and denounced by the latter. In the main he was admired and supported by editors, but there were limits beyond which his supporters would not go.

A fascinating insight into the operation of the editorial board of one of the educational journals, *Sovetskaia pedagogika*, is provided in an article by one of its former members, V.I. Malinin. Sukhomlinsky had been a regular contributor to the journal since 1952, when three of his articles had appeared in the space of seven months. The journal's editor-in-chief during the mid-sixties, F.F. Korolev, was a member of the Presidium of the Academy of Pedagogical Sciences, and, according to Malinin, an admirer of Sukhomlinsky:

> The editor-in-chief regarded Sukhomlinsky highly, though he did not agree with him on everything, did not accept everything. He valued him for his boldness, for the independence of his views, for the fact that he did not wish to cite the leading lights. Nowadays few people know that he helped Sukhomlinsky in the preparation of his doctoral dissertation. Despite an age difference of thirty years, they were close in spirit. The editor-in-chief was also a teacher from the peasantry ... [11]

During the mid-sixties scholars in West Germany were comparing Sukhomlinsky to Makarenko, seeing in their juxtaposition a confrontation between two educational systems, one "totalitarian", the other "Christian-humanistic". Sukhomlinsky was invited by the editorial board of *Sovetskaia pedagogika* to respond to these comments. Instead of the expected rebuttal, Sukhomlinsky produced *Idti vpered! [Let Us Go Forward!]*—the article on Makarenko which was cited at length in chapter five. It was an impassioned denunciation of the failure to address individual needs which was often practised in the name of collectivism. Despite the critical content of the article, Sukhomlinsky was a sincere admirer of Makarenko's work, and saw himself as defending its spirit—the "living Makarenko"—from the dogmatic interpretations which had become enshrined in Soviet educational ideology. The main object of his criticism was not Makarenko, but dogmatism and formalism in education:

> Between educational theory and the living daily practice of the school there is a breach, which I consider to be quite unique. It is a

phenomenon which one might call 'making the facts fit the theory': for decades we have been trying to prove that some theoretical proposition or other, expressed by some scholar, is true. With this aim experiments are conducted in schools, mountains of paper are covered in fine print at research institutes, dissertations are piled up in the archives.

The mechanical, mindless transformation of a theoretical proposition into an actual experience, with the sole aim of proving the truth of the proposition, empties the teacher of living ideas, turns him into an indifferent tradesman, castrates our educational work and tears out its heart and soul — the uniqueness of living phenomena, the birth of the new in the spiritual life of our pupils, in the interrelationships between people in our society and between children in particular.[12]

Korolev was delighted with the tone and content of the article, which reflected his own views on the relationship between the individual and the collective. Indeed, at one point Sukhomlinsky cites an address Korolev gave on the issue, where he maintained that Soviet educational thought could not move forward if it remained a mere commentary on Makarenko's work. Malinin gives the following account of Korolev's reaction to the article, and of the editorial board meeting at which it was discussed:

> He easily parted with the 'West German' idea. Evidently that was not what really concerned him. He kept repeating with glee: "Cop that! They should have copped that long ago!"
>
> At the editorial board meeting everyone was in favour, and only one man (he is no longer with us ...) got up and, pale with agitation, declared: if that slander on Soviet reality were published, he would resign from the editorial board and would leave the relevant authorities in no doubt as to the reasons for his departure.
>
> It was a dramatic moment in the life of the editor-in-chief. In 1952 he had been arrested on the evidence of an informer, had sat in the Lubianka, had waited for the decision of a Special Conference. The events of March 1953 had saved his life ...
>
> The dramatic nature of the moment was appreciated by everyone who attended that meeting in the spring of 1967. Yes, Vasily Aleksandrovich's article was a good one, without doubt. It was fine writing, courageous, to the point. But the approach was non-historical.

Makarenko turned out to be the guilty one, that was the problem. As far as the question of original error [in Makarenko's theory] was concerned we should have another look. Kirill Nikolaevich Volkov was right: he [Sukhomlinsky] called Anton Semenych [Makarenko] his friend, but he had not left a single stone of his friend standing. No, it was not suitable as it was... But it was a serious attempt. He was very gifted, capable... We would ask Vasily Aleksandrovich to rework it taking into account the critical comments which had been made.

The above description provides an illustration of what was happening in Soviet society at that time, and shows how difficult it was to overcome the legacy of fear inherited from Stalin's time. The end of the "thaw" had been heralded in 1966 by an article in *Pravda* which went some way towards rehabilitating Stalin. The political climate was changing, and Sukhomlinsky's article would not be published in its original form until August 1989, when it appeared in *Narodnoe obrazovanie [National Education]*. According to Malinin there were four copies of the article. One appeared in an abridged form in *Literaturnaia gazeta [The Literary Newspaper]* in 1970.[13]

Narodnoe obrazovanie was another journal in which Sukhomlinsky's articles frequently appeared. Sukhomlinsky maintained regular contact with its deputy editor-in-chief, A.E. Boim, over a period of several years, as evidenced by the publication of 26 letters from Sukhomlinsky to Boim, written between 1962 and 1970.[14] These letters present us with a picture of Sukhomlinsky the propagandist, intent on reaching his audience. They also throw light on the difficulties Sukhomlinsky had in getting his writing published, as the political climate became less favourable to his non-authoritarian approach. They show how keenly he was stung by an attack directed at him in the press, how he fought to find an outlet for his ideas through various periodicals, and where he found support.

Fourteen of the 26 letters were written in 1967, the year in which "Essays on Communist Education" appeared in *Narodnoe obrazovanie*. This series of essays marked a watershed in Sukhomlinsky's career. According to Sukhomlinsky's daughter, we find in them an expression of "the mature Sukhomlinsky, no longer a student and follower, but an original thinker".[15] The essays raised a storm of controversy, and Sukhomlinsky became the target of ideologues with authoritarian leanings. The reason for the outcry was that Sukhomlinsky was attempting to redefine the goals and methods of communist education. He wished to correct what he saw as an imbalance created by slavish adherence to certain theoretical propositions put forward by Makarenko. In the first article he writes:

> The educational ideal of the Soviet school is clearly expressed in the CPSU Programme. The human being whom we educate should combine moral purity, spiritual wealth and physical perfection. The skill and art of education consists in the educator always having before them a clear picture of the essence of this harmony ...
>
> The harmonious all-round development of the personality is unthinkable without a firm *moral hub*. The most fundamental quality of a human being in communist society is humaneness. To this moral hub must be *attached* everything which our pupils acquire in life, at school, as a result of diverse educational influences. All these influences must be refracted, as it were, through the prism of morality. Without moral purity everything loses its meaning — education, spiritual wealth, professional skills, physical perfection.[16]

Sukhomlinsky laid strong emphasis on the role of the family in the education process[17], devoting one essay in the series to the theme of "parental pedagogy". He also pointed out the changing nature of education, as human life becomes less dependent on physical strength and more determined by the subtle processes of the higher nervous system. In his view education needed to become more attuned to those subtle processes taking place in each child's mind. The work activities which formed a part of every Soviet child's schooling needed to be made more intellectually challenging and creative.

Sukhomlinsky attempted to bring about a shift in thinking on the issue of "collectivism", one of the cornerstones of Soviet educational policy. The basis of collectivism, in his view, lay in each child's need for human fellowship. Collectivism thus needed to be cultivated at the level of the individual, rather than imposed through some quasi-military discipline:

> What does it mean to say *"the school has no real collective"*? First and foremost, that in that school the pupils are not educated to seek human fellowship. The real education of the collective, in a spirit of

collectivism, in the contemporary socialist school, consists in the ability to create and instil between the pupils (especially between adolescents) relationships in which each member of the collective draws spiritual sustenance from their comrades, gives of their own wealth to others and in consequence is enriched themselves... *The skill and art of educating the collective and collectivism begins today with the educator's deep and close attention to the individuality of each pupil, to their interests, needs, inclinations and abilities.*[18]

Sukhomlinsky's anti-authoritarian stance is clearly and consciously stated:

> Attempts to govern the school collective (and in general to build the life of the collective) with orders, with a demand for unquestioning submission, through organisational dependency, are not only doomed to failure, but represent a dangerous source of hypocrisy and duplicity. Where attempts are made to build a collective on such a foundation, informing, tale-telling and deception flourish.[19]

Sukhomlinsky considers self-respect to be an indispensable precondition for moral development. The teacher should foster it by showing respect for each individual. In some instances the teacher must even protect the individual from pressures imposed by the collective.[20]

Many of the issues which Sukhomlinsky was to address during his final years of writing are raised in "Essays on Communist Education". The use of force is condemned on the grounds that it dehumanises relations between teacher and pupils and makes the operation of the conscience redundant. The emotions are to be refined through exposure to beauty and through the power of the teacher's word. Games, fairy tales, fantasy and music are considered to play an important role right up to adolescence, counterbalancing formal studies and helping to prevent the dominance of cold rationalism over the heart. Pupils are to be encouraged to constantly question and seek new knowledge, to acquire new "wealth of spirit":

> The perfection of the spirit, the constant and unending refinement of human nature—this is in essence a concern for that in the name of which we are building communism—human happiness.

It is of critical importance, in Sukhomlinsky's view, that each pupil develop a love of work by discovering that particular activity for which they are best suited. The urge to work, to create, should be fostered in each and all. This should not be the only concern of education, however. In what may be a conscious literary allusion harking back to the beginning of the "thaw", Sukhomlinsky closes the first instalment of the essay with the words "Man lives not by bread alone."

Now, however, the "thaw" was at an end, and Sukhomlinsky's interpretation of communist ideals was not to everyone's liking. The publication of the first essay was met by a harsh response. On 18 May, 1967, *Uchitel'skaia gazeta [The Teacher's Newspaper]* published an article by B. Likhachev entitled "We need a campaign, not a sermon". B. Likhachev was a relatively obscure personage at the time, a senior lecturer at the Vologda Pedagogical Institute. It was significant, though, that his article was given prominence in the most widely circulated publication for teachers: some highly placed officials must have been displeased by Sukhomlinsky's article. Likhachev accused Sukhomlinsky of departing from the guidelines laid down by the Party:

> What programme does Sukhomlinsky suggest? Instead of the concrete and precise programme outlined in the moral code of a builder of communism, he introduces a hazy concept called humanity, to which supposedly everything else can be attached.[21]

Likhachev went so far as to accuse Sukhomlinsky of encouraging "egoism and indiscipline", and generally showed a lack of familiarity with Sukhomlinsky's work. He succeeded, however, in casting doubts on the ideological correctness of Sukhomlinsky's work, and in causing personal hurt to Sukhomlinsky himself, who at the time was recovering from major surgery. On the 23 May he wrote to A.E. Boim:

> It is not just that in publishing such a sensational letter to the editor, full of conjecture, misrepresentation and distortion, *Uchitel'skaia gazeta* has caused me a deep offence which I do not merit ... My health now is such that I cannot bare to look at *Uchitel'skaia gazeta*. In May I was in the regional hospital. Before May Day I felt unwell: severe chest pains, my old wound started aching. It was so painful I lost consciousness. They took me to hospital and put me straight on the operating table. It turned out that one of two fragments which remained in my lung had begun to travel, having reached a blood vessel. They removed it. They wanted to remove the second one, but for some reason decided against it.

> … Now I feel very well, much better than before the operation. And here is the interesting bit. When I came home I was given a pile of newspapers and journals. And the first one I picked up was the 18 May issue of *Uchitel'skaia gazeta*. What sort of 'healing balm' do you think that was for my wound … Of course it was sheer coincidence, now I can relate to it with 'philosophic composure', but I will never forget that moment …
>
> … I beg you once more, not to interrupt the publication of the "Essays" … [22]

The weeks and months that followed were a particularly difficult time for Sukhomlinsky, though they helped to reveal who his true friends were. In another letter to A.E. Boim, dated 10 June, he wrote:

> … My friends give me moral support … Recently I have received many letters from teachers, from people in higher education, condemning Likhachev. I received very interesting letters from Lvov, from Gomel, from Biisk, from Baku. They all write that they are sending their letters to *Narodnoe Obrazovanie* and to *Uchitel'skaia* …
>
> *Sovetskaia pedagogika* has returned my article. I understand perfectly that now is not the time to initiate a debate …
>
> Concerning *Lit. gazeta*. Straight after the article in *Uchitel'skaia* I was approached by a woman from *Lit. gazeta* with a message (strictly confidential!!!) that they will definitely come out in my defence. By the by she asked me to give her something to publish in *Lit. gazeta*—a whole series of articles.
>
> I got out of it, I will not give her any articles, but when she came she already knew that *Sov. pedagogika* had an article of mine …
>
> While I was in the hospital I wrote part of my book 100 *Practical Pieces of Advice for Teachers*—I have already prepared 150 pages …
>
> As for other news, in April and May our school was visited by teachers and principals from Armenia, the Altai region, Belorussia, the Kalinin region, the Kirov region, the Arkhangelsk region (from the Solovki Islands no less!), from the Tartar and Mari Autonomous Republics, and of course most of all from the Ukraine. (I am convinced that I have more friends in the Ukraine than anywhere, and if I have any enemies then they are among the leadership, the devil take them!) In our school we are currently running a School of Educational Culture.[23]

This extract gives some idea of the quarters from which support for Sukhomlinsky came. The article returned by *Sovetskaia pedagogika*, to which Sukhomlinsky refers in the above letter, was undoubtably the one on Makarenko mentioned earlier in this chapter, which was published in an abridged form in *Literaturnaia gazeta* in 1970, and appeared in full in *Narodnoe obrazovanie* in 1989. While welcoming support from *Literaturnaia gazeta*, Sukhomlinsky is at pains to give the deputy editor-in-chief of *Narodnoe obrazovanie* the sense of some exclusivity in publishing his work, and to encourage him to continue with the publication of the "Essays".

On 21 June, 1967, *Literaturnaia gazeta* did in fact come out in support of Sukhomlinsky, publishing an article by A. Levshin entitled "Otpoved' vmesto spora [A rebuke in lieu of an argument]". In it Levshin (L.A. Shnaider) takes issue with Likhachev and gives strong support to Sukhomlinsky. The article was greeted by Sukhomlinsky as "an invigorating breath of fresh air".[24] Other articles appeared in favour of Sukhomlinsky. The prominent literary critic, F. Kuznetsov, had written an article entitled "Vospitanie novoi nravstvennosti [Education in a new morality]", which had appeared in *Literatura v shkole [Literature in the School]* in May of 1967. On 15 July a large and very favourable article on Sukhomlinsky's school appeared in the Belorussian teachers' newspaper. On 27 September Sukhomlinsky's own response to Likhachev was published in *Literaturnaia gazeta*.[25] It was a tactful article in which Likhachev's name was not mentioned, and was published without alteration.

Many Ukrainian party members supported Sukhomlinsky. On 30 September he wrote to Boim:

> Two days ago I was visited in the evening by five comrades: the secretary of the Aleksandria municipal Party committee, the deputy head of the Kirovograd district education office, the director of the Institute for Further Education of Teachers, the deputy head of the Department of Pedagogy at the Kirovograd Teachers College. They came to visit me and told me they had written a letter to *Pravda* ... The deputy head of the Schools Section of the District Party Committee is looking after the matter, on instructions from the first secretary of the district Party committee. And would you believe it, Aleksandr Evseevich, this is without any requests from me.

> ... I have been encouraged by the following little joys: our district newspaper devoted a whole page to me on Teacher's Day; the republic's journal *Znannia ta pratsia* [*Knowledge and Work*] (No. 8, the organ of the Central Committee of the Communist Party of the Ukraine) devoted a large article with a portrait of me; the regional newspaper published my article with a portrait; the republic's *Worker's Newspaper* (organ of the Central Committee of the Communist Party of the Ukraine) published an article about me with a portrait.
>
> ... I write about all this so that you will realise how I am viewed in the Ukraine ...
>
> Hurrah, hurrah! The book 100 *Practical Pieces of Advice* is completed. 450 typed pages. I am starting a new work—Maternal Pedagogy. It will be a practical guide for parents.[26]

While Sukhomlinsky's support was strong in the Ukraine, he was having increasing difficulty in getting work published elsewhere. *Komsomol'skaia pravda* no longer had room for his articles. In an uncharacteristically black mood he wrote to Boim:

> I have received a letter from *Komsomol'ka*. They say that due to the large quantity of official material [they have to publish] they are simply unable to publish my article (I had already signed the proofs); the article was entitled "The pedagogy of the heart".
>
> For some reason I feel very depressed. I do not know why. I confess to you, as a very close friend, that I do not feel like living.[27]

Sukhomlinsky continued to encourage Boim to press on with the publication of the "Essays" in *Narodnoe obrazovanie*, and the series of essays did appear throughout 1967. The final essay, on moral education, appeared only in part, despite Sukhomlinsky's efforts to have it published in full. It was, however, followed by an editorial rebuttal of Likhachev's attacks. The editors wrote:

> B. Likhachev has attacked the "Essays" without any foundation, in an unworthy fashion, resorting to outright distortion of Sukhomlinsky's views and statements, singling out isolated quotations and giving them arbitrary interpretations, divorced from context, with the aim of distorting the author's actual thoughts. Even greater cause for concern is the critics attempt, in the absence of convincing arguments, to cast a shadow on the actual character of the author of the "Essays" ...

The editors object strongly to Likhachev's unseemly approach, which is in contravention of the principles of the Soviet press, and fails to meet the most elementary standards required for theoretical discussion.[28]

Sukhomlinsky's health was now failing and he had less than three years to live. Throughout his remaining years he worked feverishly to to put his now mature ideas into writing, and to find avenues for publishing. He worked on several manuscripts at a time and with astonishing speed, commencing work as early as 2 am, writing till 8 am, and carrying his notebook with him at all times. In 1969 *Pavlysh School* and *My Heart I Give to Children* were published in Russian. In 1970 *The Birth of a Citizen* was published in Ukrainian. These were key works, summarising his life's work. *My heart I Give to Children* was especially important in furthering Sukhomlinsky's reputation within the Soviet Union. Of even greater significance to Sukhomlinsky, however, was a body of unpublished work completed by him during his last years.

Seven months before his death Sukhomlinsky wrote a letter to A.E. Boim in which he confided that he did not have long to live:

Dear Aleksandr Evseevich!

This is a deeply personal letter. I am writing it to you as to a close friend. My state of health at the moment is such that after a certain time two fragments of metal which remain in my chest from the war will move a few millimetres closer to some blood vessel close to my heart — and then — I assure you that I am quite sober about what will happen then, but all the same it would be better not to know about it in advance. Unfortunately I know about it. I know from my doctor. They cannot perform another operation — my heart will not take it.

In the time allotted to me by these little fragments I want to do as much as I can. I will work with all my strength to complete the most important business — several unfinished books. But I will not talk about unfinished business now.

I am writing to you, dear Aleksandr Evseevich, with a request: when something happens to me, my wife will send you several completed manuscripts in Russian. They are very dear to me. I consider them many times more valuable and necessary than everything published till now. They are lying ready to send to you. My wife knows your address. These are the books (manuscripts) of which I am speaking:

1. The methodology for educating a collective of pupils — 370 pp.

2. A teachers guide on ethics (How to educate a real human being) — 710 pp.

3. An anthology on ethics — 10 parts (one for each year level) — in total over 1200 pp.

4. The culture of educational work — 457 pp.

5. Knowledge and convictions — 293 pp.

6. The methodology of work with mentally deficient children — 453 pp.

7. Difficult children 311 pp.

8. My heart I give to children (Part III; work with senior pupils) — 378 pp. (the second part will be published in 1970 by Radianska shkola).

9. Educating aptitude for teaching among senior pupils — 213 pp.

10. Parental pedagogy, Part I — 338 pp.

11. Parental pedagogy, Part II — 413 pp.

12. The unity of the moral and the aesthetic in educational work — 189 pp.

13. Teaching as a creative art — 532 pp.

14. Directing the intellectual work during a lesson — 246 pp.

15. The theory and practice of school management — 403 pp.

I entrust them to you, dear Aleksandr Evseevich. Do what you can with them … I am only concerned that at least something should get through to the teachers … [29]

This letter reveals the extent of Sukhomlinsky's productivity during his last years, and also suggests that the public has not yet had the opportunity fully to assess Sukhomlinsky's legacy. Some of the works listed here have since been published, but many have not. It is to be hoped that future researchers will be able to gain access to unpublished material, and that more works will continue to appear in print in the coming years. Those works which have appeared have been sufficient to keep interest in Sukhomlinsky alive. Soloveichik has suggested that the continuing appearance of posthumous publications has given the impression of a writer still alive. It is certainly the case that the controversy which began with the publication of "Essays … " continued over the ensuing decades up until the demise of the communist government in August, 1991.

Erika Gartmann has given a detailed analysis of the debate which surrounded Sukhomlinsky's work during the years following the publication of "Essays ... ".[30] Sukhomlinsky's detractors, led by B. Likhachev, included L. Gordin and V. Korotov[31], F. Bondar (one of Likhachev's colleagues) and V. Kovalevsky[32]. They all expressed the view that Sukhomlinsky had an "incorrect" understanding of the role of individual and collective approaches in education, that he had erred by departing from the guidelines contained in Makarenko's legacy. They had a tendency to quote Sukhomlinsky out of context and seem not to have had a deep understanding of his work. Their approach was typical of the dogmatic interpretation of Makarenko which Sukhomlinsky had sought to counter.

Gartmann characterises Sukhomlinsky's detractors as having a "Hegelian" mind-set, a fondness for dogmatic systems of logical categories, not necessarily related to practical experience. Sukhomlinsky and his supporters, on the other hand, she sees as fitting into a philosophical framework associated with such names as Kierkegaard, Dostoevsky and Bakhtin. In such a framework the human personality is seen not as something complete, but as open-ended, in the process of becoming.

Certainly Sukhomlinsky's supporters included people of more artistic temperament than his detractors. They included the publicist S. Soloveichik, T. Samsonova[33], Yu. Azarov[34], I. Kosheleva,[35] the composer and musical educationist Dmitry Kabalevsky[36], and the painter B. Nemensky[37].

Generally speaking it may be said that Sukhomlinsky and his supporters won the day. Even during 1968, when the political climate was clearly not in Sukhomlinsky's favour, three of his articles appeared in *Pravda*, the organ of the Central Committee of the Communist Party. This seems to suggest that opposition to Sukhomlinsky's ideas was always limited to certain individuals within the Party.

The publication of archival material from Sukhomlinsky's legacy in *Novyi mir [New World]* in 1974, together with an afterword by T. Samsonova, and the appearance of an article by Yu. Azarov in *Kommunist* in 1976, rekindled the debate, and showed the extent of support now existing for Sukhomlinsky. Azarov's article was followed by a flood of correspondence to *Kommunist*, nearly all favourable to Sukhomlinsky, and with many letters coming from highly placed and highly regarded people. A summary of this correspondence was published in *Kommunist* in 1977, ten years after the appearance of "Essays on Communist Education":

> The majority of teachers writing to the editors are unanimous in considering that Sukhomlinsky's books, particularly *My Heart I Give to Children*, should, along with the works of Krupskaia, Lunacharsky, Shatsky, Makarenko, Blonsky, Vygotsky and Meshcheriaky, be on every teacher's desk.
>
> In the last ten or fifteen years millions of copies of Sukhomlinsky's work have been published, but the demand for them remains unsatisfied.[38]

The president of the USSR Academy of Pedagogical Sciences, V. Stoletov, wrote a letter to the journal strongly supporting Sukhomlinsky. In what was clearly a rebuttal of Likhachev and his associates he wrote:

> However, along with the mass of readers, who study Sukhomlinsky's articles and books with the aim of drawing some food for thought from the experience, from time to time there appear academics who study the same texts with the aim of finding some ill-conceived (in their view) formulations. They diligently juxtapose such formulations from works written years apart and — even more strikingly — on the basis of such "research" they attempt to ascribe to the author views which he does not hold. What teachers need is not arbitrary, speculative interpretation of the texts of the deceased scholar, divorced from school life, but a deep assimilation of his works in the search for concrete solutions to current problems in education ... [39]

Stoletov moreover announces the intention of the Academy to take measures to make Sukhomlinsky's work better known:

> The Presidium of the Academy of Pedagogical Sciences intends:
>
> 1) to publish a collection of the major works of corresponding member of the USSR APS V.A. Sukhomlinsky in the series "Library of Educational Classics";

2) to include in the agenda of the Scientific Council on Methodological Problems of Pedagogy the issue of the use of evidence from school practice in complex research into current teaching problems;

3) to make every effort to use experimental schools as a first stage in the testing, improvement and further development of initiatives coming from teachers in ordinary schools;

4) to make every effort to encourage and assist researchers studying the educational legacy of V.A. Sukhomlinsky and its use in solving current educational problems.[40]

This passage shows that the debate about Sukhomlinsky's work had influenced views on the role of the Academy of Pedagogical Sciences, and that of teachers, in initiating educational research and generating new ideas in education. Stoletov was instrumental in encouraging experimental work by teachers, including some who gained prominence in the 'eighties.

As anticipated in Stoletov's letter, official support for Sukhomlinsky's work was soon forthcoming in the publication of two major collections. A weighty five-volume collection (about three and a half thousand pages) was published in both Ukrainian and Russian in Kiev, during the years 1976 to 1980. The Russian language edition was issued in 100,000 copies. A three volume collection was published in Moscow from 1979 to 1981, in an edition of 150,000 copies. Both these collections contain many works written during the latter part of Sukhomlinsky's life and give a rounded picture of his mature work.

At the same time there was an upsurge of interest by researchers at pedagogical research institutes in the Soviet Union in Sukhomlinsky's work. From 1977 to 1987 more than 20 candidate's theses appeared devoted to Sukhomlinsky.

In theory, the role of the various institutes of the USSR Academy of Pedagogical Sciences was to develop the theoretical guidelines for practising teachers. The institutes were to provide the directions and the teachers were to implement them. It was expected that the ideas of creative teachers such as Sukhomlinsky would be appraised by scholars at the institutes and that appropriate guidelines for adapting their experience would then emerge.

In practice, teachers came increasingly to regard the institutes as ivory towers, out of touch with their daily experience. Educational writers such as Sukhomlinsky, who were also practising teachers, were sometimes compared to the scholars of the institutes in a way unflattering to the latter. This led some scholars to adopt a defensive attitude towards many teacher-writers, culminating in open hostility during the period of *glasnost'*, as we shall see when we turn to the question of Sukhomlinsky's successors.

One writer who played a particularly important role in promoting Sukhomlinsky's ideas was the publicist Simon Soloveichik. He 'discovered' Sukhomlinsky in 1969, through the chance purchase of a copy of the newly published *My Heart I Give to Children*. He wrote a long and passionately favourable review of it, which was published in *Komsomol'skaia pravda* on 18 September, 1969. The article apparently started a run on the book. Its meagre (by Soviet standards) run of 40,000 copies sold out within days. Sukhomlinsky wrote to Soloveichik, saying he had written a review not just of his book, but of his life.

Soloveichik never met Sukhomlinsky in person, but a few months after his death he travelled to Pavlysh, where the school made an enormous impression on him. Sitting in Sukhomlinsky's office, he wrote through the night and produced another article, entitled "Tell people about Sukhomlinsky". This panegyric was published in the magazine *Yunost'* [*Youth*] in March, 1971.[41] The article incorporates many quotations from unpublished manuscripts, so it would appear that Soloveichik had access to these while visiting the school. Soloveichik urges his readers to promote awareness of what Sukhomlinsky had achieved at Pavlysh. He suggests that it is not the outward forms of Sukhomlinsky's work which are significant, but its inner spirit and the understanding which informs it. This second passionately written article promoted further interest in Sukhomlinsky's work.

Soloveichik was also responsible for compiling an anthology of quotations from Sukhomlinsky's works.[42] This volume, first published in 1973, proved very popular, and by 1988 had gone through six editions. (The fifth edition was printed in 200,000 copies, the sixth in 100,000.) The book is in six sections, each with an introductory essay by Soloveichik. These essays include biographical material, as well as analysis of Sukhomlinsky's ideas. Each section contains a collection of quotations, thematically grouped, and ranging in length from two or three lines to half a page or so. Soloveichik urges readers to "fill in the gaps" between quotations through their own reflection and through an acquaintance with the original works.

The print media was not the only avenue through which Sukhomlinsky's influence was felt. Museums were opened in his honour, conferences were held to discuss his work, and schools adopted his name and attempted to implement his ideas. His influence was particularly strong in the Kirovograd region of the Ukraine, where many teachers had had personal contact with him.

Perhaps most important of all was the influence of other creative educators who became infected with his ideas and spirit, and whose influence was particularly strong in the 'seventies and 'eighties. One such person was Dmitry Kabalevsky, the musician and educator who was responsible for the reform of the national school music curriculum during the 'seventies. In 1977 he wrote:

> I especially felt Sukhomlinsky's great help and support at the beginning of the 'seventies, when I was caught up with the complex, but urgent task of restructuring the music curriculum, (and, more broadly, the arts curriculum) for the general school. 'Discovering' Sukhomlinsky brought me great joy. His books, with which I became acquainted as they were published, helped to strengthen my views on music education, taught me a lot, inspired me, becoming a source of my educational musings, and, if I may so express myself, of my educational emotions.
>
> As the epigraph to the new music curriculum ... I chose Sukhomlinsky's words: "Musical education is not the education of a musician, but first and foremost the education of a human being." As the epigraph to my book *How to talk to children about music* I also used his words: "The art of education includes first of all the art of talking to, of addressing the human heart". That book also closes with Sukhomlinsky's words: "Words can never fully explain the depth of music, but without words one cannot approach that subtle sphere of exploration of feelings".
>
> I consider Sukhomlinsky's idea of the unity of the ethical and the aesthetic in children's education especially valuable. In itself, of course, this idea is not new, but it permeates all the elements of Sukhomlinsky's educational conception so consistently and so compellingly, in a way that seems unprecedented in the work of earlier educators.[43]

The influence of a group of creative educators who rose to prominence during the 'eighties, and who might be considered to be Sukhomlinsky's successors will be examined in the following chapter.

Notes

1. Sukhomlinsky, V.A., "Uchitel' — sovest' naroda [A teacher is the nation's conscience]", *Narodnoe obrazovanie [National Education]*, 1988, No. 9, p. 73.
2. From a personal conversation.
3. Quoted in S. Soloveichik's conclusion to Sukhomlinsky, V.A. *O vospitanii [On education]*, 6th edition, Moscow, Politizdat, 1988, p. 261.
4. Ibid., p. 260.
5. "Iz tvorcheskogo naslediia V.A. Sukhomlinskogo [From the creative legacy of V.A. Sukhomlinsky]", *Sovetskaia pedagogika [Soviet Pedagogy]*, 1988, No. 3, p. 100.
6. Ibid., pp. 98/99.
7. See Sukhomlinsky, V.A., "Uchitel' — sovest' naroda [A teacher is the nation's conscience]", *Narodnoe obrazovanie [National Education]*, 1988, No. 9, p. 73.
8. See Tartakovsky, B.S., Povest' ob uchitele Sukhomlinskom [The Story of the Teacher Sukhomlinsky], Moscow, Molodaia gvardiia, 1972, pp 160–163, 172–176.
9. Malinin, V.I., "Sukhomlinsky o Makarenko — nezavershennyi trud [Sukhomlinsky on Makarenko — An uncompleted work]", *Sovetskaia pedagogika [Soviet Pedagogy]*, 1990, No. 3, p. 86.
10. See "Obsuzhdenie knigi V.A. Sukhomlinskogo 'Formirovanie kommunisticheskikh ubezhdenii molodogo pokoleniia' [A discussion of V.A. Sukhomlinsky's book 'The formation of communist convictions in the younger generation']", *Sovetskaia pedagogika [Soviet Pedagogy]*, 1962, No. 9, pp. 156–160.
11. Malinin, V.I., "Sukhomlinsky o Makarenko — nezavershennyi trud [Sukhomlinsky on Makarenko — An uncompleted work]", *Sovetskaia pedagogika [Soviet Pedagogy]*, 1990, No. 3, p. 88.
12. Sukhomlinsky, V.A., "Idti vpered! [Let us go forward!]", *Narodnoe obrazovanie [National Education]*, 1989, No. 8, pp. 70/71.
13. Sukhomlinsky, V.A., "Pedagog — kollektiv — lichnost' [The teacher — the collective — the individual]", *Literaturnaia gazeta [The Literary Newspaper]*, 28 October, 1970.
14. See Sukhomlinsky, V.A., "Uchitel' — sovest' naroda [A teacher is the nation's conscience]", *Narodnoe obrazovanie [National Education]*, 1988, No. 9, pp. 73–81.
15. From personal correspondence.
16. Narodnoe obrazovanie, 1967, No. 2, p. 39.
17. Ibid., p. 41.
18. Ibid., p. 42.
19. Ibid.
20. Ibid., p. 43.
21. Quoted in Soloveichik, S., "Pedagogika zastoia [The pedagogy of stagnation]", *Uchitel'skaia gazeta [The Teacher's Newspaper]*, 1987, 19 May, p. 2.

22 Sukhomlinsky, V.A., "Uchitel' — sovest' naroda [A teacher is the nation's conscience]", *Narodnoe obrazovanie [National Education]*, 1988, No. 9, p. 75.
23 Ibid.
24 Ibid., letter dated 24 June.
25 "Vizhu cheloveka [I see a human being]", *Literaturnaia gazeta [The Literary Newspaper]*, 27 September, 1967.
26 Sukhomlinsky, V.A., "Uchitel' — sovest' naroda [A teacher is the nation's conscience]", *Narodnoe obrazovanie [National Education]*, 1988, No. 9, pp. 73–79.
27 Ibid., p. 77.
28 "Ot redaktsii [From the editors]", *Narodnoe obrazovanie [National Education]*, 1967, No. 12, p. 43.
29 Sukhomlinsky, V.A., "Uchitel' — sovest' naroda [A teacher is the nation's conscience]", *Narodnoe obrazovanie [National Education]*, 1988, No. 9, pp. 78–79.
30 Gartmann, E., *Padagogik zwischen Menschen-und Güterproduktion. Zur Sittlichkeitserziehung V.A. Suchomlinskys*, München: 1984., pp. 13–45.
31 Gordin, L., Korotov, V., Likhachev, B., "Pis'mo v redaktsiiu [A letter to the editor]", *Yunost'*, 1972, No. 4, p. 90.
32 Letters from Kovalevsky and Bondar appeared in *Sovetskaia pedagogika[Soviet pedagogy]*, 1975, No. 4: 147–149.
33 Samsonova, T., "Konkretnyi gumanizm vospitatel'noi sistemy V.A. Sukhomlinskogo [The concrete humanism of V.A. Sukhomlinsky's educational system]", *Novyi mir [New world]*, 1974, No. 8, pp. 184–194.
34 Azarov, Yu., "Grazhdanstvennost' i chelovechnost' [Civic sense and humanity]", *Kommunist*, 1976, No. 8, pp. 64–73.
35 See *Novyi mir [New world]*, 1976, No. 9, p. 271.
36 Kabalevsky, Dm., "Bol'shoi rezerv v pedagogicheskom arsenale [A great reserve in the pedagogical arsenal]", *Kommunist*, 1977, No. 13, pp. 90–92.
37 See *Kommunist*, 1977, No. 13, pp. 84–85.
38 Ibid., pp. 78/79.
39 Ibid., p. 80.
40 Ibid.
41 *Yunost'*, 1971, No. 3, pp. 78–85.
42 See Sukhomlinsky, V.A. *O vospitanii [On education]*, 6th edition, Moscow, Politizdat, 1988.
43 Kabalevsky, Dm., "Bol'shoi rezerv v pedagogicheskom arsenale [A great reserve in the pedagogical arsenal]", *Kommunist*, 1977, No. 13, p. 91.

CHAPTER 8

Sukhomlinsky's Successors

> Having read Sukhomlinsky's books [this teacher] became enthused with his ideas. He decided not to play around with his quotations, but to see for himself, to relive his experience in himself. From this position he began to evaluate and enrich his practice. Each lesson and each encounter with his pupils he planned as a process of self-development and perfection of the art of teaching.[1]
>
> (Sh.A. Amonashvili — "teacher-innovator".)

DURING the 'eighties a new constellation of teacher-writers emerged who, in some respects, may be considered to have been Sukhomlinsky's successors. They included Sh.A. Amonashvili, V.F. Shatalov, S. Lysenkova, I.P. Volkov, V. Karakovsky, E.N. Ilyin and others. Each worked in relative isolation until they were invited by the editorial board of *Uchitel'skaia gazeta [The Teacher's Newspaper]* to attend a two day meeting at Peredelkina, on the outskirts of Moscow, in October of 1986. Through the publicity given them by the newspaper they became widely known as the "teacher-innovators". It is not possible to give a detailed account of their writings in the confines of this chapter, but an attempt will be made to show the thematic continuity between their work and Sukhomlinsky's, and to show why their work was likely to appeal to the same audience.

Perhaps the closest in spirit to Sukhomlinsky was Sh.A. Amonashvili, a corresponding member of the USSR Academy of Pedagogical Sciences and director of the Ya.A. Gogebashvili Scientific Research Institute of Pedagogical Sciences in Tbilisi, where he worked as a class teacher in an experimental school. Like Sukhomlinsky, he combined the activities of teacher, administrator and writer. Like him, he was interested first and foremost in the moral development of each child, and in developing teaching methods which would allow all children to develop their unique potential. He writes in a similar genre to Sukhomlinsky, giving an account of his actual teaching experience, interspersed with observations and conclusions based on that experience.

He has acknowledged his debt to Sukhomlinsky (see the epigraph to this chapter), whom he clearly reveres.[2]

Just as, in *My Heart I Give to Children*, Sukhomlinsky had written about his experiences teaching six-year-olds and primary school children, so Amonashvili wrote about his experience teaching children of the same age. He did so in a sequence of three books. *Hello Children!* tells of his work with a class of six-year-olds during their first year at school. *How are you living, Children?* describes his continuing work with the same group of children during the ensuing two years, and *Singleness of Purpose* completes the sequence with an account of the class's fourth and final year of primary schooling.

Like Sukhomlinsky, Amonashvili called on teachers to enter into the inner world of each child, to study each child's life in detail:

> Teachers should read educational theory, psychology, methodology, they should read the educational classics and draw wisdom from them, they should keep up to date with the latest developments in theories of teaching and upbringing, they should study the experience of the innovators. All of this is excellent, it is a good way of shortening the winding road that leads to the unlocking of the secrets of education … But that is not all. Until teachers become researchers into the lives of their little children, they will not have sufficient knowledge of them. Teachers truly grasp only those secrets of education which they have discovered for themselves in their creative laboratory, even though they follow in the tracks of thousands and millions of other teachers. In this laboratory Marika must be discovered as a unique life, Bondo must be discovered as the result of a concrete set of circumstances, all the others must be discovered as individuals, but taking into account their collective life.
>
> People live for each other, and in this is contained the highest meaning of their humanity. But in order to indeed live in this way, for each other, giving joy to each other, together, each of us must have our own life and our spiritual world.[3]

The central concern of Amonashvili's work is the education of a truly humane personality—that aspect of Sukhomlinsky's work which was discussed in the fifth chapter of this study. He is especially concerned with the relations between class members, and with what is happening in children's families. Like Sukhomlinsky, he hopes to have a favourable influence on family relationships. One aspect of family life in which he took a special interest was the relationship between children and their grandparents. He writes:

> My observations have convinced me that a greater mutual understanding arises between children and their grandparents, than between children and their parents. Perhaps this comes about because grandparents, as a rule, do not base their relationships with their grandchildren on some remote educational aims, incomprehensible to children, but rather on the children's immediate interests and needs. Grandparents are quick to become involved in a game with their grandchildren, and happy to carry out their wishes. Children have more secrets with their grandparents. Grandparents protect them in their pranks, jokingly forgive them their misdeeds and never betray them to their parents. Grandparents are an impenetrable refuge from parental anger. Children have faith in their grandparents' devotion, and so they are not afraid of them and do not always obey them. But when grandmothers are upset and angry with them, children experience it painfully and rush to give them hugs and kisses, apologising and showing their remorse.
>
> So do we need a special pedagogy to show grandparents how to educate their grandchildren? I think it would be wonderful to have such books. Grandparents enrich the golden age of childhood, filling it with love, care and wisdom ...
>
> I shut my eyes and go back to my distant past, when the sound of artillery reached us from the nearby mountains of the Caucasus, and I, burying my head in my pillow, waited deep into the night for my grandmother to return from the collective farm bakery, where she worked. Grandma used to come back, bringing with her a delicious-smelling loaf of hot rye bread, putting me at ease and telling me stories, and I would go to sleep with a sense of security and hope. And this sense of security, acquired thanks to the heart-felt kindness and affection of one who was dear to me, was for me nothing less than the impregnation of my heart with humanity.[4]

The last paragraph of this passage could almost have been written by Sukhomlinsky, so close is it in spirit to his work. Amonashvili goes on to describe how he invited grandparents into his classroom and involved them in the children's education. This aspect of his work is reminiscent of the way in which Sukhomlinsky fostered relationships between his pupils and old people. There are also passages in Amonashvili's books where he offers advice to parents.[5]

Amonashvili considers teaching to be an art, and develops the idea of the lesson as an art form. In his books we see a lot more of what happens in the classroom than we do in Sukhomlinsky's writings. Often a chapter is devoted to a description of a single day's lessons, with reflections on various incidents. Amonashvili is particularly fond of musical imagery. When preparing a lesson he produces not a plan, but a 'score', to be interpreted with sensitivity. The teacher's chief instrument, in Amonashvili's view, is his voice, which should be trained to express a wide range of feelings and attitudes.

In the closing chapter of *Singleness of Purpose* Amonashvili proposes three principles which should govern a teacher's work:

> The *first* principle is to love the child. Love is the human sun. The sun radiates warmth and light, without which there would be no life on earth. A teacher should radiate human kindness and love, without which it is impossible to educate a humane soul in a person. A child becomes happy as soon as he senses that his teacher loves him, loves him sincerely and selflessly. Love facilitates education, since it is the only kindly force capable of bringing the child harmony of soul, of stimulating his growth towards maturity, mutuality and a kindly attitude to those around him. In the pedagogy of love there is no place for rudeness, for pressure, for damaging the self-respect or ignoring the life of the child. These constitute the dark forces of education, educational evil, which at times is capable of crushing and poisoning the life of a child, hitherto illuminated and warmed by love and kindness, of introducing confusion, disillusionment and bitterness.
>
> The *second* principle (it flows from the first) is to humanise the environment in which the child lives. Humanising the environment means paying attention to all the child's spheres of social contact, with a view to ensuring psychological comfort and equilibrium. Not one sphere of social contact should disturb the child, giving rise to fear, lack of confidence, depression or sense of inferiority. A disharmony

between the various spheres of social contact gives rise educationally to an uncertainty in the soul of the child, who becomes confused and may easily develop an embittered state of mind. Then he begins to behave maliciously towards others, even towards his father, mother or teacher. It is precisely at this time that he may find shelter in the "devil's workshop". Who can bring all the child's spheres of social contact into harmony? Who else but the teacher? He should bring clarity to all these spheres, transforming them in the interests of educating the child.

The *third* principle is to relive one's childhood in the child. This is a reliable way of ensuring that the child trusts the teacher, appreciates his kindness of soul, accepts his love. It is also the way to come to know the child's life. A deep study of the child's life, of the movements of his soul, is possible only when the teacher becomes aware of the child within himself.[6]

In the fifth chapter of *How are you living, Children?* Amonashvili discusses a particular methodology developed by him for educating humane qualities. He quotes Sukhomlinsky:

Vasily Aleksandrovich Sukhomlinsky used to say that the basic subject in school should be the study of human beings. He meant this in the widest sense of the word, intending that the whole education process should be permeated with the fostering in a young person of a need for human fellowship. But he also meant that there should be a special subject which would incorporate and generalise the school's concern for educating the human within a human being.

So in my class I have opened a "school in humanity", and I conduct activities twice a week. Vasily Aleksandrovich's words have become the motto for our school ... "You were born a human being, but you have to become human."[7]

Amonashvili's methodology made use of the dramatisation of scenes from the children's lives. The children were put in an imagined testing situation and were asked to show how they would react. Particular attention was drawn to language and intonation, and the effect that these produced. The teacher might deliberately place a child who often hurt others' feelings in a role where he or she was on the receiving end of someone else's hurtful remarks.

The "school of humanity" had a particular thematic structure, with 16 themes being covered in the course of 64 lessons. This experimental course utilised booklets prepared at Amonashvili's institute. These contain drawings illustrating contrasting approaches to family and public life, and a series of texts and questions. The aim was to develop certain ethical concepts, to assist children to identify with those approaches which were socially desirable, and to encourage them to reflect on how they should behave in a variety of situations they would be likely to encounter in the future.

Language lessons were also often given a moral orientation. The reading of children's literature, such as St Exupéry's *The Little Prince*, was often combined with exercises to develop the children's imagination, inwardness and empathy. Like Sukhomlinsky, Amonashvili worked at the level of both consciousness and action:

> These are the sort of assignments I give the children in class and for homework:
>
> - Put your heads down, shut your eyes and think what you would do in his place …
>
> - Think about why you feel sympathy for him (or her) …
>
> - Think about what you do not like in your own character, and how you will improve yourself …
>
> - Shut your eyes and imagine you are performing some heroic act …
>
> - Shut your eyes and perform some good act in the school corridor during recess (at home when your elders are out, etc.) …
>
> - Shut your eyes and do something good for your friend … For your classmates … For your family …
>
> … Giving these assignments I aim for each child to learn to go deep within themselves, to immerse themselves in their inner world, to rehearse their future life and activity. And then I try to create a situation where they will actually behave as they have imagined, where they will actually perform a noble act.[8]

Amonashvili's work was subjected to considerable scrutiny by the press, television, and by the many visitors to his classroom. He was highly regarded both popularly, and by academics, amongst whom he was known principally for his experimental work with six-year-olds.

What impressed visitors to his school most, was the degree of affection between Amonashvili and his pupils, and the degree of autonomy of the young children, who were actively involved in evaluating the success of each lesson. They had become the teacher's partners in the education process, and, as they grew older, were given responsibility for conducting 'mini-lessons'.

Like Sukhomlinsky, all the teacher-innovators were concerned to ensure that each child participated actively in all lessons, and worked at his or her optimum level. This resulted in the development of particular teaching techniques. In Amonashvili's case the blackboard was used skilfully to present material in an attractive and stimulating way (he includes samples of blackboard presentation in his books), and its dramatic impact was enhanced by the addition of curtains, which could be drawn with a flourish. When Amonashvili put a question to the class, rather than have a single pupil answer aloud, he walked from one to another as they whispered their answers in his ear. In this way a correct answer from one pupil did not interrupt the train of thought of the others. Sometimes he deliberately made mistakes in order to encourage critical attention. Like Sukhomlinsky, Amonashvili wrote his books for practising teachers, and found an enthusiastic audience.

In one matter Amonashvili went further than Sukhomlinsky. Sukhomlinsky would never give failing grades to primary school pupils, preferring to defer the awarding of a grade until they had reached the required standard. Amonashvili altogether abandoned the practice of awarding grades in the primary school. His final reports issued to pupils at the end of grade four were accounts of personal growth and scholastic achievement, but not grades on a scale of one to five, as was the common practice. Indication was also given in the reports of where further work was needed. The development of character was clearly made the top priority, though Amonashvili suggests that achievement was very high in consequence. His descriptions of the children's work do indicate a high standard of work, resulting from the development of a moral orientation, independence, responsibility, critical thought, imagination and creativity.

Another teacher-innovator given considerable publicity during the period of *perestroika* was Igor Pavlovich Volkov, a teacher of drawing and draftsmanship at School No. 2, Reutova, near Moscow. If the central theme in Amonashvili's work is the development of humane qualities, the key issue in Volkov's work is the uncovering of each child's unique talents and the development of a vocation. Like Sukhomlinsky, Volkov achieves this through a broad range of extracurricular activities held during the second half of the day, which effectively constitute a "second curriculum". His unique contribution is the development of a formal record of pupil's participation in extracurricular activities, a so-called "record of creative work". This served as a vocational guide of interest to teachers, career advisers and future employers.

Volkov describes his approach thus:

> In our view the school should work through two main avenues. The first is the study of the compulsory state program, in which, rather than breaking the material for study into strict units with a prescribed number of hours for each theme, only the required result at the end of each year of study should be indicated. It is the teacher's job to decide what system to follow and in what order to present the material for study. The second avenue is to offer possibilities for children to manifest, develop and take account of their talents and abilities (outside class time). In consequence the pupil, on graduating from school, will receive two equally valid documents. One—the school leaver's certificate—would reflect his knowledge of the basic disciplines. The other—the "Pupil's Creative Record"—would record independent work, carried out on his own initiative in addition to the school program, and give a description of the personal qualities manifested in such activity.[9]

At Volkov's school the idea of undertaking extracurricular activities was introduced by the class teacher in the context of a discussion on the choice of a future vocation. Pupils were encouraged to undertake independent work in any school subject or any area of technology, art or work in which they had an interest.[10] Subject teachers regularly suggested the possibility of such work to their pupils, and showed the class samples of completed projects. Sometimes teachers also read out entries from a pupil's "Record of Creative Work".

In order for a project to be entered in a pupil's record it had to meet certain objective criteria and was checked by a teacher with competence in that area. Written projects, for instance, were expected to be in the order of 12–15 pages in length, though length was not considered important in appraising a poem or a literary prose composition. A translation from a foreign language was expected to be at least 200 lines in length, though a translation into a foreign language need be only 50 lines. Participation in a drama group was entered in the book if it continued for a year and involved taking part in three productions. The composition of a piece of music would be entered, as would a musical performance with a duration of ten minutes. The setting of such objective criteria was considered necessary to give the entries a certain status and to ensure that the pupils perceived the whole process to be fair. It helped to eliminate arguments about whether a pupil's efforts merited being recorded or not.

Each entry contained a description of the work undertaken. For example:

> Botany. Written project on the topic "The morphology and metamorphosis of a leaf", based on materials from a tertiary course. 34 pages. 6 drawings. 2 photographs. Year 7 …
>
> French Language. Written project. Translation into Russian. 320 lines (10 pages) from a work of literature.

Following such a description an analysis was given of the way in which the pupil went about the task, the degree of creativity, independence, consistent application and so on.

When a pupil left the school a summary was prepared of all the extracurricular work undertaken and of the personal characteristics manifested during its execution.

Teachers were generally discouraged from creating a fanfare about the extracurricular work, or from holding competitions or conferences about the results, as it was thought that this would corrupt the motivation of the pupils. One of the key aims was to develop independence.

Volkov recommended setting up special rooms for extracurricular work in each school. Any classroom could be used as such at the end of the school day. Each room was to specialise in a particular area, such as modelling, creative writing or music.

In Volkov's experience, the development of a comprehensive extracurricular program was of great assistance in helping pupils determine their career path. We have already seen how a similar program functioned at Sukhomlinsky's school in Pavlysh. Volkov formalised such a program and developed guidelines for it which met with the approval of the Academy of Pedagogical Sciences and the Ministry of Education. In so doing he facilitated the introduction of similar programs in other Soviet schools.[11]

Perhaps the most publicised of all the teacher-innovators was V. Shatalov. The keynote in his work is the attempt to give every pupil the joy of success in study. Once again this echoes a theme in Sukhomlinsky's work. Shatalov worked as a mathematics teacher at School No. 5 in the Ukrainian city of Donetsk. In his view the underlying reason for most children's failure to master work was loss of faith in their ability, resulting from past failures:

> It is only a young teacher, lacking adequate educational experience during his first years of work, who just cannot understand why his pupils cannot quote a rule which has been repeated at lessons five or six times, why the children cannot solve problems which have been worked through more than once in class, why he is nearly driven crazy by the same mistakes in dictations being repeated thousands of times. So what do we have—the teacher's irritation, children's mute despair, insulting reproaches and mutual alienation, at times giving rise to direct enemy attacks on the part of certain desperate pupils. And there is one simple reason: loss of faith in one's ability, a depressing sense of hopelessness and of there being no way out. Who other than the teacher should lead children out of this state of mind?[12]

Shatalov developed a system of methodological procedures for ensuring that no pupil became excluded from active participation in learning. He achieved spectacular, albeit sometimes disputed, results. His classes often completed two years' work in a single year, with some pupils able to master material several years beyond that stipulated for their age. He was particularly successful in encouraging pupils with poor scholastic records. Some critics, however, accused him of oversimplifying the material to be studied.

At the heart of Shatalov's methodology was his method of assessing children's work:

> If we turn now to the work of the Donetsk experimenters, we must note that the essential element is not the supporting diagrams [a type of schematic teaching aid—see below] which have received so much

attention over the years, but a new, extremely elegant and effective *system of assessing the work of teachers and pupils*. Objective and mobile, it completely eliminates any conflicts at home or at school and makes the pupil an active and interested participant in his own instruction and education.[13]

Shatalov shared Sukhomlinsky's view that a student's work should not be given a grade until it had been brought to a successful conclusion. In his mathematics classes each student was given the whole year to complete all the exercises in the textbook — at his or her own pace. Of course it was necessary for teacher and parents to encourage students in their work, but this was done without resorting to fear as the motivating factor. Like Sukhomlinsky, Shatalov was able, through the influence of his personality, to foster an atmosphere in which each wanted to do their best.

The quantity of homework completed each night was left to the pupils, but every exercise successfully completed was recorded and on view for all to see. No record was kept of unsuccessful attempts. Assessment was far more comprehensive than in most classrooms, as the children were trained to assess each other's work. At the end of a period of study each pupil was given responsibility for assessing a particular question, and over a period of a couple of weeks every student successfully answered every question, as more than one attempt was permitted. The result of such a 'friendly' approach to assessment was to free pupils from the fear of failure, and to foster a joy in learning.

Another method associated with Shatalov's name was the use of a particular form of teaching aid which was called in Russian *opornyi signal*, which might be loosely translated as "a supporting diagram". This was usually a diagram which represented, in a graphic and easily decoded form, a summary of the main elements covered under a given topic. With the support offered by these graphic aids, students of lesser ability were able to attempt the same work as those of greater ability. They simply made greater use of the charts which were on display for all to see. With practice all students mastered the required syllabus and the need for referring to the charts disappeared.

All of Shatalov's methods were aimed at increasing pupils' confidence in their ability, and at encouraging persistence, so that all could experience the rewards of achieving success through their own efforts.

The work of S.N. Lysenkova, another teacher-innovator, is in many ways similar to that of Shatalov, though she worked in the primary school. Like Shatalov, she used "supporting charts", and like him she evolved a variety of techniques to keep all pupils actively involved in learning.

One of these techniques she calls "direction with commentary". A standard technique used by Soviet teachers at all lessons was the question session — which usually involved summoning a pupil to the blackboard to answer a question. It was a way of checking homework and revising past work, and of awarding grades to pupils. Lysenkova gives this procedure a twist. She calls on the pupil not to answer a question, but to lead the class in an exercise. While this effectively amounts to the same thing, it creates a different mental attitude in the pupil and allows the whole class to be involved. Pupils summoned to the blackboard to work through an exercise carefully describe each step as they work, while the rest of the class copies each step into their work books. This encourages a responsible attitude on the part of the child leading the class, who is, for the time being, the 'teacher'. The children develop good diction and gain confidence. Should the child who is leading the class make an error, it will generally be corrected immediately by the rest of the class.

Another feature of Lysenkova's work which she shares with Shatalov is what she calls *operezhenie* (getting in front). She decided, paradoxically, that in order for pupils to have more time to master material, it was necessary to introduce it earlier than indicated in the program. To do this she needed to gain time, which she did by increasing the tempo of work with the aid of supporting charts and by the use of "direction with commentary":

> Supporting charts and direction with commentary ensure that the whole class works harmoniously and that all the children advance rapidly in their studies. In consequence there is spare time at every lesson, which means there is an opportunity to carry out a large number of varied exercises for reinforcement and revision of ground covered, and also for generalising knowledge and developing sound skills. Moreover, and no less importantly, it allows us to work on future topics in the program, to take a forward-looking or anticipatory approach to their study.[14]

Another of the teacher-innovators was Evgeny Ilyin, a teacher of literature at school No. 307 in Leningrad. The theme which dominates his work is the "art of communication", especially communication between a teacher and his pupils. In his view the teacher of literature must understand the lives of his pupils in order to teach in a way that they find relevant:

> The art of communication consists in the resourceful combination of study material with material from real life in our contacts with our pupils. Knowledge which is only about books and based on books will not strike a chord with the majority of children. Books will lead the study of literature into a dead end if they are studied independently of real life.[15]

For him a school literature lesson should be first and foremost a lesson about life, in which the author under study emerges as a living person. The study of literary devices, genres and so on, should be secondary, and should not inhibit the direct response of the pupils to the author's work of art:

> The life experience of the characters, and not how they are 'made', is is what excites the children first and foremost ...
>
> Yet how often it happens that, for instance, the genre, hyperbole and metaphor of Gogol's *Dead Souls* are subjected to detailed analysis, while Gogol himself is absent from the lesson![16]

Like other teacher-innovators, Ilyin developed particular methodological devices which he describes in his writing. One of these is to focus on some seemingly insignificant detail in a work of literature, and to see the whole work refracted in that detail, "to see the world in a grain of sand" as it were.

> When one catches a glimmer of the *big* in the *small*, there arises a curiosity about both, and generally about the links between them. It is as if one's interest is doubled by the premonition of something important. All children, without exception, find small detail psychologically accessible. It is their pathway to Art ...
>
> The unravelling of a detail gives the lesson a plot, an idea, it teaches the children how to work on the sub text. Problem, imagery, a subject for analysis, are all to be found in a detail, in that distinctive little knot

of text where many threads meet. In essence it is these threads which link the teacher with the children and the children with the book.[17]

Ilyin favours the intensive study of a few representative works, rather that the attempt to make a comprehensive, and necessarily superficial, study of Russian and Soviet literature. He would rather pupils have the time to read widely of their own initiative, having learnt the art of appreciation on the basis of selected material.

Like Sukhomlinsky, Ilyin considers the central concern of education to be the study of human nature, and of ethical issues. Like Sukhomlinsky, he sees poets and writers as friends from whom one should draw strength and insight, rather than merely as objects of study.

By now it should be apparent that there is a thematic continuity between the work of the teacher-innovators and that of Sukhomlinsky. In their writings we find more attention given to the techniques of classroom instruction than we find in Sukhomlinsky's writings, but they are working to an agenda which had been elaborated by him in the 'sixties.

In the 'eighties the teacher-innovators became the leaders of a grass roots movement for educational reform. They produced four educational manifestos, which were published in *Uchitel'skaia gazeta* over the space of two years. The first, a summary of their meeting in Peredelkina in October 1986, was entitled "The pedagogy of cooperation". This became the slogan under which their ideas were promoted by the newspaper. The second manifesto, entitled "The Democratisation of Personality", was published on 17 October, 1987. The third, "The Methodology of Renewal" was published on 19 March, 1988, and the fourth, entitled "Let us Enter the New School", on 18 October in the same year. In a curious way history appeared to repeat itself, as Simon Soloveichik, now working as a journalist with *Uchitel'skaia gazeta*, played a key role in promoting the teacher-innovators, and B. Likhachev, who had led the attack on Sukhomlinsky two decades earlier, was one of the most vocal of a group of academics and educators who conducted a sustained attack on the teacher-innovators from the pages of *Narodnoe obrazovanie* and *Sovetskaia pedagogika*. The resulting debate was far more heated than that which had arisen over Sukhomlinsky's work, conducted as it was during the period of *glasnost'*.

Avril Suddaby has written a valuable essay on the contribution of the teacher-innovators to Soviet educational reform in the latter half of the 'eighties. She has also explained the opposition to them which came from some members of the educational establishment. In her view the academicians were reacting to what they saw as a usurpation of their role as the formulators of educational theory and policy:

> In *Pedagogy of Cooperation* there had been an implicit challenge to the Academy of Pedagogical Sciences. Rather than accepting the recommendations of the APN [the Academy], the innovators were devising and proposing not only their own teaching methods, but also a new educational theory.[18]

It is clear from surveys conducted by *Uchitel'skaia gazeta* that during the period of *perestroika* many teachers were dissatisfied with the guidelines offered by the Academy and extremely receptive to the ideas of the teacher-innovators. It also appears from published materials that many creative teachers met resistance from the educational bureaucracy. The resistance encountered by V. Shatalov, for instance, was discussed on the pages of *Uchitel'skaia gazeta*, and was also the subject of a play by Soloveichik entitled *Pechal'nyi odnoliub [Unfortunate obsession]*. The degree of publicity which surrounded the debate about the teacher-innovators was extraordinary. Some of the teachers appeared on television giving demonstration lessons and generating much comment. *Uchitel'skaia gazeta*, which itself had a circulation of one and a half million, received thousands of letters in support of the teacher-innovators and conducted surveys of teachers' attitudes to them.

Even Gorbachev had his say on the matter. At a Central Committee plenum held on 18 February, 1988, he weighed in on behalf of the teacher-innovators:

> We need to change our attitude to teachers at the root, without any strings or hesitation. To free them from petty surveillance, to shed our suspicious attitude towards exploration and discoveries. To take away the burden of non-educational duties, to free their time and energies for their main task. To take away all the barriers to innovation in education, to create material conditions worthy of the creative work of teachers. This is the duty of the Party and administrative organs.

In the multinational Soviet school remarkable teacher-innovators are working, seeking their own ways to instruct and educate children. Their names are well known. And the more there are of such highly qualified teachers, the more there arise unique teaching collectives of like-minded people, the sooner our schools will be freed of hum-drum routine, formalism and the spirit of stagnation. This will benefit our children, our grandchildren, and the whole cause of revolutionary reconstruction.[19]

It should be noted that the debate about the teacher innovators took place in the context not only of *perestroika*, but also of a reform of the education system initiated in 1984. This was one of a series of cyclic reforms in education undertaken during the post-Stalin era. Previous reforms included the Khrushchev polytechnical labour reform of 1958–64, the reform of 1966, which sought to reinstate a more academic approach, and the reform of 1977, which sought to correct the excesses of the 1966 reform and reasserted the importance of vocational training in the school. These reforms have been the subject of a number of excellent studies[20] and will not be treated in detail here.

The 1984 reform has also been subjected to detailed scrutiny.[21] Its main thrust was further to strengthen the vocational strain in secondary education with a view to creating a closer match between pupils' skills on graduation and the needs of the economy. Universal secondary education had served to raise young people's expectations of receiving higher education and of moving into a high-status white-collar occupation. Industry, on the other hand was still relatively primitive, and suffered from a shortage of unskilled labour.

Another avowed intention of the reform was to raise the quality of education and upbringing, and it was clear that the highest echelons of the party were deeply concerned about deteriorating attitudes towards education and lack of ideological commitment among the young. Zajda has noted the increasing incidence of delinquency in the 'eighties[22], and the priority given to the education issue by the Politburo may be gauged by the standing of the people involved in its committee on educational reform. Andropov had launched the reform process, Chernenko had headed the committee appointed to review education, and Chernenko's successor in the post had been Gorbachev. Szekely was tempted to suggest that Kremlin watchers should take note of the next appointee to the post, as he might prove to be Gorbachev's successor.[23]

The 1984 school reform was overtaken, however, by the much more sweeping reforms of *perestroika*. The policy of *glasnost'* led to an open airing of teachers' grievances and brought to the surface issues even more fundamental than the relative mix of vocational and general studies. The whole ethos of the education system was called into question. Just as Gorbachev was seeking to dismantle the centralised 'command' structure of the economy, so educators called for a dismantling of the 'command' structure in education, and sought greater room for initiative by teachers and schools.

The education system in 1985 still owed its character, in large part, to the Stalinist legacy. All pupils in the Soviet Union were expected to follow a uniform syllabus through to the final year (10 or 11). Text books, programs and even lesson plans were standardised, albeit with some allowances for national differences. The style of teaching was authoritarian in the extreme, with little tolerance of independent thought. There was a standard answer for every question asked in class.[24] Such a mode of operation was clearly not up to the task of encouraging the soul-searching, critical thought and creative initiative demanded by *perestroika*.

The deepest problem of all in the education system, as in the society at large, was a crisis of faith which became more and more evident throughout the 'eighties, and which ultimately led to the disintegration of the Soviet Union. Many factors contributed to this crisis of faith. The economy was stagnating. The centrally controlled economic system, which earlier in the century had achieved spectacular 'extensive growth' in heavy industry, seemed unable to produce further 'intensive growth' in the way that Western economies had. There was a general awareness of a gulf between official Party rhetoric and reality. Genuine achievements in raising the general level of education had contributed to a lessening of respect for the ideologically constrained ideas emanating from the Party. Corruption was endemic and the black economy was of enormous proportions. The war in Afghanistan was also responsible for undermining the morale of young people, as graphically shown in the film *Legko li byt' molodym? [Is it easy to be young?]*. In some respects the war played a similar role in Soviet society to that played by the Vietnam War in America. The crisis of faith deepened during the period of *perestroika*, as new revelations about the Soviet past continually appeared in the media.

The societal malaise was reflected in the school system, where children frequently showed open disrespect for the ideology which the teachers were required to promote. Privately, many of the teachers, too, had ceased to believe in it. They were often further demoralised by having to work in poor conditions, with inadequate housing and remuneration.

A major problem in education was the phenomenon of 'percentomania'. This was the practice of awarding 99% of pupils passing grades, regardless of their level of achievement. Not to do so would lead to accusations of incompetence and to condemnation by parents and administrators. Students realised that they would be given a pass regardless of how they worked. All students, without exception, were expected to complete secondary schooling, and all, regardless of ability, were expected to cover the same syllabus. The pressures on teachers created by this situation can be imagined.

During the latter half of the 'eighties the policy of *glasnost*' allowed all these problems in education to be brought to the surface and openly discussed. The editorial board of *Uchitel'skaia gazeta* and its journalists (most notably Simon Soloveichik) took up a particularly radical stance in this discussion. Soloveichik, with editorial backing, accused the Ministry of Education and the Academy of Pedagogical Sciences of incompetence and corruption, and suggested that teachers should expect no solutions from them, but look elsewhere for guidance:

> The trouble with educational scholarship is not that it is directed to the wrong ends, but that it is experiencing a drought. No matter which way you direct a half-dried river, no good will come of it. It will not become navigable or irrigate any fields.
>
> ... The existence of the Academy [of Pedagogical Sciences] introduces an element of immorality into all the pores of educational scholarship. The ambition to receive a cherished title prompts some people to act in a way incompatible with a scholarly conscience. Once having become a corresponding member or academician, such a person becomes rooted to the spot, and he is the one, frozen stiff and barren, who is named head of a research institution or proclaimed as the

highest scholarly authority. How can a living discipline develop under such a compacted layer of asphalt?

... Let us survey the combined result of academic activity during the past two decades: educational psychology is experiencing great difficulties, methodology is in a bad way, theory of character education is in such a catastrophic state, and has spawned so many victims, that it is high time we appointed a government commission to identify the guilty parties.[25]

The alternative was, to *Uchitel'skaia gazeta*, clear: the pedagogy of cooperation developed by the teacher-innovators.

Not surprisingly, many in the educational establishment took exception to the stance adopted by *Uchitel'skaia gazeta*. They voiced their views on the pages of *Narodnoe Obrazovanie* (the organ of the Ministry of Education) and *Sovetskaia pedagogika* (the organ of the Academy of Pedagogical Sciences). Some of those who published articles of protest in these journals addressed their criticisms not so much at the teacher-innovators, the value of whose work they recognised[26], as at the attempt by *Uchitel'skaia gazeta* to scuttle the whole of Soviet pedagogical science in favour of the "Pedagogy of Cooperation". Others showed hostility to one or more of the teacher-innovators, as well as to Soloveichik and the newspaper.

It was a debate which generated more heat than light, and it is difficult for an outsider to fully assess the merits of each side's arguments. The more extreme participants on each side seemed blind to the legitimate concerns of their antagonists, and adopted a tone of abusive self-righteousness. Interestingly, both sides frequently cited Sukhomlinsky in support of their position.

The fact that *Uchitel'skaia gazeta* received such strong support from its readership suggests that there was indeed a need to break free from the rigidity of thought imposed by bureaucratic control of the education process through the Ministry and the Academy of Pedagogical Sciences. Soloveichik justified the newspaper's stance thus:

Each one of us has probably seen a class where the children's faces bear a numbed expression, and benumbed staff rooms, where no-one dare say a bold word. This numbed state of mind is just what the opponents of *perestroika* long for. They create the pedagogy of stagnation, because they need stagnation in education and stagnation in society, because that is the only way they can remain on top. Any movement forwards holds hidden dangers for their career. Whatever shortcomings there are in the newspaper sheet entitled "The Pedagogy of Cooperation", it has already performed and will continue to perform its task. It helps people to cast off their numbness; it has shown that it is possible to think, to speak, to write and to publish, taking into consideration only the interests of our common cause, the communist education of children.[27]

It is questionable, though, whether it was necessary to resort to such sweeping condemnation of all academicians and public servants. In the article from which the above quotation was drawn, for instance, Soloveichik ridicules Yu. Babansky for making vague general statements on educational policy without naming the names of those with whom he agrees or disagrees. This is a little harsh, as Babansky had in fact been instrumental in getting many of the teacher-innovators' works published.[28]

Uchitel'skaia gazeta may also have erred in the degree of support they offered to M. Shchetinin, one of the "teacher-innovators" promoted on the pages of the newspaper. Some of the material published about him in *Narodnoe obrazovanie* appears quite damning, and suggests that, however good his intentions, his work was undisciplined and ineffectual.[29] He was given charge of a school in the area where Sukhomlinsky had worked (at Zybkovka), and received very considerable support from the Party, the Ministry and the Academy. In spite of this he appears to have alienated most of his staff, and to have brought the school to a ruinous state. It would seem that some of the criticisms voiced on the pages of *Narodnoe obrazovanie* were valid, and that the editors and journalists of *Uchitel'skaia gazeta* were tendentious in their approach and deaf to any criticism of their views.

To some extent the disharmony between the main educational journals and the newspaper may have been due to a clash of genres, as publicist and academic met head on. As a publicist, Soloveichik was used to highly emotive forms of expression, to hyperbole and the voicing of moral indignation. He saw himself as a mouthpiece for millions of long-suffering teachers and pupils. The very same forms of expression were

Sukhomlinsky's Successors 201

an affront to academic sensibilities, to a scholarly sense of balance and objectivity.

Yu. Azarov, who had played a key role in stimulating interest in Sukhomlinsky during the 'seventies, was one of those to come out in favour of the teacher-innovators. He took the view that Soviet pedagogical science, which in the 'twenties had been rich in experimentation and creativity, had been shackled by repressive measures in the 'thirties:

> In the 'thirties all experiments, such as that conducted by Shatsky, were banned, many organisers of such enterprises were compromised, and some paid for their educational ideas with their lives.
>
> This barred the way to creative enquiry, to the development of the optimum forms for the content and methods of instruction. But now the time has come to speak of far-reaching reform of education, of reinstating Leninist ideas in schooling, of fundamental restructuring of the education system.[30]

In his view, the Soviet school system under Stalin had been based on the Prussian model, which had inspired the Tsarist gymnasia. He suggests it would have been more fruitful to have followed the American model, as, he suggests, Krupskaia, Lunacharsky and others had wished to do:

> Krupskaia, following Ushinsky, stood up for the American model, that is to say, for one where independent activity was developed, where such methods as work activities, games, drama, art, psychoanalysis and [psychological] testing were widely used.[31]

Azarov sees the teacher-innovators as having thrown off the shackles of repressive control, and having returned to the creative experimentation of the 'twenties.

With the passage of time it became clear that public opinion and the support of the Party were, for the most part, on the side of the teacher-innovators. The Communist Party's Central Committee Plenum of February 1988, at which Gorbachev spoke out in favour of the teacher-innovators (see above), also heralded dramatic changes in the school system and an abandonment of a significant part of the 1984 reform guidelines. No less conservative a Party stalwart than Yegor Ligachev urged a more differentiated and individualised approach:

It is necessary to decisively intensify the education process, to integrate study courses, reducing the number of subjects, to differentiate instruction, to develop the students' urge to acquire knowledge beyond the compulsory programme. In a word, to direct our *main attention to the development of the individual abilities of the students*.[32]

The vocational orientation of the reform guidelines was rejected and it was decided to make a universal general education the basis for further vocational specialisation. Ligachev suggested that there was a need for more schools with a special profile in order to achieve higher academic standards amongst university applicants.

The Plenum was followed by two years of unprecedented reform activity which has been well documented by Sutherland.[33] *Uchitel'skaia gazeta* was encouraged by the tone of the Plenum to become even bolder in organising educators to develop new practical initiatives. A Creative Union of Teachers was formed under the auspices of the newspaper. There was a marked increase in the activity of the Eureka Clubs and the Commune Movement, also heavily promoted by the newspaper. The Eureka Clubs gave rise to the formation of experimental schools headed by reformers and called "author schools".

These grass roots movements were accompanied by new state initiatives. A State Committee for Public Education, headed by G.A. Yagodin, was created to coordinate and give direction to the various ministries responsible for education. One of its initiatives was to found, in June 1988, a new type of research base known as the "School" Interim Research Collective (VNIK — "Shkola"). This was headed by E.D. Dneprov, who was destined to play an important role in furthering the reform movement, ultimately becoming the first Minister for Education in Yeltsin's post-putsch government. In August 1988 a commission was set up to investigate the Academy of Pedagogical Sciences and to make recommendations for its reform. In December of the same year a Congress of Workers in Education took place:

> The chairman of the State Committee for Education, G.A. Yagodin, spoke for humanisation and democratisation. He said that he proposed to carry out serious revolutionary changes in both the structure and the content of secondary education. The present system aimed to create a 'normal' child, extinguishing inquisitiveness, liveliness and

unconventionality. This suppressed creativity, initiative and boldness of thought and deed.[34]

State policy was increasingly coming to resemble the ideas of the reform movement which had been led by the teacher-innovators and *Uchitel'skaia gazeta*. Such an impression was strengthened by the election of Amonashvili and I. Ivanov as full members of the Academy of Pedagogical Sciences in January 1989. Ivanov was the founder of the Commune movement which had been strongly promoted by Soloveichik and *Uchitel'skaia gazeta*.

In May 1989 the first national conference of the Creative Union of Teachers was held. It elected a Central Council of 27 members, among whom were Soloveichik, V. Matveev (editor of *Uchitel'skaia gazeta*), E. Dneprov and Deputy-President of the Academy of Pedagogical Sciences V.Davydov. Amonashvili was elected President. He held the view that the Union should have closer ties with the Academy, the Party and the State Committee on Education.

The State Committee, meanwhile, continued the reform process. In August 1989 it issued a decree establishing school councils, with the intention of making schools more independent and democratic. The councils were to be made up of staff, pupils, parents and community representatives, and were to be given authority over significant issues such as choice of subjects taught, timetabling and whether pupils started school at age six or seven. In September the State Committee approved a new model curriculum. This was to reduce standardisation and the need for rote learning, and to allow greater flexibility in the choice of subjects. There was a shift towards the humanities, from 41% to 50%.

In the light of the above developments it is not surprising to find that by November 1990 the leading article in *Sovetskaia pedagogika* contained a sympathetic summary of the contribution of the teacher-innovators to Soviet education. The article also noted the similarity between them and Sukhomlinsky:

> ... it is quite clear that there is an indissoluble link, a continuity, between the creativity and practical activity of the teacher-innovators and the theoretical contributions and legacy of Krupskaia, Makarenko, Sukhomlinsky and other Soviet educators.

... V.A. Sukhomlinsky saw in front of him a human being first and foremost, and only secondly a pupil. The teacher-innovators promote the same faith.

The teaching methods of Shatalov, for example, are based on an approach to character education: one should make judgements about a child not on the basis of his knowledge, but according to his attitude to work and to people, on the basis of his moral qualities ...

Influencing the individual child's personality via a working, creative collective, as a general educating principle, is an integral part of the creative quest of other teacher-innovators. I.P. Volkov, a work and drawing teacher from the outskirts of Moscow, building on the experience of the "universal free workshop" of the F.E. Dzerzhinsky Commune, promoted and gave practical expression to the extremely important idea of early detection and development of the talents and abilities of pupils. To achieve this, he considers, it is necessary to give all pupils from grade one up the opportunity to try their hand at a range of varied activities.

... Each of the authors in the "Educational quest" series is a person who thinks and lives with intense creativity, each has developed their own original methodology, permitting them to significantly enhance the effectiveness and quality of the education process.

Sh.A. Amonashvili scientifically developed and tested in practice curriculum content and principles for working with six year old children, with young pupils, conducive to the establishment of a strong motivation to study, and to the humanisation of the learning process ... Moscow school teacher ... S.N. Lysenkova developed an effective system for managing the learning of young pupils, giving each child the joy of success in study, arming children with learning skills and an ability to self-regulate the study process ...

The Leningrad language and literature teacher E.N. Ilyin found a way to accelerate the personal development of his pupils, turning language and literature classes into lessons in life and self-knowledge, lessons in moral perception and the study of human nature.[35]

The acceptance of the ideas of the teacher-innovators may also be seen as the triumph of that humanistic trend in education which Sukhomlinsky had promoted in the 'sixties.

The events of the 'nineties were even more dramatic than those of the 'eighties. The disintegration of the Soviet Union and of the myths upon which it was founded led to a situation of crisis at all levels: spiritual, moral, economic and political. The creative potential of the education reform movement seemed to have been thwarted by lack of unity and lack of funding, the preoccupation of the majority being with survival.

The educational periodicals of the Soviet period experienced difficulties in continuing publication, and it became difficult to know the fate of the teacher-innovators. The education system became more privatised, and communist ideals were seen to have been discredited. New educational institutions with a more commercial orientation sprang up.

In the assessment of Sukhomlinsky's daughter, her father was still highly regarded by many as a humanist and as the propagator of a non-authoritarian approach to education. He was seen as one who resisted the totalitarian orientation which dominated Soviet education for many years. Some, however, considered his loyalty to communism a weakness, and wished to make a complete break with the past.[36] As the situation stabilises educators will undoubtably reexamine Sukhomlinsky's work and reassess it in the light of new attitudes. A study of his work may help a new generation of Russian educators reconcile their past and their present.

Notes

1 Amonashvili, Sh., *Edinstvo tseli [Singleness of purpose]*, Moscow, Prosveshchenie, 1987, p. 13.
2 See also Amonashvili, Sh., *Kak zhivete deti? [How are you living, children?]*, Moscow, Prosveshchenie, 1986, pp. 73/74.
3 Amonashvili, Sh., *Edinstvo tseli [Singleness of purpose]*, Moscow, Prosveshchenie, 1987, pp. 165/166.
4 Amonashvili, Sh., *Kak zhivete deti? [How are you living, children?]*, Moscow, Prosveshchenie, 1986, pp. 155/156.
5 See, for instance, *Kak zhivete deti? [How are you living, children?]*, Moscow, Prosveshchenie, 1986, pp. 83/84.
6 *Edinstvo tseli*, Moscow, Prosveshchenie, 1987, p. 167.
7 *Kak zhivete deti?*, Moscow, Prosveshchenie, 1986, pp. 137/138.
8 Ibid., pp. 117/118.
9 Volkov, I.P., "Proektirovanie protsessov obucheniia [Planning the processes of instruction]", *Sovetskaia pedagogika [Soviet pedagogy]*, 1987, No. 12, p. 22.
10 See Volkov, I., "Vyiavlenie i razvitie sklonnostei i sposobnostei uchashchikhsia [uncovering and developing the interests and abilities of students]", *Narodnoe obrazovanie [National Education]*, 1987, No. 6, p. 57.

11 Ibid., p. 56.
12 Shatalov, V.F., *Tochka opory [Fulcrum]*, Moscow, Pedagogika, 1987, p. 45.
13 Ibid., p. 32.
14 Lysenkova, S.N., "Kogda legko uchit'sia [When it is easy to study]", in *Pedagogicheskii poisk [Pedagogical Quest]*, Moscow, Pedagogika, 1987, p. 72.
15 Ilyin, E.N., "Iskusstvo obshcheniia [The art of communication]", in *Pedagogicheskii poisk [Pedagogical Quest]*, Moscow, Pedagogika, 1987, p. 205.
16 Ibid., p. 206.
17 Ibid., pp. 209/210.
18 Suddaby, A., "An Evaluation of the Contribution of the Teacher-Innovators to Soviet Educational Reform", *Comparative Education*, Vol. 25, No. 2: 247.
19 Gorbachev, M.S., "Revoliutsionnoi perestroike — ideologiiu obnovleniia [For revolutionary restructuring — the ideology of renewal]", *Uchitel'skaia gazeta*, 1988, 20 February, p. 1.
20 See, for instance, Zajda, J., "Recent Educational Reforms in the USSR: their significance for policy development", *Comparative Education*, Vol. 20, No. 3, 1984, pp. 405–420, and Dunstan, J., "Equalisation and Differentiation in the Soviet School 1958–1985: A Curriculum Approach" in his, *Soviet Education under Scrutiny*, Glasgow: Jordanhill College Publications, 1987.
21 See Zajda, op. cit., Dunstan, J., "Soviet Education Beyond 1984: a commentary on the Reform Guidelines", *Compare*, Vol. 15, No. 2, 1985, pp. 161–187, and Szekely, B.B., "The New Soviet Educational Reform", *Comparative Education Review*, Vol. 30, No. 3, August, 1986, pp. 321–343
22 Zajda, J., "The Moral Curriculum in the Soviet School", *Comparative Education*, Vol. 24, No. 3, 1988, pp. 389–404.
23 Szekely, B.B., "Mobilization for Implementation of the New School Reforms", *Soviet Education*, Vol. XXVIII, No. 1, pp. 3–7.
24 For a description of typical Soviet teacher-pupil interaction, see Muckle, J., "Classroom Interactions in some Soviet and English Schools", *Comparative Education*, Vol. 20, No. 2, 1984, pp. 237–251.
25 Soloveichik, S., "Uroki peremeny [Lessons of change]", *Uchitel'skaia gazeta [The Teacher's Newspaper]*, 1987, 13 October, p. 3.
26 Amonashvili's and Volkov's work, for instance, was recognised by the Academy of Pedagogical Sciences and the Ministry of Education. In the same issue of *Narodnoe obrazovanie* in which a scathingly critical article on Shchetinin was published, one of Volkov's articles appeared with official endorsement. Other articles by Volkov were published in *Sovetskaia pedagogika* in 1987 and 1988. These publications are evidence that the educational establishment was not totally hostile to the teacher-innovators.
27 Soloveichik, S., "Pedagogika zastoia [The pedagogy of stagnation]", *Uchitel'skaia gazeta [The Teacher's Newspaper]*, 1987, 19 May, p. 2.
28 See Khelemendik, V.S., "Splav traditsii i novatorstva [A blend of tradition and innovation]", *Sovetskaia pedagogika [Soviet pedagogy]*, 1990, No. 11, p. 7.
29 See Tselishcheva, N., "Granitsy novatorstva i bezgranichnost' prozhekterstva [The limits of innovation and the limitlessness of day-dreaming]", *Narodnoe obrazovanie [National education]*, 1987, No. 6, pp. 37–46.

30 Azarov, Yu., "Uchit'sia, chtoby uchit' [Let us study in order to teach]", Novyi mir [New world], 1987, No. 4, p. 239.
31 Ibid., p. 238.
32 Ligachev, Ye.K., "O khode perestroiki srednei i vysshei shkoly i zadachakh partii po ee osushchestvleniiu [On the progress of restructuring secondary and tertiary schooling and the Party's role in its completion]", Uchitel'skaia gazeta, 1988, 18 February, p. 2. (Emphasis appears in text.)
33 Sutherland, J., "Perestroika in the Soviet General School: From Innovation to Independence?", in Dunstan, J., ed., Soviet Education under Perestroika, London: Routledge, 1992, pp. 14–29.
34 Ibid., p. 14.
35 Khelemendik, V.S., "Splav traditsii i novatorstva [A blend of tradition and innovation]", Sovetskaia pedagogika [Soviet pedagogy], 1990, No. 11, pp. 7–9.
36 From personal correspondence.

CHAPTER 9

Sukhomlinsky's Relevance to the West

> I am firmly convinced that the human personality is inexhaustible; each may become a creator, leaving behind a trace upon the earth. This is really what we are building communism for. There should not be any nobodies — specks of dust cast upon the wind. Each one must shine, just as billions upon billions of galaxies shine in the heavens.[1]

IT MIGHT be alleged that Sukhomlinsky's circumstances and personality were so unique that his work can have little relevance to educators in English-speaking countries. He was working in a rural community where he enjoyed enormous personal authority. This enabled him, among other things, to make recommendations to parents about children's daily routines and habits which would be regarded as unduly intrusive by most parents in Western countries. He was working within an ideological framework alien to the West. Even in the Soviet Union, his experiment was unique, a testimony to his dedication and strength of will, but unlikely to be duplicated by others lacking his exceptional qualities.

Such comments have a certain validity, but do not necessarily mean that Sukhomlinsky's work has no relevance to Western educators. It is true that one could never hope to duplicate his approach in its outward forms, and that one might reject certain national and ideological aspects of his educational philosophy. In spite of all this, however, his work is likely to attract attention as a significant attempt to realise ideals shared by many educators: the ideals of holism, humaneness and social responsibility.

When we examine Sukhomlinsky's educational ideas we should not ask whether we could adopt his system in its entirety. We should rather ask whether his holistic conception of education might stimulate teachers and parents to develop parallel approaches.

Sukhomlinsky thought a new era was dawning, that we were on the threshold of the "age of humanity":

> "The age of mathematics", one hears all the time, "the age of electronics", "the space age". These are all catchy phrases, but they do not reflect the real essence of what is happening in our times. The world is entering the age of humanity — that is what is important …
>
> More than ever before, we are obliged to consider what we are contributing to the human soul. I am very concerned that for the majority of students the end of secondary school marks the end of their education in the humanities. I mean the broad humanitarian education of young people — emotional and aesthetic education, the education of sensitivity and refinement, of an impressionable nature, of a responsive and sensitive heart.[2]

This concern with the humanising role of education may strike a chord with many Western educators. James Bowen, in the concluding section of his historical study of Western education, wrote:

> It does not seem feasible for us ever to develop a radical alternative to the process of education per se; certainly we shall continue to evolve strategies of teaching and learning, especially as electronic developments occur; certainly the curriculum will continue to respond to changes in needs and in knowledge; certainly we shall continue to improve all aspects of administration, student evaluation and support systems. Yet, for all these improvements, the process of education must retain its central purpose since society began, namely the humanizing of each new generation … Education retains, as its central purpose, the utopian aspiration of producing genuinely human persons … [3]

In the same work Bowen suggested that the approach of natural holistic education, which found expression in the work of Pestalozzi and Froebel, was subverted sometime in the middle of the nineteenth century. In his view subsequent social and educational development was "dominated by positivism and the exploitative approach".[4] In the current social climate we might say that the ideal of humanism in education explored in this study is under siege from the spirit of "economic rationalism", commercialism and crass materialism — even within the education system itself. Educational decisions are made largely on the basis of economic, rather than ethical criteria, investments in education being justified on the basis of the needs of the economy. Whatever the "ideal culture" of our society, its "real culture", its ethos, is dominated by the spirit of capitalism and consumerism. In such a climate the humanities are under threat, unable to justify their existence in economic terms.

Allan Bloom, in his searing analysis of the state of American education in 1987, drew attention to the danger of our losing touch with our cultural heritage, to a widespread debasement of popular culture. He suggested that the coherence of the Western liberal tradition was being lost, and that educators had developed such an abhorrence of moral prescriptiveness as to have lost touch with the ethical core of that tradition. He bemoaned the parlous state of the humanities:

> The humanities are like the great old Paris Flea Market where, amidst masses of junk, people with a good eye found castaway treasures that made them rich. Or they are like a refugee camp where all the geniuses driven out of their jobs and countries by unfriendly regimes are idling, either unemployed or performing menial tasks.[5]

A study of Sukhomlinsky's work may lead us back to the spirit of holism which informed Pestalozzi's endeavours, and illumine what Bowen has defined as the central purpose of education, "the humanizing of each new generation".

The theme of Gartmann's doctoral study of Sukhomlinsky is that of "human production" versus the "production of goods". In all industrial societies, capitalist and Soviet, human beings have found themselves subordinated to the tasks of material development. Sukhomlinsky envisaged a society in which the ultimate value would be enshrined in human beings, and all resources would be at the service of human development. Each individual in society would then shine like the multitudes of stars in the heavens. It is in this light that we should consider his statement that "pedagogy should be studied by everybody". Society as a whole was to have an educational orientation.

What goals did Sukhomlinsky have in common with Western educators? On the basis of the material examined in previous chapters we could suggest several goals which most humanistic educators might share with Sukhomlinsky. At a personal level all might wish that their pupils would acquire health and vitality, self-discipline and strength of character, empathy for their fellows, reverence for life, and a thirst for knowledge. They would wish them to acquire a social conscience and a concern that natural resources be preserved for future generations. They would hope that each pupil would find, during the course of their education, a natural vocation providing an avenue for service to the community and for self-fulfilment. On all of these issues they could find material of interest in Sukhomlinsky's educational legacy.

Let us focus on a few of the issues raised by a study of Sukhomlinsky's holistic approach to education. His interest in pupils' health as the foundation for all personal growth, and the thoroughness with which he pursued health goals, are worth considering. There are a number of features in his approach to health education which might be relevant to educators and parents in English-speaking countries. There is the provision of medical examinations for preschool children, together with advice to parents on diet, exercise and daily routines. There is the attention given to creating a healthy environment (including outdoor study areas at school and at home) and to providing many opportunities for outdoor activities. There is the attention to posture and to the provision of desks and seating on an individual basis. There is the way in which the curriculum was timetabled to ensure that the most intellectually demanding subjects were programed early in the day when pupils were fresh, and the practice of encouraging pupils to do homework in the morning rather than the evening. There is the question of the quantity and type of vegetation in the school environment. We may have some difficulty with the notion of "phytoncides", but with an extremely high proportion of children suffering from asthma and various allergies, we might do well to pay more attention to the role of plants in the environment where children are working and playing. There is the very conception of health not merely as an absence of disease, but as a feeling of inexhaustible energy capable of sustaining an optimistic and creative approach to life.

Another feature of Sukhomlinsky's holistic approach is the priority given to the moral and aesthetic context within which intellectual development and vocational training take place. Sukhomlinsky projects an ideal of human development which excludes no one, as all have the potential for moral growth, for developing empathy and rendering service to others. All are involved in creating an optimal educational environment. The spirit of collective endeavour fostered by Sukhomlinsky is in stark contrast to the competitiveness of our current system with its inevitable casualties. This is not to suggest that the Soviet system was not competitive. Sukhomlinsky, though, was moved by a deep concern that there be no casualties in the process of schooling, and he viewed education, like medicine, as a most humane calling.

Another key feature of Sukhomlinsky's educational approach is the provision of a great variety of extra-curricular activities. The experience of many excellent schools in English-speaking countries supports the notion that extra-curricular activities offered through school clubs and societies can form an integral and extremely valuable part of school life. Drama circles, school newspapers, technical clubs and the like can offer many opportunities for pupils to uncover their unique talents. The experience of Sukhomlinsky and of Volkov (with his "record of creative work") may prompt us to question whether it is possible for any school to provide pupils with adequate vocational orientation without such a program. One cannot legislate to create enthusiasm, but it would be possible to encourage such programs by funding equipment and facilities and possibly extra staff. In the current climate such funding might need to be undertaken by parent bodies.

Any educational ideal is based on ideals of individual and social development, education having both a humanising and a socialising function. The ideals of individual and social development implicit in an educational philosophy must complement each other, must be in harmony, if the individual's growth is to be integrated and harmonious. Bowen has suggested that "education, and the school, are part of a much wider social and political process"[6], and Price considers that schooling is the smaller part of education, the family, the media and the general cultural milieu making up the greater part.[7] Sukhomlinsky's notions of unconscious educational influences and of dissonance are relevant in this context.

The ideal of social development implicit in Sukhomlinsky's work has its origins in Plato's Republic and Thomas More's *Utopia*, and is one in which individualism, so dear to people in English-speaking countries, is severely curtailed. As suggested in Chapter 6, each society needs to find its own balance in attempting to satisfy both individual and collective needs and desires. A study of Sukhomlinsky's work may assist in working towards such a balance, by offering a different perspective.

Soviet, post-Soviet and capitalist societies all seem to offer a dissonant setting for the implementation of Sukhomlinsky's educational ideals. Urban industrial societies are generally far more impersonal than the rural town in which Sukhomlinsky worked. There is a widespread loss of the sense of community and of oneness with Nature. Sukhomlinsky's work will appeal to those who feel this loss.

The moral core of Sukhomlinsky's holistic approach is the practice of humaneness. This ideal is very close to the Christian ideal of love or charity found in the gospels and in St Paul's epistle to the Romans. Unless we are to ignore this key element of our own "ideal culture", we should be interested in any practical methods for training our young people to practise a humane approach.

Dmitry Kabalevsky wrote that he knew of no educator who had combined moral and aesthetic education so forcefully and comprehensively as Sukhomlinsky. An attempt was made in Chapter 5 to elucidate this aspect of Sukhomlinsky's work. In this sphere the teacher needs to become an artist, and one is reminded of Amonashvili's statement that teaching is an art based on science. Two thousand years of Christian civilisation have yet to produce a truly charitable society, though the welfare state might be seen as a giant step forward. Perhaps what has been lacking is a humane educational methodology based on adequate psychological insight.

Pestalozzi, following Rousseau, made steps in the direction of developing such a methodology. Sukhomlinsky's work may be seen as a continuation of that tradition. In studying the methods developed by Pestalozzi and Sukhomlinsky, we should pay attention to the priority they gave to developing the imaginative and creative faculties, to freeing children from the fear of failure, and to seeking out each child's unique potentialities. It was within such a holistic framework that intellectual development occurred.

Above all, we should note the crucial importance of the teacher's own love for children. Sukhomlinsky and Amonashvili, following Tolstoy, suggested that the teacher's love is of prime importance in educating the child. This seems to imply that methods of teacher selection, training and induction which rely almost exclusively on intellectual criteria need to be questioned. At present, success in studies is generally the only condition for admission to teacher-training courses, and once a student has graduated, he or she is in most cases appointed to a school through bureaucratic procedures.

Teaching is so much a question of human relations that a person's ability to empathise and to relate to others should be taken into account in the processes of teacher training and induction. At the very least, there should be some process of counselling and preliminary work experience prior to undertaking training. In the light of Sukhomlinsky's work with young teachers, something resembling an apprenticeship might form a part of teacher-training. During training greater attention should be given to communicative skills. Sukhomlinsky talks of the importance of the teacher's word in character development, and Amonashvili suggests that all teachers should have undertaken some sort of training of the voice.

One concern voiced by educators in Australia is that the best teachers are often promoted out of the classroom into administration, where their talents may be wasted. Sukhomlinsky's experience prompts us to reflect on the role of the school principal. Perhaps by providing trained administrative assistance to principals, they could be allowed to continue working as educators, and train their staff in the art of good teaching.

Sukhomlinsky's experience seems to suggest that a good school is the product of a gradual process of development, during which the principal develops an *esprit de corps* among the staff and fosters a dedicated approach to teaching. Such a process might be facilitated if principals were given the power to appoint staff, and if staff played a role in the appointment of principals, as was the case at Pavlysh. Parents may also be involved in this process, possibly through a school council. Such a policy might initially be given a trial at selected schools where the principal and staff were receptive to such an idea.

Another aspect of Sukhomlinsky's work which might be of interest to Western educators is the manner in which he fostered relations between home and school. While most parents in English-speaking countries would not welcome the degree of direction which emanated from the school at Pavlysh, there is room for the provision of some sort of support for parents in the task of educating their children. The breakdown of the extended family, together with the increasing mobility of families, has meant that many parents raise their children in relative isolation, and have little contact with others who have already gone through the experience.

Support for parents need not take an authoritarian form. At the School of Total Education in Warwick, Australia, for instance, parents attend weekly discussions at the school in groups chaired by teachers. They may raise any issues concerning their children's lives at home or at school, such issues being addressed through a collective pooling of experience. Occasionally guest speakers are invited to talk on relevant matters. Parents, teachers and children all benefit from the regular contacts afforded by these meetings, which serve a similar function to the twice-monthly meetings at Pavlysh.[8] The school in Warwick offers an example of a carefully developed model of holistic education adapted to the conditions of Western society. It is interesting to note, though, that, like Sukhomlinsky's school, it could hardly exist without the support of a closely-knit community.

An interesting issue raised by Sukhomlinsky's work and that of the teacher-innovators is the importance of educational research conducted by practising teachers. Russia is not the only country where teachers have had difficulty in applying theoretical educational research. While it is counterproductive to negate the value of theoretical research, there is also a need for what Evelina Orteza y Miranda has called "practical applied research", in which teachers play a crucial role. Such research is necessary, she suggests, because the life of a classroom or school, linked to that of society, is too complex to be encompassed by any single academic discipline or paradigm.[9]

Echoing sentiments expressed in the Soviet Union during the debate about the work of the teacher-innovators, she writes that "practical applied research" can only be promoted if teachers are respected as active agents in the education process, capable of critical inquiry and of making decisions on matters of policy and practice:

> ... The kind of relationship required among research centers, colleges of education and schools, promoted by practical applied research, is that of membership in a community of inquirers, working together on mutual concerns. It places practising school teachers, not in a subordinate position to colleges of education or other agencies, but in an active and cooperative role in determining and developing educational aims, objectives and school policies, and in inquiring into matters of curricular interest.[10]

Sukhomlinsky's work is an outstanding example of a teacher working in such a responsible and creative way. The question teachers need to ask is whether education is to be merely the handmaiden of industry, subservient to the needs of the market, or whether it is to be a force for renaissance and reform. Are we to preserve the humanistic ideals of the Western tradition, or are we, like the sorcerer's apprentice, to stand helplessly by as the magic woven by our technological prowess gets out of hand?

Sukhomlinsky's educational system, nourished by folk culture, calls on us to revive the traditional wisdom of reverence for the land and for life, to nurture the creative, life-sustaining powers of each individual, and to build a society that is truly humane. It was not his fault that the Soviet Union was not such a society. The significance of his work lies in its deep moral impulse, in its utopian vision, and in the practical methods that were developed in attempting to realise universal humanistic ideals.

In the conclusion of his history of Western education, James Bowen writes:

> The task ahead is surely to transcend the persisting, destructive doctrines of nineteenth century industrial capitalism, with its theory of mind over nature, of the external world as the object of man's exploitation ...
>
> ... The way ahead is surely to fulfil Robert Owen's vision of the "new moral world", reconstructed now on the basis of the recognition of the totality of mankind as a part of nature, and therefore to develop

a new unitary theory of knowledge and morals in the interest of producing a genuinely humane world. This, surely, is the highest purpose we can assign to education.[11]

It is hoped that this study has shown how an examination of Sukhomlinsky's work might contribute to the realisation of such a purpose.

Interest in Sukhomlinsky's work is growing in countries outside the former Soviet bloc. An international society devoted to the evaluation and propagation of his ideas was formed in 1990.[12] Its annual conferences have attracted scholars from Germany, Greece, China and Japan, as well as from former Eastern bloc countries. The headquarters of the society were established in Marburg, Germany, where a school bears Sukhomlinsky's name and an attempt has been made to implement his educational philosophy. An experimental kindergarten in Greece is also implementing his ideas. A conference of the International Sukhomlinsky Association, held in Kiev and Pavlysh in October of 1993, was devoted to the theme: "European Education and Vasily Sukhomlinsky as a Contemporary Humanist Educator". In the USA, an educational institute in Oregon — Medford Education International — is examining Sukhomlinsky's ideas and using them as a basis for an educational model to be promoted in schools.

Only time will tell what Sukhomlinsky's relevance to English-speaking educators will be. If teachers are to evaluate his ideas, adequate translations of his major works will need to be undertaken. There are several possibilities for further research into the Sukhomlinsky phenomenon. A more detailed study of Sukhomlinsky's work as a school principal could be made on the basis of archival material held at the school in Pavlysh and elsewhere. His methodology of conducting "lessons in thinking" in natural settings would seem to be worthy of more detailed study. This could possibly be done by looking at the experience of other schools in the Kirovograd region where such a methodology has been widely used. A carefully researched biography would be an interesting undertaking, and the appearance of hitherto unpublished works, such as his book on helping children with learning difficulties, may in the future provide material for further research.

No matter what books are written on education, each teacher has to discover through experience the art of teaching. The value of Sukhomlinsky's books, and of those by other dedicated practising teachers,

Sukhomlinsky's Relevance to the West

is that they provide a window into this creative process. They help to break down the isolation within which many teachers work, and provide support in what Sukhomlinsky held to be the most demanding of all professions.

Notes

1. Sukhomlinsky, V.S., *Pis'ma k synu [Letters to my son]*, Moscow: Prosveshchenie, 1987, p. 53.
2. Ibid., p.37.
3. Bowan, J., *A History of Western Education*, Vol. 3, London, Menthuen, 1983, p. 554.
4. Ibid., p. 556.
5. Bloom, A., *The Closing of the American Mind*, New York: Simon and Schuster, 1987, p. 371.
6. Bowan, J., *A History of Western Education*, Vol. 3, London, Menthuen, 1983, p. 553.
7. Price, R.F., *Marx and Education in Late Capitalism*, Croon Helm, London, 1986.
8. On the School of Total Education see Yogendra, V., *Total Education: The Urgent Need*, Centre Publications, Warwick, 1983.
9. Orteza y Miranda, E., "Broadening the Focus of Research in Education", *Journal of Research and Development in Education*, Vol. 22, No. 1, Fall 1988, p. 34.
10. Ibid., p. 37.
11. Bowan, J., *A History of Western Education*, Vol. 3, London, Menthuen, 1983, p. 557/558.
12. See Sukhomlinskaia, O., "V.A. Sukhomlinsky v Oberkhauzene [V.A. Sukhomlinsky in Oberhausen]", *Sovetskaia Pedagogika*, 1991, No. 4: 156–158 and Sukhomlinskaia, O., "Mezhdunarodnoe obshchestvo posledovatelei Sukhomlinskogo [The International Sukhomlinsky Society]", Pedagogika(Moscow), 1993 1977.

SELECTED BIBLIOGRAPHY

A. Works by Sukhomlinsky

1. English language publications

Sukhomlinskii, V. "Conversation with a Young School Principal", *Soviet Education*, Vol. 8, No. 4: 3-17; No. 7: 3-18; No. 9: 3-13; No. 11: 30-43. Vol 9, No. 3: 30-46; No. 4: 31-42; No. 5: 34-41; No. 7: 34-47.

Sukhomlinsky, V.A. *On Education*, Moscow: Progress Publishers, 1977.

———. *To Children I Give My Heart*, Moscow: Progress Publishers, 1981.

———. *The Singing Feather*, Moscow: 1984.

2. Key Russian Language Sources

Sukhomlinsky, V.A. *Izbrannye proizvedeniia v piati tomakh [Selected works in five volumes]*, Kiev, Radianska shkola, 1979-80.

Vol. 1: Problemy vospitaniia vsestoronne razvitoi lichnosti [Issues in the all-round education of the personality]
Dukhovnyi mir shkol'nika [The spiritual world of a school pupil]
Metodika vospitaniia kollektiva [Methodology for educating a collective]

Vol. 2: Formirovanie kommunisticheskikh ubezhdenii molodogo pokoleniia [The formation of communist convictions in the younger generation]
Kak vospitat' nastoiashchego cheloveka [How to educate a true human being]
Sto sovetov uchiteliu [100 pieces of advice for school teachers]

Vol. 3: Serdtse otdaiu detiam [My Heart I Give to Children]
Rozhdenie grazhdanina [The birth of a citizen]
Pis'ma k synu [Letters to my son]

Vol. 4: Pavlyshskaia sredniaia shkola [Pavlysh school]
Razgovor s molodym direktorom shkoly
[Conversation with a young school principal]

Vol. 5: Stat'i [Articles]

Sukhomlinsky, V.A. *Izbrannye pedagogicheskie sochineniia v trekh tomakh [Selected pedagogical works in three volumes]*, Moscow, Pedagogika, 1979-81.

Vol. 1: Serdtse otdaiu detiam [My Heart I Give to Children]
Rozhdenie grazhdanina [The birth of a citizen]

Vol. 2: Pavlyshskaia sredniaia shkola [Pavlysh school]

Vol. 3: Razgovor s molodym direktorom shkoly
[Conversation with a young school principal]
Mudraia vlast' kollektiva [The wise power of the collective]
Roditel'skaia pedagogika [Parental pedagogy]

———. "Etiudy o kommunisticheskom vospitanii [Essays on communist education]", *Narodnoe obrazovanie*, 1967, No. 2: 38-46; No. 4:44-50; No. 6: 37-43; No. 8: 51-56; No. 9: 28-33; No. 10: 54-59; No. 12: 40-43.

———. *Kniga o liubvi [A book on love]*, Moscow, Molodaia gvardiia, 1983.

———. *Pis'ma k synu [Letters to my son]*, Moscow, Prosveshchenie, 1987.

———. *O vospitanii [On education]*, 6th edition, Moscow, Politizdat, 1988.
Compiled and with introductory essays by S. Soloveichik.

———. *Mudrost' roditel'skoi liubvi [The wisdom of parental love]*, Moscow, Molodaia gvardiia, 1988.

———. "Iz tvorcheskogo naslediia V.A. Sukhomlinskogo [From the creative legacy of V.A. Sukhomlinsky]", *Sovetskaia pedagogika*, 1988, No. 3, pp. 97-102.
Text of Sukhomlinsky's letter to Khrushchev, 13 July, 1958.

———. "Uchitel' — sovest' naroda [A teacher is the nation's conscience]", *Narodnoe obrazovanie*, 1988, No. 9, pp. 73-79.
Sukhomlinsky's correspondence with A.E. Boim, deputy editor of *Narodnoe obrazovanie*. Gives insights into the controversy surrounding the publication of "Etiudy o kommunisticheskom vospitanii".

———. "Idti vpered! [Let us go forwards!]", *Narodnoe obrazovanie*, 1989, No. 8, pp. 70–78.
Sukhomlinsky's criticism of slavish adherence to Makarenko's theories of education through the collective.

———. *Kak vospitat' nastoiashchego cheloveka [How to educate a true human being]*, Moscow, Pedagogika, 1989.
This edition, prepared by Sukhomlinsky's daughter, is closer to the author's original conception than that which appears in the five volume collection.

———. *Khrestomatie po etike [An anthology on ethics]*, Moscow, Pedagogika, 1990.
This anthology, prepared for publication by Sukhomlinsky's daughter, is intended to accompany the 1989 edition of *Kak vospitat' nastoiashchego cheloveka*.

B. Bibliography and Biography

Sukhomlinskaia, A.I. Sukhomlinskaia, O.V., "*Biobibliografiia [Biobibliography]*", Kiev, Radianska shkola, 1987.
By far the most comprehensive bibliography of works by and about Sukhomlinsky. 254 pages. Over 2000 entries.

Tartakovsky, B.S. *Povest' ob uchitele Sukhomlinskom*, Moscow, Molodaia gvardiia, 1972.
The most comprehensive and authoritative biography of Sukhomlinsky.

C. Other Works in English

Amonashvili, Sh.A. "Hello, Children! A Teacher's Guide. Excerpts.", *Soviet Education*, April & May, 1988, Vol. 30, Nos. 4 & 5.

Andreeva, E.K. "From Ecological Upbringing to Understanding the Noosphere", *Soviet Education*, January, 1991, Vol. 33, No. 1: 23–36.

Ilyin, E.N. et al. "And Suddenly a Lesson is Born", *Soviet Education*, February, 1988, Vol. 30, No. 2: 9–26.

Lysenkova et al. "The Pedagogy of Cooperation", *Soviet Education*, February, 1988, Vol. 30, No. 2: 82–98.

Shatalov, V.F. "Give Me a School!", *Soviet Education*, February, 1988, Vol. 30, No. 2: 54–67.

Soloveichik, S. "Letter to a Teacher about a Teacher", *Soviet Education*, February, 1988, Vol. 30, No. 2: 27–53.

———. "A Man with Ideas", *Soviet Education*, February, 1988, Vol. 30, No. 2: 68–81.

———. "The Amonashvili Principle", *Soviet Education*, March, 1988, Vol. 30, No. 3: 46–53.

———. "The School of Trust", *Soviet Education*, March, 1988, Vol. 30, No. 3: 71–76.

Suddaby, A. "An Evaluation of the Contribution of the Teacher-Innovators to Soviet Educational Reform", *Comparative Education*, Vol. 25, No. 2, 1989, pp. 245–256.

INDEX

A

Academy of Pedagogical Sciences, 20, 67, 81, 87, 88, 155, 156, 160/161, 162, 174/175, 181, 190, 195, 198, 200, 202, 203.
Aesop, 113.
aesthetic education, 27, 95–98.
Afghanistan War, 197/198.
Akishina, 83.
Aleksandria, 169.
'all-round development', 25, 54, 71.
Amonashvili, Sh.A., 156, 181–187, 203, 204, 214, 215.
Andersen, Hans, 113.
Andreeva, E., 150.
Andropov, Yu.V., 196.
Anna Karenina, 114.
Arseniev, A.M., 160.
Ashton-Warner, Sylvia, 80.
atheism, 66–68.
Azarov, Yu. 173, 201.

B

Babansky, Yu., 200.
Bach, 112.
Bakhtin, 173.
Beethoven, 112.
Billington, J.H., 138.
Birth of a Citizen, The, 22, 41, 104, 105, 111, 171.

'blank shots', 31.
Blok, Alexander, 4.
Blonsky, 174.
Bloom, Allan, 211.
Boguslavsky, M.V., 81.
Boim, A.E. (Sukhomlinsky's letters to), 22, 164, 167–172.
Boldyrev, N.I., 161.
Bolshevism, 139.
Bondar, F., 173.
Book about Love, A, 22.
Borishpolets, G.M., 160.
Borisovsky, A.M., 23.
Bowen, James, 210, 211, 213, 217.
brain, the, 60, 81–84.
Brezhnev, L.I., 141, 144.
Bulgaria, 20.
Bushlia, A.K., 160, 161.

C

Chavdarov, S.Kh., 160.
Chernenko, K.U., 196.
Christianity, 2, 3, 4–5, 147, 156, 161, 162, 214.
civic responsibility, 5, 137–153.
collective education, 92–94, 120–125, 162–166.
collective research, 16, 37/38.
collectivisation, 8, 140.
Comenius, 2, 3, 76, 126.
Commune Movement, 202.

communism, 3, 29/30, 54, 137–141.
Communist Party, 12, 15, 29, 66, 139, 140, 141, 145, 156, 161, 170, 200.
Cuba, 20.
Czechoslovakia, 143.

D

Davydov, V., 203.
De Jure Pacis et Belli, 3.
Dead Souls, 193.
Dewey, 84.
Diesterweg, 126.
diet, 53.
'dissonance', 41/42.
Dneprov, E.D., 202.
Donetsk, 1, 190.
Dostoevsky, F.M., 104, 173.
Dunstan, John, 66, 68.
Dzeverin, A.G., 160.

E

East Germany, 20.
'economic rationalism', 4, 211.
'educability', 56/57.
education:
    aesthetic, 27, 95–98.
    collective, 92–94, 120–125, 162–166.
    emotional, 33/34, 103–132, 185/186.
    environmental, 150–152.
    health, 35, 38, 49–54.
    intellectual, 27, 51, 71–85.
    moral, 9/10, 27, 30/31, 34, 49, 54–68, 103–132, 165, 185/186.
    music, 96/97, 109–114.
    physical, 27, 49–54.
    work, 27, 52, 85–94, 187–190.
emotional education, 33/34, 103–132, 185/186.

'emotional memory', 112/113, 128.
environment at school, 41–44, 150–152.
environmental education, 150–152.
Erasmus, 2.
"Essays on Communist Education", 21, 93, 164–168, 173.
'Eureka Clubs', 202.
extra-curricular activities, 33, 40, 45/46, 88, 91–94, 187–190, 213.

F

Formation of Communist Convictions in the Younger Generation, The, 20.
Forwards! (Idti vpered!), 121–125, 162–164.
Franko, Ivan, 80.
Froebel, 210.
Fromm, Erich, 149.

G

Gartmann, Erika, 173, 211.
Gogol, 193.
Goncharov, N.K., 160, 161.
Gorbachev, M.S., 74, 138, 156, 195, 196, 197.
Gordin, L., 173.
Gorky, Maksim, 152.
'green classrooms', 53.
Grieg, 110, 112.
Grotius, 3.
Gurevich, S.A., 160.

H

'harmony of educational influences', 28, 42, 114.
health, 35, 38, 49–54, 118/119, 212.
Hello Children!, 182.

holism, 5, 25–29, 98/99, 209/210.
homework, 51, 191.
How are You Living, Children?, 182, 185.
How to Educate a True Human Being, 22, 56, 117, 142, 143, 147.
humaneness, 5, 103–132, 181–187.
humanism, 2–6, 147, 149, 156, 162, 212.
humanitas, 5.
Hundred Pieces of Advice for School Teachers, A, 22, 157, 168, 170.
Hungary, 20, 143.

I

ideology, 2, 73–76, 137–153.
Ilyin, E.N., 181, 193–194, 204.
immortality, 67/68.
intellect, education of, 27, 51, 71–85.
Issues in the All-round Development of the Personality, 22, 29.
Ivan IV, 138, 139, 140.
Ivanov, I., 203.

J

'journeys into nature', 9, 76–79, 81–83, 85.

K

Kabalevsky, D.B., 97, 173, 177, 214.
Kairov, I.A., 161.
Karakovsky, V.A., 157, 181.
Keller, Helen, 80.
Khrushchev, N.S., 32, 60, 74, 141, 144, 155, 156, 157–160, 196.
Kierkegaard, 173.
Kiev, 218.
Kilpatrick, 84.
King, Martin Luther, 138.

Kirovograd, 169, 177, 218.
Kitaigorodskaia, 83.
Kommunist, 173.
Komsomol'skaia pravda, 155, 170, 176.
Korczak, Janusz, 106, 126.
Korolev, F.F., 162–164.
Korotov, V., 173.
Kosheleva, I., 173.
Kovalevsky, V., 173.
Kozol, J., 32.
Kramskoy, 114.
Kremenchug, 8, 10.
Krupskaia, N., 86, 126, 174, 201, 203.
Kuznetsov, F., 169.

L

learning difficulties, 20, 83/84.
Lenin, P.I., 66, 86, 139, 146.
Leningrad, 193.
Leonardo da Vinci, 114.
Leontiev, A.N., 131.
Lermontov, 80.
Letters to My Son, 19, 22, 30, 67, 144.
Levitan, 114.
Levshin, A., (Shnaider, L.A.), 169.
Ligachev, Yegor, 201/202.
Likhachev, B., 20/21, 167, 169, 170/171, 173, 174, 194.
Literatura v shkole, 169.
Literaturnaia gazeta, 164, 168, 169.
Little Prince, The, 186.
love, 126–129, 184.
Lunacharsky, 174, 201.
Lysenkova, S., 181, 192, 204.

M

Makarenko, 1, 10, 21, 55, 92/93, 121–124, 126, 162–166, 169, 173, 174, 203.

Malinin, V.I., 162, 163, 164.
Manukian, M., 157.
Marburg, 218.
Marx, 72/73, 86, 89, 139.
Marxism, 75, 86, 137–141, 149.
Matveev, V., 203.
Medford Education International, 218.
Meshcheriaky, 174.
Methodology for Educating the Collective, 22.
Monoszon, E.I., 160.
moral education, 9/10, 27, 30/31, 34, 49, 54–68, 103–132, 165, 185/186.
More, Sir Thomas, 2, 152, 214.
Morgan, Lyndall, 74/75.
Murray, Gilbert, 2/3.
music education, 96/97, 109–114.
My Heart I Give to Children, 13, 22, 26, 28, 57, 76, 81, 105, 106, 108, 171, 174, 176, 182.

N

Narodnoe obrazovanie, 21, 22, 164, 168, 169, 170, 194, 199, 200.
Nekrasov, 80.
Nemensky, B., 173.
New Economic Policy, 139.
Nicholas I, 138.
Nikitin, B.P., 52.
Novyi mir, 173.

O

O'Dell, 91.
Onufrievka, 9, 10, 11, 14.
Orteza y Miranda, Evelina, 216/217.
Owen, Robert, 86, 217.

P

Parental Pedagogy, 18, 64.

parenting, 18/19, 32, 40, 64–66.
Pavlov, 60.
Pavlysh, 6, 9, 10, 14, 15–23.
Pavlysh School, 22, 26, 29, 35, 36, 38, 55, 92, 129, 131, 171.
Pavsysh school:
  environment, 41–44.
  facilities, 45–46.
  philosophy, 29–36.
  staff, 36–41, 129–132.
'percentomania', 35, 198.
Peredelkina, 181, 194.
perestroika, 155, 187, 195–204.
Pestalozzi, 2, 126, 210, 211, 214.
Peter I, 138, 139, 140.
Petrarch, 2.
physical education, 26/27, 49–54.
'phytoncides', 43, 212.
plants in the school environment, 43, 212.
Plastov, 114.
Plato, 3, 5, 112/113, 214.
Poltava Pedagogical Institute, 10, 11.
Povsha, Vera, 13.
'practical applied research', 216/217.
Pravda, 155, 164, 169, 173.
Price, R.F., 73, 86, 213.
Pushkin, 80.

R

Raphael, 114.
Renaissance, the, 2, 5, 137.
Republic, The, 5.
Rimsky-Korsakov, 97, 110.
Rousseau, 57, 77, 126, 214.
Rzhev, 13.

S

St. Exupery, 186.

Sakharov, 156.
Samsonova, T., 173.
Sasaki, Sadako, 148.
Savrasov, 114.
School of Total Education, 216.
Schumacher, E.F., 149.
sex education, 61–66.
Shatalov, V.F., 156, 181, 190–191, 192, 195, 204.
Shatsky, 126, 174, 201.
Shaw, George Bernard, 129.
Shchetinin, M., 200.
Shishkin, 114.
Singleness of Purpose, 182, 184.
Skovoroda, 58.
Soloveichik, Simon, 17, 22, 23, 75, 85, 156, 172, 173, 176, 194, 195, 198–200, 203.
Solzhenitsyn, 156.
Sovetskaia pedagogika, 157, 162, 168, 169, 194, 199, 203.
Soviet press, 74/75, 155, 156, 161–177.
Stalin, 73/74, 93, 138, 139, 140, 144, 146, 155, 156, 164, 196, 197, 201.
State Committee for Education, 202/203.
stoicism, 3, 5.
Stoletov, V., 174, 175.
Suddaby, Avril, 194.
Sukhomlinskaia, Anna Ivanovna, 7, 14.
Sukhomlinsky:
  biography, 7–23.
  controversy, 12, 160–175.
  health problems, 10, 22, 167–168, 171.
  travel, 20.
  wartime experiences, 12–14, 21, 142.
Sutherland, J., 202.

Szekely, B.B., 196.

T

Tartakovsky, B.S., 10, 14, 23, 44.
Tchaikovsky, 110, 112.
'teacher-innovators', 181–204.
Tolstoy, 16, 18, 27, 55, 65, 80, 108, 114, 126, 148, 160, 215.
Tucker, R.C., 138, 139.
Twelve, The, 4/5.

U

Uchitel'skaia gazeta, 21, 150, 167, 168, 181, 194, 195, 198, 199, 200, 202, 203.
Ukraine, 1, 8, 13, 168, 170, 177.
Ukrainian Educational Research Institute, 17, 160.
Ukrainian folk influence on Sukhomlinsky's work, 19, 59, 111, 113, 160.
Ukrainka, Lesia, 80.
Ushinsky, 80, 126, 201.
Uva, 13, 14.

V

Vasilievka, 8, 9, 10.
Vittorino da Feltre, 2.
vocational education, 27, 52, 85–94, 187–189.
Volkov, I.P., 181, 187–190, 204, 213.
'vospitanie', 25.
Vygotsky, 174.

W

War Communism, 139.
What is to be Done?, 139.
work education, 27, 52, 85–94, 187–189.

Wright Mills, C., 149.

Y

Yagodin, G.A., 202.
Yeltsin, Boris, 202.
Yuon, 114.
Yunost', 176.

Z

Zajda, Joseph, 1, 196.
Znannia ta pratsia, 170.
Zubkovsky, V.V., 11.
Zybkovka, 9, 10, 200.

www.ingramcontent.com/pod-product-compliance
Lightning Source LLC
Chambersburg PA
CBHW070603300426
44113CB00010B/1378